How to Do Everything
Adobe® InDesign® CS4

About the Authors

Donna Baker is a freelance graphic designer and the author of many books about design software and Web design. You can read tips and tutorials from her many books through Adobe Design Center and on numerous Web sites for creative professionals. Donna writes a monthly column and serves on the Experts' Panel for acrobatusers.com. She is both an Adobe Community Expert and an Adobe Certified Expert. Donna facilitates an InDesign course through an online company, and recently published her first video InDesign course through designprovideo.com. Contact her via the Baker Communications website at www.donnabaker.ca.

Laurie Ulrich Fuller has personally trained more than 10,000 people to make better and more creative use of their computers. She has written and co-written more than 25 nationally-published books on computers and software, including several titles on Adobe products. She currently teaches InDesign at the Pennsylvania College of Art & Design, and in the last few years, she's created several video training courses and put her graphics and editorial expertise to work for online and print news publications. She runs her own company, Limehat & Company, offering graphic design, marketing and promotion, training, and web development services. She invites you to contact her at help@limehat.com.

How to Do Everything

Adobe® InDesign® CS4

Donna Baker
Laurie Ulrich Fuller

New York   Chicago   San Francisco   Lisbon
London   Madrid   Mexico City   Milan   New Delhi
San Juan   Seoul   Singapore   Sydney   Toronto

The McGraw·Hill Companies

Cataloging-in-Publication Data is on file with the Library of Congress

McGraw-Hill books are available at special quantity discounts to use as premiums and sales promotions, or for use in corporate training programs. To contact a special sales representative, please visit the Contact Us page at www.mhprofessional.com.

How to Do Everything: Adobe® InDesign® CS4

1234567890   DOC DOC   019

ISBN   978-0-07-160634-9
MHID   0-07-160634-3

Sponsoring Editor	Roger Stewart
Editorial Supervisor	Patty Mon
Project Manager	Vasundhara Sawhney, International Typesetting and Composition
Acquisitions Coordinator	Joya Anthony
Technical Editor	Erica Gamet
Copy Editor	Lisa McCoy
Proofreader	Paul Tyler
Indexer	Karin Arrigoni
Production Supervisor	George Anderson
Composition	International Typesetting and Composition
Illustration	International Typesetting and Composition
Art Director, Cover	Jeff Weeks
Cover Illustration	Pattie Lee

For my little model, Avery. You go, girl.

—Donna

Contents at a Glance

Contents

Acknowledgments

Thanks to the great folks at McGraw-Hill for the opportunity. Heartfelt thanks to my co-author, Laurie Ulrich Fuller, for stepping in, and to our agent, Margot Hutchison, for making it work. It's been a great pleasure to get to know our editor, Roger Stewart. Some of those e-mails should be framed! And finally, thanks to Erica Gamet for her amazing tech edit. Her grasp of the technology and what it means to a user was invaluable.

Thanks to my hubby Terry for his support (and my new art studio), and to my girls—Erin, Deena, Daisy, and Benni—for being there. A special thanks to my "model" Avery and to my sister and brother-in-law, April and Rob, for accommodating my incessant photo needs. Finally, as always, thanks to Tom Waits for the music I live by.

—Donna

Introduction

InDesign CS4 has come a long way in its years as a successor to Adobe PageMaker. It's been interesting to watch the program develop from InDesign version 1 in 1999 to the latest release in 2008, CS4. In this book, you'll learn about existing and new features in InDesign CS4.

InDesign CS4

InDesign CS4 is part of the Adobe Design Suite of graphic and design products. Our aim was to cover the program in this book from opening InDesign to producing commercial print-ready content but still maintain the publication's requirements.

It's not an easy task to balance interesting detail with practical realities. Our approach to emphasizing one tool or process over another is based on what the average user would turn to for assistance in designing and managing their InDesign publications.

Information about the Book

You'll see a liberal sprinkling of short Notes and Tips throughout the book that offer a tidbit of information pertaining to the current topic or references to other areas in the book.

You'll find two types of sidebars in each chapter. Some are "How To" sidebars that explain an aspect of an InDesign CS4 feature or tool in depth. For example, the sidebar "Save Print Settings" in Chapter 17 describes how to store a group of settings configured for a print job to reuse in the future.

The "Did You Know?" sidebars, on the other hand, offer branching topics or in-depth information about the current subject, although the information isn't required to use InDesign. For example, the sidebar in Chapter 3, "InDesign Has Your Data Covered in Case of Emergency," describes the different ways in which InDesign defines and displays recoverable data. You don't need the information for general use of the program, but it's good to know.

How the Book Is Organized

We approached the book's structure based on how you use the program and the frequency with which the average user would experience a particular concept or feature. That is, the beginning of the book illustrates universal concepts, such as getting around the program and creating new publications, while the last section deals with Portable Document Format (PDF), Shockwave (SWF) files, and other types of interactivity that aren't features every InDesign user may experience.

The book contains five parts:

Part I: Get Up to Speed in InDesign CS4   The first part of the book comprises Chapters 1-4. You'll learn about the InDesign program interface and its component parts in Chapter 1. Chapter 2 is all about Adobe Bridge. Chapters 3 and 4 go into detail about creating new documents, configuring their component parts such as master pages and links, and navigating and viewing an InDesign document.

Part II: Tell the Tale in Text   The longest section of the book, Part II covers the realm of text, tables, formatting, styles, and working with long documents, such as books. In Chapter 5, see how to add and format text, how to thread text frames, and get a new perspective on the text using the Story Editor. In Chapter 6, you'll see how to use fonts, specify their features, and handle paragraph items such as indents and drop caps.

Chapter 7 leads you into style design for paragraphs and characters. You'll see how to design the styles and then how to use and manage a document's styles. Next, Chapter 8 shows how to work with specific text-based features, such as lists and tables. You'll see how to add these features, how to work in their respective panels, and how to work with their styles. Finally, in Chapter 9, you'll learn how to define a book file, how to create and manage its component parts, and how to work with ancillary features, such as tables of contents and indexes.

Part III: A Picture Is Worth a Thousand Words   As the section title states, a picture is worth a thousand words, and if you don't have a handle on using images and drawing features, a picture can be worth a thousand headaches. Chapter 10 looks at the basics of placing images and graphics into a document, along with basic manipulations like frame fitting and paste into features. In Chapter 11, learn to handle files and their contents, including linked content, snippets, and library files.

Chapter 12 takes you into the InDesign drawing tools and program features for layout, such as align and distribute options. Lucky Chapter 13 gives you the inside scoop on working with layers and effects, working with multiple effects, and using transparency.

Part IV: Use and Manage Color   Chapters 14-16 let you get up close and personal with color in all its Technicolor glory. From the basic processes of creating and storing colors and tints in Chapter 14, to specifying and managing colors using mixed and spot inks in Chapter 15, you'll get a good understanding of how to handle color for different types of documents. Chapter 16 takes the discussion to the program level, demystifying color management and color profiles, in addition to some document-specific features, such as color separations.

Part V: Outputs and Exports   In the final section, learn about different ways in which to prepare and export content from InDesign. Chapter 17 describes preflight and packaging, as well as printing and exporting PDF files. Chapters 18 and 19 look at designing and using interactive content. In Chapter 18, learn about using tags, transitions, hyperlinks, and bookmarks for navigation and interest. Chapter 19 describes the ways in which you can now work with InDesign and SWF files in concert, exporting files directly to SWF or in the new Flash-ready eXtended Formula Language (XFL) format. Finally, Chapter 20 winds up the book with descriptions on using content online as web pages or images.

Installation on Windows

Minimum requirements to run InDesign CS4 on Windows include:

- 1.5-GHz or faster processor
- Microsoft Windows XP with Service Pack 2 (Service Pack 3 recommended) or Windows Vista Home Premium, Business, Ultimate, or Enterprise with Service Pack 1 (certified for 32-bit Windows XP and Windows Vista)
- 512MB of RAM (1GB recommended)
- 1.8GB of hard-disk space for installation
- 1024 × 768 display (1280 × 800 recommended) with 16-bit video card
- DVD-ROM drive
- QuickTime 7 software

Macintosh Installation

Minimum requirements to run InDesign CS4 on Mac OS include:

- PowerPC G5 or multicore Intel processor
- Mac OS X v10.4.11–10.5.4
- 512MB of RAM (1GB recommended)
- 1.6GB of available hard-disk space for installation
- 1024 × 768 display (1280 × 800 recommended) with 16-bit video card
- DVD-ROM drive
- QuickTime 7 software required for multimedia features

What's New?

Some of the changes in InDesign CS4 are enhancements to previous program features, while others are new and ready for your experimenting pleasure. I'm sure you'll find that many integrate into your regular workflow.

We've included highlights in this introduction and pointed out where you can read about them in the book. To make sense of the myriad changes, the changes are organized into several categories.

User Interface

Changes to the user interface give you quicker access to features and settings. You can read about the features in Chapter 1. One of the most obvious new features is an Application bar at the top of the program window that offers access to many common settings, such as workspaces, document views, and searches. You can now work with multiple documents, each open in individual tabs, and arrange the documents using a selection of *N*-up views.

Add some power to your zoom using the new Power Zoom. The Hand tool and mouse work in concert to zoom in and out of pages, spreads, and across pages.

Productivity

New features offer substantial savings in time and effort on your part, with more onscreen information tracking and assisting your work. Once you start working with Live Preflight, you'll wonder how you worked without it! Specify your requirements and track problems in real time. Use the Preflight panel features to locate and view errors for on-the-fly corrections.

A collection of Smart features helps you align, space, resize, and rotate multiple objects onscreen. You'll see dynamic guides identifying matching dimensions, spacing, and rotation, and Smart Cursors show X and Y locations and object dimensions.

The Links panel has expanded substantially, letting you find, sort, organize, and manage placed content. You can review details on the placed content and relink, update, or embed as needed.

Text and Tables

Several new features in the realm of text and tables help save time in construction and customization of your documents, ranging from highly advanced conditional text (not covered in the book) to the ability to use InDesign like a word processor, automatically adding pages and adjusting text flow.

One new timesaver lets you create a style in dialog boxes where you can select a paragraph or character style right from the dialog box, such as working in the Find/Change dialog box. And, speaking of timesavers, you can check out the contents and structure of your tables in the Story Editor.

Graphics and Drawing

Graphic and drawing changes are designed to make your actions more efficient. For example, if you draw a frame with an image loaded in the cursor, the frame uses the graphic's dimensions.

Quickly create a contact sheet by placing multiple images in a grid arrangement. When placing multiple images, hold down CTRL-SHIFT (Windows) or COMMAND-SHIFT (Mac OS) to drag a grid of images. Use the arrow keys to control the number of rows and columns in the grid.

Interactivity

Interactive features are substantially expanded in InDesign CS4. Look for features you can include in your InDesign publications, designed for export to PDF and SWF. Read about the new features in Chapters 18 and 19 (Part V).

Work with hyperlinks and cross-references in new ways. Build a wide range of hyperlinks to Uniform Resource Locators (URLs), e-mail, documents, or anchors, and verify the links in InDesign CS4. The new Button panel lets you design multiple button states, specify events, and apply actions. Design your own buttons, or use buttons from the new Button library.

Use page transitions for individual pages or an entire publication. Customize transitions by setting speeds and direction for exported SWF and PDF files.

You can design dynamic content in InDesign for export to SWF files and open exported files directly in Flash Player. Export a document in the new XFL format for use in Flash CS4 Professional. XFL automatically reformats images for onscreen use, reuses assets, and maintains editable text.

Design dynamic documents for PDF export. Include media like sound, QuickTime, and SWF movies, and features like transitions and buttons. Export hyperlinks, bookmarks, and cross-references.

Files for Download

Many of the files shown as examples or projects in the book are available for download. The downloads include readme.txt files describing the contents of the chapter's material:

1. Open www.mhprofressional.com in your browser.

2. Click the Computing link to open the Osborne home page.

3. Look for the Downloads link about halfway down the left side of the page.

4. Click the link for How to Do Everything: InDesign CS4 to download the files automatically.

PART I

Get Up to Speed in InDesign CS4

1

Get Around the Interface

How to...

- Locate program features and areas
- Find the tools
- Customize a workspace
- Set up custom menus and shortcuts

InDesign Creative Suite 4 (CS4) is one of those programs that gets more useful the more you work in it. As your expertise increases, you're sure to find new techniques, shortcuts, and program features that accommodate your need for speed and accuracy.

Use the first part of this book to get your bearings in InDesign CS4, its surroundings, interface, and documents. Chapter 1 first offers a general orientation to the program's interface and components, such as panels. Then check out some customization features, such as workspaces, menus, and command shortcuts.

Chapter 2 takes you out of InDesign per se for a tour of Adobe Bridge. File management is always a big issue, regardless of your workflow. You'll discover how Bridge helps in organizing, previewing, and locating files and their metadata.

Then it's on to Chapter 3 for a look at the ins and outs of starting new publications. InDesign includes different methods for creating, saving, and opening files for a variety of purposes. We'll dig into master pages to check out how they provide consistency and timesaving benefits in your project design and development.

Use Chapter 4 as a guide to getting around and viewing content in InDesign. You'll read about different methods for setting up visual assists such as rulers and guides. InDesign CS4 introduces a number of *Smart* features that you're sure to appreciate.

Interpret Commands for Use on Mac

For ease of reading, this book displays Windows commands in the descriptions and functions, rather than displaying both Windows and Mac commands, unless the commands are unique. Here are some common examples.

- On Windows, to accept a dialog box or start a new line, you press the ENTER key, while on Mac, you press RETURN. In the text, you'll see ENTER only, rather than ENTER (Windows)/RETURN (Mac).

- On Windows, you locate files in Windows Explorer; on Mac, you use Finder.

- For the most part, Windows keystroke combinations using CTRL-keystroke equate to COMMAND-keystroke on Mac; ALT-CLICK commands on Windows equate to OPTION-CLICK commands on Mac.

- On Windows, choose Edit | Preferences to display program preferences, while on Mac, use the InDesign | Preferences command.

- For a complete list of platform-specific commands, please consult the program Help files.

Take a Tour of InDesign CS4

InDesign CS4 shares many similarities with other CS4 products. If you're accustomed to working in another program, such as Adobe Photoshop or Illustrator, you'll find it easy to get around the InDesign interface.

In this chapter, we'll check out the InDesign CS4 interface in depth. After an introduction to the program components, the rest of the chapter is dedicated to customizing the functionality and appearance of the program to suit your work style.

Start from the Welcome Screen

Launch InDesign CS4 for the first time, and you're greeted with the Welcome screen, a feature that serves as an InDesign switchboard.

Links to online resources

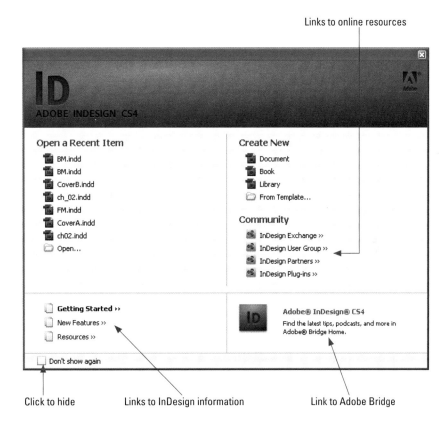

Click to hide   Links to InDesign information   Link to Adobe Bridge

Use the links on the Welcome screen to access various program areas, web sites, and folders on your system, including:

- **Open a Recent Item**   The last few InDesign files you've worked with are listed here. To open another file, click Open and follow the prompts to locate and select your file.

- **Create New**   Click one of the options to start a new publication. You can also choose from dozens of templates, displayed in Adobe Bridge.

- **Community**   Use the Community links to access different areas at Adobe. The links lead to extras such as tips and tutorials, user groups, and more.

- **Links to Help Features**   These links open different areas of the Help menu to offer assistance for new users and to locate online InDesign resources.

■ **Adobe Bridge** This link brings you to the Adobe Bridge home page. Adobe Bridge is a separate program and opens in its own window. Read about Bridge in Chapter 2.

■ **Don't show again** Select the check box at the lower-left corner of the window to bypass this screen when you open the program in the future. If you'd like to see the Welcome screen again, choose Help | Welcome Screen.

Take It from the Top

Once you close the Welcome screen, you're into the program proper. InDesign displays several control and management features at the top of the program window, including the Application bar, program menus, and Control panel.

Control Your Views in the Application Bar

New in InDesign CS4, the Application bar brings together various display management features. The Application bar across the top contains a workspace switcher and other application controls, as shown in Figure 1-1.

Aside from the self-evident InDesign program icon, the Application bar includes the following:

■ Click Go to Bridge to open Adobe Bridge. Press ALT-CLICK to open Bridge behind InDesign, or press CTRL-CLICK to maximize the Adobe Bridge window.

■ Zoom Levels has moved from its previous location on the Status bar to the Application bar. Click the Zoom Levels drop-down arrow to open a list of magnification options.

■ Click View Options to open a drop-down menu of several onscreen items. Select/deselect the options to show features such as hidden characters, rulers, guides, and frame edges.

FIGURE 1-1 Manage program display and other settings from the Application bar.

Zoom Levels   Screen Mode   Workspace Switcher

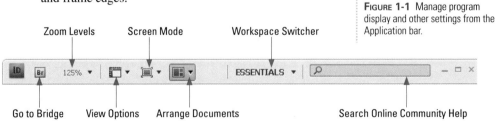

Go to Bridge   View Options   Arrange Documents   Search Online Community Help

- Click Screen Mode to display the four screen modes found at the bottom of the Toolbox and its submenu (read more about screen modes in Chapter 4).

- Click Arrange Documents to display a panel of *N*-up options for tiling open files in a single window. The available choices depend on the number of open files. For example, with three open files, you'll have 3-up options active, and so on.

- Instead of using menu commands, click Workspace Switcher to open a list of InDesign workspaces. Any custom workspaces you save are included on the list.

- To search Adobe Community Help from the Assistance bar, type a search term in the field and click Search.

Look into the Control Panel

The Control panel conveniently displays horizontally across the top of the document window by default. Here you'll find options, settings, and commands for a selected item on your page.

What displays in the Control panel varies according to the object selected in the document. In all cases, if you hold your mouse over an icon or label, you'll see information in a tooltip. Each Control panel display includes a panel menu and a Quick Apply button.

The three Control panel displays bring together settings from a variety of panels, which the following sections describe in detail.

Selected Text   If you select text in a frame, you'll see either character or paragraph options, depending on which icon is selected at the left edge of the Control panel. For active character formatting controls, you'll see some paragraph options along with the character choices. With active paragraph formatting controls, as you see here, the paragraph options display along with some character options on the right.

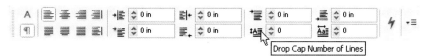

Selected Frame A frame selected on the page displays options for size; position; transformations, such as rotating and skewing; and object styles in the Control panel.

Selected Table Cell The Control panel displays options for modifying row and column dimensions, aligning text, adding strokes, and merging cells when you select a table cell on the page.

Control panel icons are associated with dialog boxes. ALT-CLICK an icon on the panel to open its corresponding dialog box.

Scan the Program Menus

InDesign contains nine program menu headings. To save time finding menu items, not all commands are shown by default. Sometimes, you'll open a program menu expecting to find a particular command, and it's nowhere to be found. You don't need Sherlock Holmes or a hound dog; you simply need to choose a couple of commands.

Depending on your circumstances, some suggestions include:

- Open your menu and select Show All Menu Items at the bottom to expand the menu.

- Change to the Advanced workspace, which shows all menu items by default.

- If items are hidden due to your custom menu design, press CTRL and click the menu's name to display hidden content.

Read about customizing program menus in the upcoming section "Serve Up Tailor-Made Menus."

Rummage Through the Toolbox

The Tools panel, or Toolbox, is shown vertically at the left of the program window by default. Click the double arrows at the top of the panel to change the configuration, which cycles through single then double vertical columns. Drag the panel away from its docking location to include a horizontal row display in the toggle choices (see Figure 1-2).

You can't rearrange the tools in the Toolbox.

Toggle Toolbox display   Type tools   Gradient tools   Navigation tools   Display modes

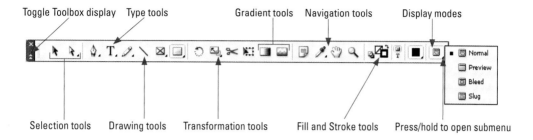

Selection tools   Drawing tools   Transformation tools   Fill and Stroke tools   Press/hold to open submenu

FIGURE 1-2 The Toolbox (shown in horizontal configuration) contains several groups of tools.

The tools and their functions are discussed in depth throughout the book, although they share a few general features, which the following sections describe.

Tool Selections   Click a tool to select it. An arrow at the lower-right corner of the tool's icon indicates a submenu of similar tools. Click and hold to display the submenu (shown in Figure 1-2).

Display Tooltips   Hold your mouse over a tool in the Toolbox to display the tool's name and its keyboard shortcut in a tooltip. The default tools offer single-stroke shortcuts. For those tools with submenus, the alternate tools usually have different keystrokes with a modifier.

View Tool Options   Several tools offer configuration dialog boxes. Double-click the tool to display a dialog box for the Eyedropper, Pencil, or Polygon tool. Configure the settings and click OK.

You Can Frame Up Elements on Mac

The Application frame on Mac groups your program elements into one window that you can manipulate as a single unit. Move or resize the Application frame, and its elements obligingly rearrange themselves so they don't overlap. Panels remain visible, even if you change the focus to another program and then back to InDesign. If you prefer traditional onscreen actions, choose Window | Application Frame to toggle it off.

Check Out the Document Window

Your InDesign publication occupies a large portion of the program window. Like most programs, the display for the actual work allows for change in magnification, positioning of content in the window, and horizontal and vertical scrollbars. InDesign CS4 includes other features as well (see Figure 1-3).

For example, you can tab open documents and display content in an *N*-up layout, based on a selection from the Arrange Documents list in the application.

Reveal Your Document's Status

The Status bar shows information about the file at the lower-left corner of the document window (shown in Figure 1-3). Click the drop-down arrow to display a list of your document's pages and master pages. The arrows on either side of the page list let you navigate the document by spread.

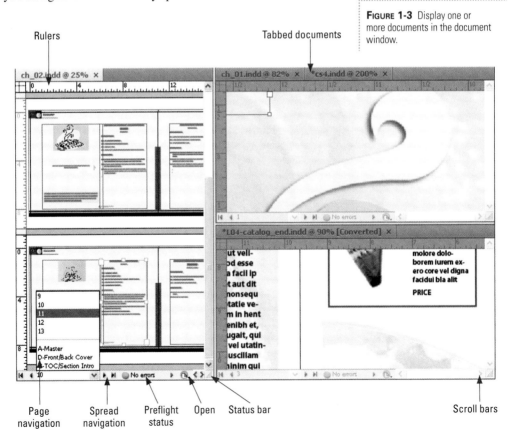

FIGURE 1-3 Display one or more documents in the document window.

Rulers

Tabbed documents

Page navigation

Spread navigation

Preflight status

Open

Status bar

Scroll bars

Also on the Status bar, you can view any document errors in the preflight notification, or click the arrow to view a menu for opening the Preflight panel or defining profiles. (Read about preflight in Chapter 17.)

Finally, click Open to reveal a menu where you can choose other versions of the file, or you can locate the file in your system by choosing Reveal In Explorer (Windows) or Reveal In Finder (Mac). If you're working with a new file that hasn't been saved, the tooltip reads *Never Saved,* and the menu options are unavailable.

Take a Shortcut (Menu)

Unlike the menus that appear at the top of your screen, context-sensitive, or shortcut, menus display commands related to the active tool or selection. For example, right-click a graphic frame to choose from a variety of fitting, content, and transform commands. When you right-click a text frame to display the shortcut menu, you'll reveal text and text frame options in addition to the commands shown for a graphic frame.

Organize Your Efforts with Panels

Modify, monitor, and manage your work in the panels at the right of the program window. The panel configuration changes according to the selected workspace. Choose Window and select other panels to open them as well or to close existing panels.

Each panel includes a menu, accessible by clicking the Menu icon at the upper-right edge. Most panels include a toolbar along the bottom (see Figure 1-4).

Experiment with Panel Behaviors

Panels behave in the same ways, along with sharing common features. The best way to learn about panels and how they function is through experimentation. Like other CS4 programs, the InDesign panels may be docked, grouped, moved, and so on.

Dock Panels for Safekeeping   By default, panels are *docked* at the right of the program window, meaning they are stationary. Dock or undock a panel by dragging its tab. For a panel group (several panels tabbed together) drag from the *title bar,* the empty bar above the tabs.

Tip   To prevent a panel or panel group from docking, press CTRL while moving it.

Panel group   Panel menu   Panel group   Toggle expand/collapse

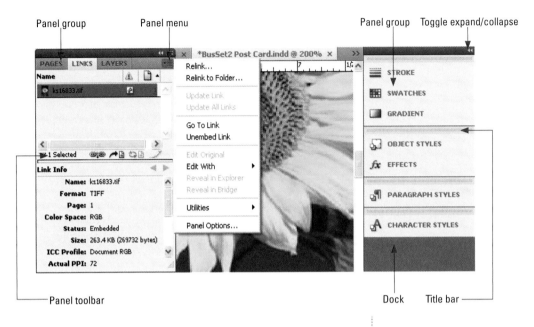

Panel toolbar   Dock   Title bar

FIGURE 1-4 Manage and control panels in a number of ways.

Move and Reorder Panels   Move panels either to combine them in groups or out of existing groups by dragging up or down in the panel dock. Drag a panel by its tab or a panel group by its title bar. Drag a panel or group away from the dock area to float it in the document window. Change the order of a panel in a group by dragging its icon up or down in the group when closed or by dragging its tab left or right when the panels are open.

Resize and Reveal Panels   Resize panels by dragging from any side. Double-click a tab to minimize or maximize a panel or panel group. Collapse panels to icons by decreasing the width of the dock. Icons can show labels or the icon only. Click a panel's icon to open it again.

Hide and Seek Panels

A computer screen (or two) has a finite amount of space. Use these simple tips to hide combinations of panels.

- To hide or show all panels, press TAB.
- To hide or show all panels with the exception of the Tools and Control panels, press SHIFT-TAB.

▦ To maintain panels in their hidden states but reveal them temporarily, move your mouse to the edge of the InDesign program window in Windows or to the edge of the application frame used by default in Mac. As you hover your mouse in those locations, the corresponding panels display. Move the mouse away, and they're hidden again.

Make the Program Work for You

Like most programs, there are plenty of basic tools and default settings when you first embark on your adventures in InDesign-land. However, as your expertise and familiarity increase, so does your need to customize how you work.

InDesign lets you configure and save *workspaces,* or program configurations, that offer a convenient way to start your work sessions. If you notice over time that you're continually looking for a command where it doesn't exist, look into designing a custom menu. And speaking of custom, why not devise your own set of shortcuts for faster access to commands and actions?

 On Mac, the OWL (OS Widget Library) component controls how windows and panels work.

Pick Your Workspace

InDesign includes a number of workspaces that display specific arrangements of panels and menu settings tailored for different types of work. For example, the Book workspace includes panels like Index, Conditional Text, and Bookmarks, while the Interactivity workspace includes Buttons, Page Transitions, and Hyperlinks.

Here's a brief rundown of the workspaces:

▦ **Getting Started**   This is a minimal workspace, including Pages, Links, Stroke, Color, and Swatches—enough to get you started on a letter or basic document.

▦ **Essentials**   This workspace is similar to the Basic workspace seen in InDesign CS3, and is the workspace used as the program default workspace.

- **Advanced** Based on the default workspace used in InDesign CS3, you'll find a variety of style and color application panels in this workspace.

- **Book** Use the Book workspace for long documents and InCopy workflows.

- **Interactivity** Use the Interactivity workspace to facilitate working with the new interactive features in InDesign, including Shockwave Flash (SWF), Editable Flash Format (XFL), and interactive Portable Document Format (PDF).

- **Typography** This workspace is the only workspace where you'll see the Glyphs panel and other panels designed for those working in typesetting.

- **Printing & Proofing** Carried over from CS3, this workspace includes Preview and Presets panels, as well as the Preflight panel.

- **What's New** This workspace highlights new features and custom panel arrangements. New and altered menu items and commands are colored blue, as you see here.

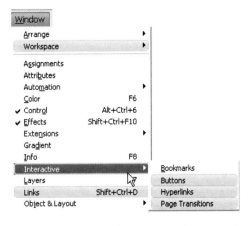

 Check out the "What's New" section in the book's introduction for a look at program changes and modifications.

Save Your Own Workspaces

Although InDesign offers a collection of different workspaces, you're sure to make changes to them. The more you work in a program, the more you need it to show a particular arrangement of panels and displays. Fortunately, InDesign lets you save a custom workspace that includes your panels arranged in your choice of configuration, size, location, and position.

With the interface arranged to your satisfaction, choose Window | Workspace | New Workspace. Type a name in the field, and click OK. You can access your custom workspace from the Workspace Switcher in the Application bar or the Window menu.

Clear Program Preferences

As you make, change, and revise preferences on an ongoing basis, your settings are stored in a program preference file. If you find InDesign mishandles your shortcuts and other preferences, it's time to delete your preferences file and start over. Close InDesign and then restart it. As the program restarts, press the keystroke combination SHIFT-CTRL-ALT-CLICK (Windows) or SHIFT-OPTION-COMMAND-CONTROL (Mac)

As the program boots up, you'll see a dialog box asking if you want to delete preference files. Click OK to close the dialog box. You'll have to rebuild your preferences.

Change Interface Preferences

Choose Edit | Preferences | Interface to open the preference panel. Many of the preferences you'll use are active by default, such as showing tooltips and showing the thumbnail in a loaded graphic cursor.

Some features described in this chapter are available in the Interface preferences as well. For example, select the Auto-Show Hidden Panels option to display panels temporarily when you hold your cursor over the edge of the document window, or select the Open Documents as Tabs check box to tab all open documents in the program window.

Customize the Control Panel

Working with the Control panel definitely makes configuring options and settings easier. You can make the Control panel even more functional by adding or removing features from its displays.

Pay attention to what you're looking for as you work. You may find, for example, that you always use the Distribute tools after using the Align tools. The default Control panel layout doesn't include both tool groups, but you can change that by activating the Distribute tools in the Object settings.

Click the Control panel's menu, and choose Customize to open the Customize Control Panel dialog box. There are five customizable categories of settings in the Customize Control Panel dialog box, including:

- **Object**   The Object choices include the usual transform, stroke, and effects tools. If you do a lot of text wraps or want to keep Object Styles at hand, make those selections in this category.

- **Character**   Character settings toggle with the paragraph settings in the Control panel. By default, only Character Fonts and Character Attributes are selected. Add other features such as kerning, scale, and styles here.

- **Paragraph**   Paragraph settings toggle with the character settings. You'll find alignments, indents, spacing, hyphenation, and bullets/numbering active by default. In this category, find other options, such as Paragraph Styles and Baseline Grid.

- **Tables**   The Tables category includes common formatting, such as alignments, merging options, and so on. You can select Cell Options and Table & Cell Styles, among others.

- **Other**   The only choice in the Other category is the Quick Apply button.

Serve Up Tailor-Made Menus

Custom menus are a great way to remove distractions and screen clutter. InDesign offers custom menu options for all menu levels, including the main program menu, context (or shortcut) menus, and panel menus.

Follow these steps to set up a custom menu:

1. Choose Edit | Menus to open the Menu Customization dialog box.

2. Click Save As to open a dialog box. Type the name for your menu set (or leave the InDesign *Defaults copy* name), and click OK. As you make changes, (*Modified*) is appended to the name; click Save to update the stored file.

3. Click the Category drop-down arrow and choose the type of menu for customization. You can select Application Menus or Context & Panel Menus.

4. Scroll through the list to find the specific menu you want to modify, and click to open its command list. Toggle the visibility, and click None to display a drop-down box. You can click the drop-down arrow and choose a background color for the commands.

5. When you're finished, click OK to close the dialog box. Open the menu to see your customizations in action, as shown here.

Specify Shortcuts

InDesign includes a wide range of shortcuts, ranging from the utilitarian H to activate the Hand tool, to the slightly more exotic SHIFT-CTRL-ALT-Y to show the Overprint Preview.

There are several preconfigured sets of keyboard shortcuts. The [Default] set is the application default. If you are moving into InDesign from another program, you'll find shortcuts for Adobe PageMaker 7 and QuarkXPress 4 in the Set drop-down list.

Choose Edit | Keyboard Shortcuts to open the Keyboard Shortcuts dialog box. Rather than using the default shortcut set, select another preconfigured set from the Set drop-down list.

Follow these steps to create a set of custom shortcuts:

1. Click New Set to open a dialog box where you name the shortcut set and choose a preexisting set as a starting point. The program preselects *Default* for you. Click OK to close the dialog box and return to the Keyboard Shortcuts dialog box. As you see here, the custom name shows in the Set field.

Don't modify the Default or QuarkXPress shortcuts sets, as InDesign stores your custom sets in a different hard drive location (see the sidebar "You Can Share Shortcut Sets").

2. Select a program area or menu from the Product Area drop-down list to display the options in the Commands list.

3. Scroll through the list and locate the command you'd like to access via shortcut.

4. Type the key/keystroke combination you want to use in the New Shortcut field. If it's used elsewhere, the action is shown below the field and the Command list scrolls to the existing command location. Pick a new shortcut or change the preexisting shortcut.

5. Select an option from the Context drop-down list to specify a shortcut for a particular type of work. For example, you can set a shortcut to manipulate text and use the same shortcut keystrokes in a table. Think carefully before defining a shortcut's context—Default

You Can Share Shortcut Sets

InDesign stores shortcut presets as .indk files in the Presets folder in the main application folder. Copy your custom shortcut set—saved as an *.indk file—from one computer and install it on another computer in the appropriate folder.

Custom keyboard shortcut sets are stored in different locations, depending on your operating system.

- In Windows XP, custom presets are located at Documents and Settings\[username]\Application Data\Adobe\InDesign\[version]\[language]InDesign Shortcut Sets.

- In Windows Vista, look for presets at Users\[username]\AppData\Roaming\Adobe\InDesign\[Version]\[Language]\InDesign Shortcut Sets.

- In Mac OS X, your presets are stored at Users/[username]/Library/Preferences/Adobe InDesign/[version]/[language]/InDesign Shortcut Sets.

applies a shortcut, regardless of the document's environment; a shortcut specified in a particular context overrides a default shortcut.

6. Click Assign to complete the new shortcut. When you're finished, click OK to close the dialog box.

 Don't waste time clicking and scrolling through the Product Area and Commands areas. Instead, click Show Set to display all the commands and those with assigned shortcuts in a Notepad/Text Edit window. Save and print the file, and design your killer set of shortcuts at your leisure.

Summary

The first part of this chapter serves as a tour guide to help you make your way around InDesign. You saw how the different components make up the InDesign interface. The new Application bar at the top of the program window brings together a variety of common view and organization tools and features. Menus offer access to different categories of menus.

The second part of the chapter deals with customizing the interface for the way you like to work. Starting with existing workspaces, you saw how to create and save your own workspace. You were introduced to interface preferences and ways to customize the Control panel. The chapter finished off with more customizations—this time, for menus and shortcuts.

In the next chapter, see how to manage and control the assets you use in InDesign as you read about Adobe Bridge.

2

Tap into Adobe Bridge

How to...

- Find and view assets
- Download and manage digital images
- Organize your work
- Use keywords and filters

If your vocation (or avocation) includes digital design work, one of your biggest sources of pleasure and interest is undoubtedly collecting assets, such as images, audio, and video. On the other side of the coin, one of your biggest sources of irritation can be managing those assets. I'm sure most of us have finished a project only to realize that we'd forgotten about a particular image or clip that would have been *perfect*.

Fortunately, the Adobe Creative Suites and components include Adobe Bridge. Bridge started life as the File Browser in Photoshop 7 and has evolved into a separate program bundled with Creative Suite programs. Use Bridge to track down, organize, and manage both Adobe and non-Adobe assets.

A common use for Bridge is managing downloads from a digital camera. In this chapter, follow a simple workflow for downloading and handling images from a digital camera.

 Bridge may also include assets managed by Adobe Version Cue, which is not covered in this book.

Make Your Way Around Bridge

Start Adobe Bridge from any Creative Suite application by clicking its icon, like the one at the top of the InDesign program window; using the File | Browse In Bridge command; or, from

InDesign, press CTRL-ALT-O to open Bridge; use the same shortcut keys to return to InDesign.

The Bridge Interface

The Bridge program displays content in three panels by default. At the left, you'll find different ways to locate, filter, and collect assets. The central panel displays the Content tab, while the right panel shows visual previews of your assets in the Preview tab. In any preview, click the image with the cursor (a magnifying glass by default) to see a magnified area. Drag it over the preview to see detail, and click the X at the lower-right corner to close it. Also in the Essentials workspace, you'll find metadata and keywords in their respective tabs (see Figure 2-1).

FIGURE 2-1 Arrange folders in different display modes, with tools and features surrounding the content views.

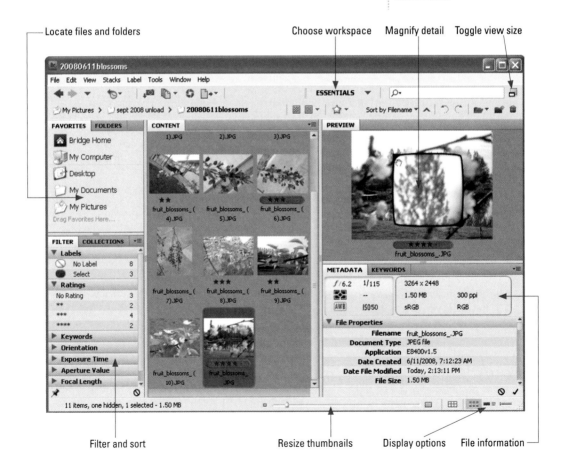

Locate files and folders   Choose workspace   Magnify detail   Toggle view size

Filter and sort   Resize thumbnails   Display options   File information

Workspace	Use
Essentials	General file organizing and managing.
Filmstrip	Evaluate individual assets in a folder, such as a group of images.
Metadata	Compare features in groups of images, such as resolutions or color profiles.
Output	Define document and layout features for output as Portable Document Format (PDF) or web gallery.
Keywords	Search for assets using assigned keywords and assign keywords to items.
Preview	Evaluate a group of images.
Light Table	Assess a group of images and select subgroups for labels or ratings.
Folders	Check the contents of folders for reorganization, renaming, and so on.

TABLE 2-1   Workspace Choices Defined by Task

Change the Program Layout

Bridge functions in multiple ways for multiple workflows. For that reason, you'll find the interface offers a number of arrangements, available as *workspaces*. Like the workspaces you've used in InDesign and other Adobe programs like Photoshop, the Bridge workspaces are configurable.

When you open Bridge, the Essentials workspace shows by default, indicated by the Essentials label (shown in Figure 2-1). Click Essentials to open a drop-down menu containing a variety of workspaces, detailed in Table 2-1.

Modify Your Program Display

A Bridge workspace—like that in InDesign—isn't a static layout. That is, you can open and close tabs, resize panels, and change their orders.

Choose a Display Option

Regardless of the workspace you're working with, you can modify the way the thumbnails are displayed in the Content area of the window. At the lower-right edge of the Bridge window, click an icon to display thumbnails (shown in Figure 2-1), or choose from two additional layouts.

Store a Custom Workspace

Bridge lets you save a custom workspace, just as in other Creative Suite products. Organize the program window and panels as you like, and then follow these steps to save your workspace:

1. Click the visible workspace label on the Bridge toolbar to open the list, and choose New Workspace. The New Workspace dialog box appears.

2. In the Name field, type a descriptive name rather than the default *Workspace 1* name. The following options should be selected by default:

   ■ Save Window Location as Part of Workspace. Use this option if you characteristically have Bridge open in a specific location on your screen.

   ■ Save Sort Order as Part of Workspace. Use this option if you have used sort filters, such as keywords or ratings, that you'd like to maintain from session to session.

3. Click OK to close the dialog box and save the workspace, now accessible from the list of workspaces.

Click View Content as Details to show information about each image along with its thumbnail (top), or click List to show thumbnails and the assets' information in a spreadsheet-like display (bottom).

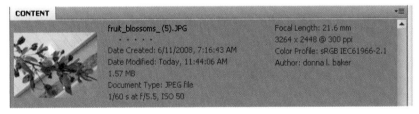

At any time, to return to the default workspace display, click the workspace button and choose Reset Workspace.

Compact Your View

Suppose you want to add a general scenery image to your InDesign publication but aren't sure which one is best. You can place and remove a few until you find the right one, or pick before you add the files using the Compact view.

FIGURE 2-2 Compact the program window to view thumbnails only.

Rather than showing the entire Bridge interface, click Use Compact Mode to shrink it to a compact view. The program collapses to show minimal tools, the folder hierarchy, thumbnails, and the thumbnail resize slider (see Figure 2-2).

For the ultimate in miniaturization, click Collapse to the right of the Search field to collapse Bridge into a single row of tools. In that view, your actions are limited to navigation using the arrows or history drop-down lists.

Note   The four images shown in Figure 2-2 aren't in sequential numbered order. You can manually drag-and-drop the thumbnails in the Content tab in Bridge and then shrink the program window to view only those image thumbnails under consideration.

Navigation arrows   Common locations   Recent folders and files

Use Bridge as a Locator

Rather than looking for files in Windows Explorer or Finder, use the Folders feature in Bridge to track down your files. Once you find them, consider adding them to your Favorites list for ongoing work, or make collections for assembling content for a current project.

Hunt for Files in the Folders Tab

Most of the Bridge workspaces include the Folders tab, which shows your files in a typical folder hierarchy format. Locate your files by opening folders in various drive locations. You'll see the path for folders or locations shown above the Folders tab.

■ You can have more than one Bridge window open at a time. If you're planning to reorganize some files in your folder structure, choose File | New Window to open an additional window. Then all you have to do is drag-and-drop content from one window to another. If you're reorganizing using this method, use the Folders workspace for maximum visibility of your files.

- Use the navigation features above the Folders tab to move through your files and folders. Click the left and right arrows to move back and forth through the views in a selected tab, or click the drop-down arrow next to the navigation arrows to display a list of common locations, such as Bridge Home, My Computer, or Desktop.

- If you don't recall where you last viewed a file, click the watch icon to open a drop-down menu. Here you'll find lists of files from Creative Suite programs, such as Adobe Illustrator, InDesign, and Photoshop, as well as a list of the last ten folders you've explored.

Make It a Favorite

Rather than opening sequences of hard drive locations and folders to locate assets you want for a project each work session, specify the location as a Favorite once.

Use the Folders workspace, which separates the Favorites and Folders tabs. Locate the folder you want to designate a Favorite, and drag it into the Favorites panel. If you're working in another workspace, right-click the folder and choose Add to Favorites from the shortcut menu.

How to... Save Time Collecting Files

Sometimes, collecting assets for a large or complex project can be downright time-consuming. Rather than creating a Favorites folder, make a collection. That way, you can select files from various folders and collect them into a single location.

Click New Collection at the bottom of the Collections tab. A listing shows on the tab with an active text field. Type the name for your collection. Then drag content into the folder for storage and future use.

Make Your Collection Smart

What a super feature! Rather than collecting assets manually to store in a collection, let Bridge do the work for you. Bridge Creative Suite 4 (CS4) includes a Smart Collection feature that allows you to define criteria and collect files that comply with the criteria.

Follow these steps to set up a Smart Collection:

1. Click Smart Collection on the Collections tab toolbar to display a new listing named *New Smart Collection* by default. Type your collection's name.

On Mac, when you click Smart Collection, the dialog box appears immediately. After you're finished adding content, you're asked to name the collection.

2. In the Smart Collection dialog box, click the Look in drop-down arrow and choose the location where you want to collect the assets.

3. Specify the criteria for the search:

■ Click the first drop-down arrow and choose the value used as the basis for the default criterion, ranging from document types to dates, bit depths to general metadata.

■ Click the center drop-down arrow and choose a condition, which varies according to the value selected in the first field.

■ Click the right drop-down arrow and choose or type the parameters.

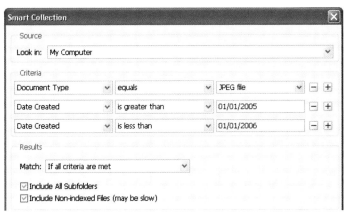

4. Define how the results are matched and whether to use subfolders and nonindexed files, as you see here. Bridge warns that nonindexed files add to the search time, and they do—considerably!

5. Click Save to close the dialog box. Bridge starts a search and displays the results in the Content tab.

Use a Multi-image Workflow

Now that you've had a tour of Bridge and how it looks, what's next? Sometimes it's difficult to know what to do with a program, even if you're aware of some of its features. In this section, follow a simple workflow for downloading and handling images from a digital camera. You can perform the tasks without opening the files themselves.

Download and Process Camera Files

Before downloading, connect your camera to your computer or enable your wireless image transfer. Once you're connected, choose File | Get Photos from Camera or click the camera icon on the toolbar to open the Adobe Bridge CS4–Photo Downloader dialog box, and select your camera from the Source drop-down list. Specify import settings, such as storage location, folder name, and so on (see Figure 2-3). Click Get Photos to close the dialog box, download the images, and display their thumbnails and storage location.

Processing image files can include many actions far beyond the common choices in this project. For example, your workflow may include tasks such as creating digital negative (DNG) or RAW data files for manipulation in Photoshop.

Batch-Rename the Images

Digital images are named by your camera, such as *DSCN9882 .jpg*. While you can tell one image from another by its thumbnail, you certainly can't simply by reading the name.

Here's how to batch-rename files in Bridge:

FIGURE 2-3 Specify settings for downloading images from your camera.

1. Select the folder's name from the Folders tab, or select all the thumbnails on the Content tab.

2. Choose Tools | Batch Rename or use the keyboard shortcut CTRL-SHIFT-R to open the Batch Rename dialog box.

3. Specify whether to rename the files and save in the same folder, move the files, or copy them to another folder. Click Browse to select a destination for copied or moved files.

4. In the New Filenames section, choose options from the drop-down list to define the name. The example project uses images of Banff, Alberta, so the filenames start with the word *Banff.* To add additional elements to the name, click the plus sign (+), select a parameter, and type a value.

 Add additional operating system compatibility if you like, along with your current operating system (OS), which is selected by default. Select the Preserve Current Filename in XMP check box to store the original filename with other file information.

5. Review the preview of your new naming scheme, and click Rename to close the dialog box and rename your files.

Apply Keywords

To include tailor-made search terms, assign keywords to your assets that are included in the files' metadata. For convenience, switch to the Keywords workspace, which shows the Keywords panel at the left and the images showing detail at the right. The simplest way to assign keywords is from general to specific. The example shows 12 images, all shot in Canada. You can select all 12 images and click *Canada* in the *Places* keywords. Then you can select a subgroup for another keyword, such as forest, and so on.

 **Assign Stars and Labels**

Often, you assemble a few similar items to pick from when you're working. One way to keep track of these items is with a star rating. Bridge lets you assign from one to five stars. To assign a star rating, select the image (or images) to receive a particular rating. Choose Label and select the rating. You'll see the stars below the thumbnail.

For a production workflow, use the labels offered in Bridge in the Label menu. Choices range from *To Do* to *Approved,* each of which assigns a color to the star area under the thumbnail. To make a definite statement, choose Label | Reject to overlay the word *Reject.*

To add new keywords, right-click a keyword heading and choose New Sub Keyword from the shortcut menu. Type a name for the heading in the blank line that displays in the active keyword group. In the same way, right-click any item on the keyword list to open the shortcut menu, and choose New Keyword to open a blank line. Type a name, and it's ready for nesting subkeywords.

Search Using Keywords

There's not much point to adding keywords if you don't do something with them, such as filtering your images. It's simple to find what you want from a dozen or two shots, but much more work when you're dealing with hundreds. To perform a sort, click the Filter tab, next to the Keywords tab in the Keywords workspace.

Select the items you want to apply as a filter. In addition to metadata you've added, you can filter by camera settings, such as focal length. The more choices you make, the smaller the probable returns. As you see here, there's only one image in the Banff collection with both a five-star rating and a foreground interest keyword.

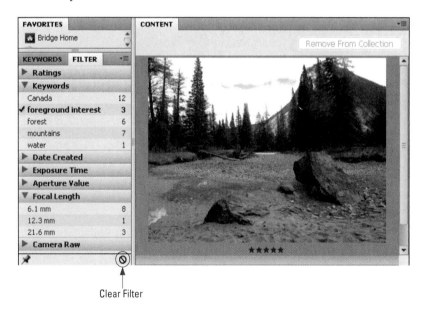

Clear Filter

When you're finished, click Clear Filter at the bottom-right corner of the Filter tab.

Tidy Up the Folder

At any time, you can select images you'd like to cull. There's no advantage to saving and storing multiple versions of poor-quality images, particularly if you do not intend to correct them.

Thumbnail selected   Stack selected

On the other hand, if you have similar shots that you want to keep, use the Stack feature to collect their thumbnails. Select the files and choose Stack | Group as Stack. The last file selected is shown as the top thumbnail by default. To view the top thumbnail, click the stack in the Contents panel. If you want to see all the items in a stack, click the lower frame of the stack as well or click the number (see Figure 2-4).

Note If you'd like to drop a stack of images into an InDesign project, press ALT and click the stack's thumbnail to select the entire group. Otherwise, you'll only select the top thumbnail.

Review File Metadata

Managing assets in Bridge depends on metadata, which is simply information about the file. Metadata ranges from the asset's creation date to the frame rate of a video clip to its color palette. Bridge uses the stored metadata as a means of organizing, searching, and filtering your assets. The content shown in the Metadata panel in Bridge varies with the file format.

In Bridge, manage content in the Metadata panel or through the File Info dialog box, duplicated in InDesign. The Metadata panel contains some default read-only data, as well as configurable content. Saving an InDesign file also saves the default metadata, including a thumbnail preview, color swatches, links, and fonts used in the document. Check out Chapter 3 for more information on metadata and the File Info dialog box.

Note Adobe products, such as Bridge, Illustrator, InDesign, and Photoshop, share the same metadata standard, called the eXtensible Metadata Platform (XMP). Writing data in the same format allows for data exchange across publishing workflows. Other forms of metadata, such as Tagged Image File Format (TIFF) or Exchangeable Image File Format (EXIF), are synchronized and described with XMP for sharing.

Summary

This chapter looked at using Adobe Bridge as a method for organizing and managing assets. Although I featured images in the examples, the processes work equally well with other assets, such as audio and video.

There's much more to working with Bridge than what's included in these few pages; look for additional information in other chapters, including:

- Find out how to start a new document from a prepared InDesign template in Chapter 3 and how to add and edit file information.

- Learn how to review and place files in your documents from Adobe Bridge, drag assets from Bridge into InDesign to create snippets, and use metadata in the File Info dialog box in Chapter 10.

- Discover how color settings are synchronized using Bridge across color-managed Creative Suite components in Chapter 15.

Coming up next—in addition to using Bridge to track down templates for starting a new document—see how to start, save, and reopen InDesign documents; work with document presets; and handle master pages.

3

Start a New Publication

How to...

- Start a new document
- Add and change pages
- Work with master pages and templates
- Save and reopen files

The fundamental purpose of InDesign CS4 is building documents of varying types. The wide range of available options seems almost overwhelming until you reach a certain comfort level.

At its core, we're looking at several principal functions in document construction. First, creating a new document, either from scratch or based on a template. Second, including the pages for your project, whether a one-page letter or a ten-page brochure. Third, assigning recurring elements to master pages, which are then attached to the document pages. These master pages save time and provide consistency in your layouts. And, finally, saving and reopening the files for further use.

In this chapter, you'll see how these functions are performed and discover many ways InDesign assists in producing consistent and attractive publications.

Create New Documents

Take a few minutes to plan ahead before starting a new project. At a minimum, decide on your page size and the type of document planned. For example, the configuration for a newsletter requires a different setup than that for a web page.

Pick Your Settings

Regardless of the sort of document you are planning, all new documents start the same way. Follow these steps to start a new document:

1. Choose File | New | Document to open the New Document dialog box.

2. Select a page size and other document items, described in the following section.

3. Choose margins and columns settings if desired. If you intend to use bleed and slug areas, click More Options and choose the extension dimensions (see Figure 3-1).

4. Click OK to close the dialog box and start the new document.

Customize Your Options

Specify settings for the new document in the dialog box, described in the preceding set of steps. The options are listed in Table 3-1.

FIGURE 3-1 Choose settings to start a new document.

Reuse Your Settings

One way to save time, maintain consistency, and prevent errors is through document presets. When you're finished working in the New Document dialog box, click Save Preset prior to starting your document. You can define a preset whenever you like, not only when starting a new document. Choose File | Document Presets | Define, and click New in the Document Presets dialog box.

In the resulting dialog box, name your new preset and choose the layout options. Click OK to close the dialog box. To use your new preset, choose File | Document Presets to open the list, now including your custom preset, as you see here. Press SHIFT and click the name of your custom preset. A new document opens based on your preset, bypassing the New Document dialog box.

Setting	Use
Facing Pages	Use this default selection for double-page spreads, such as a magazine or book, where the document contains left and right pages. Deselect for single-page documents, such as letters and posters.
Master Text Frame	Choose this option (deselected by default) to place a text frame the full size of the page within the margins on the A-Master.
Page Size	Choose one of the preconfigured page sizes from the drop-down list.
Width and Height	Type alternate values or use the arrows to reset the Width or Height setting. Page Size renames to *Custom* as soon as you change the value.
Orientation	Portrait and Landscape orientation icons display according to the Page Size settings. Click the nonselected orientation icon to swap values.
Columns	Specify the number of columns for the document and the width of the *gutter*, the margin between the columns.
Margins	Change the value for one or all margins, which are identical and linked by default (read more in Chapter 4).
Bleed and Slug	Click More Options at the upper-right area of the dialog box to display bleed and slug settings, set at 0 by default. *Bleed* specifies an area beyond the margins where objects at the edges of the page should extend to prevent misalignment errors during printing. *Slug* refers to the outer edge of the page, trimmed after printing (read more in Chapter 17).

TABLE 3-1   Settings You Can Choose for a New Document

You Can Add Custom Page Sizes

Well, you certainly can. If you regularly use a custom page size, edit an InDesign preset file to include your desired dimensions. In the InDesign application folder on your hard drive, open the New Doc Sizes.txt file located in the Presets | Page Sizes | [language] | folder. Follow the instructions in the file to include your custom document size. Once you save the new information in the file, your custom size is listed in the New Document and Document Settings dialog boxes.

Start from a Template

Many InDesign documents are variations of other documents, such as letterhead or a newsletter. Instead of starting from scratch, assemble the content and save it as a reusable template.

A template offers everything in the file at the time it's saved as a template, including all of the layout features, images, text, graphics, and fonts. Save the file as an INDT (InDesign template) file. The next time you want to start a new version of your document, choose File | Open to locate and select the template file, which opens as an unnamed InDesign file.

You access the dozens of templates that ship with InDesign in a slightly different manner. Choose File | New | Document from Template to open Adobe Bridge, displaying the template folders in the Contents panel. Locate the template you want to use, and double-click its thumbnail to open it in InDesign, still as a template file. Be sure to save the template as an InDesign file to prevent overwriting the original template.

Handle Document Pages

InDesign sets pages as individual pages or as parts of spreads if you specify Facing Pages in the document setup. You're looking at a spread right now, in fact. A spread refers to a pair of pages—left and right—that you view in a book. Each individual page or spread overlays its own pasteboard, a handy area for placing objects for your project.

FIGURE 3-2 Customize the layout of the Pages panel for convenience.

Customize the View

Maybe you work with presentation-type materials that include page transitions, or you need to keep track of when a page uses transparency. Or what if you work with a single master and dozens of pages? Instead of leaving the Pages panel in its default layout showing small thumbnails, customize it to suit your project and work style, like the example shown in Figure 3-2.

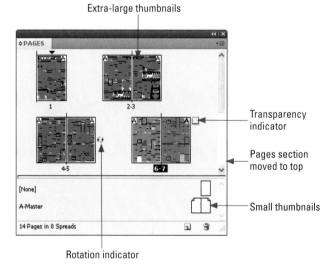

Extra-large thumbnails

Transparency indicator

Pages section moved to top

Small thumbnails

Rotation indicator

Choose Panel Options from the Pages panel's menu to open the Panel Options dialog box. Make your selections, and click OK to close the dialog box and apply the changes. Your modification choices include:

- Choose a page icon size from the Pages and Master sections. Also, specify whether to show the pages vertically and whether to show thumbnails of the actual content. By the way, *Extra Small* and *Small* size icons can't show thumbnail content.

- Specify the icons to show next to the page thumbnails, including transparency, page transitions, and spread rotation.

- Choose whether Master (the default) or Pages appears on top in the Pages panel.

- Specify whether Pages and Master sections of the panel resize as you change the panel's dimensions. You can choose both, or fix one of the sections.

Wrangle Document Pages

Like most programs, you aren't restricted to the page or item you start with in InDesign. Several useful techniques help organize, reorder, and modify the number of pages in your document.

Make sure you're selecting the right element. If you select an item on a page or its pasteboard, the corresponding page or spread auto-selects in the Pages panel. To select a page in the Pages panel, click its icon; to select a spread, click the page numbers below the spread icon in the Pages panel. To show a page in the document window, double-click the page icon in the Pages panel.

Do the Shuffle

How you go about managing your pages with a minimum of irritation and unpleasant surprises depends on a few rules, the biggest of which is page shuffling.

When you design a new document, the pages shuffle by default, meaning a story on Page 3 can move to Page 4 if you insert another page after Page 2. On the other hand, if the content on Pages 2–3 is meant to display together, and only together, then the pages shouldn't shuffle.

To specify page shuffling for an entire document, choose Allow Document Pages to Shuffle from the Pages menu (or right-click anywhere on the Pages panel and choose the command from the shortcut menu). You'll see the Allow Selected Spread to Shuffle command active as well.

Tip If you have a circumstance like the previous example, where Pages 2–3 must stay together, select the spread, and then deselect the Allow Selected Spread to Shuffle command from the shortcut or Pages panel's menu.

Adjust Page Orders, Counts, and Contents

Adding, deleting, duplicating, and moving pages in InDesign involve more than you might find in other programs. In addition to simply adding more pages to the document, InDesign lets you control how the pages are redistributed according to whether you allow page shuffling.

The following sections describe common page manipulations, the quickest way to perform them, and things to watch out for.

Add One or More Pages Select the page or spread to precede the new content. Click New Page on the Pages panel's toolbar to add the page using the same master as the active page. To add multiple pages, choose Insert Pages from the shortcut or Pages panel's menu to open the Insert Pages dialog box. Specify the number of pages, where you want to start, and which master to apply.

Change the Page Order Select a page or spread and drag it to a new location. As you drag, notice the vertical bar that designates the page's position when you release the mouse. The vertical bar may show in the middle of a spread or between spreads. Specialized icons show where the page is inserted (Figure 3-3 shows a composite of several actions). The placement of the page when you release the mouse depends on page shuffling.

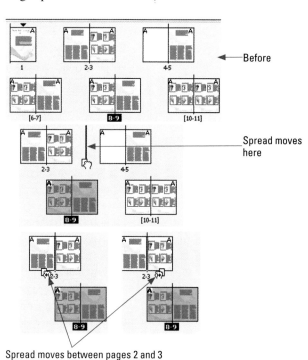

FIGURE 3-3 Move pages in and out of spreads.

Before

Spread moves here

Spread moves between pages 2 and 3

Threads between text frames are preserved. When you have objects that span multiple pages, the object stays where it covers the most area.

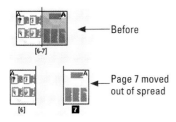

◄──── Before

Page 7 moved
out of spread ◄────

Move a Page out of a Spread   You can also move a page out of a spread. First, deselect Allow Selected Spread to Shuffle in the shortcut or Pages panel's menu. Then, drag the page out of the spread and drop it when the vertical placement bar is away from other page icons. You'll have two single-page spreads as a result.

Duplicate Pages or Spreads   Select the page, spread, or range of pages you want to duplicate. Press ALT and drag the duplicate set from the selection. Drop the duplicate content in its new location. All of the objects on the duplicated page or spreads are duplicated. If there are text threads on the original pages, they are included on the duplicate pages, but the originals aren't threaded to the duplicates.

Control Publications Using Master Pages

If you've ever had to duplicate the layout of a document several times, substitute content, and force all versions to look the same, you'll appreciate working with a master page. In a production situation, master pages are even more useful due to their portability. You can save a set of master pages, apply them repeatedly, and then updates made to the masters automatically are reflected in the documents containing those masters when you reopen them.

Every document you create has a default master page, whether or not there's any content. The master page has its own component of the document's structure, fundamentally serving as a background layer for the document. Master pages offer a considerable amount of manipulation, as you'll see in this section.

Build a Master Page

There are several ways to design a master page. The optimal method depends on what you're designing and how far your design process has evolved.

Start a New Master

In many projects, you'll find the best
way to start a new master is from scratch.
To get started, choose New Master from
the Pages panel's menu to open the New
Master dialog box, shown here.

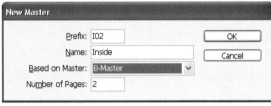

Specify a prefix and name for the
master. A basic document names the master *A-Master* by
default; in the New Master dialog box, InDesign assigns *B* as
the default prefix and *Master* as the default name. You can use
up to four characters for the prefix and type any name you like,
useful for complex parent/child master structures.

By default, the Based on Master setting specifies *None*.
However, you can select an existing master in your current
document from the drop-down list. Finally, specify the number
of pages in your new master (up to ten) and click OK to close
the dialog box and add your new master page(s).

Modify an Existing Master

Any existing master page can be modified. Select the name of
the master in the Pages panel, and choose Master Options For
[*name*] from the shortcut menu or the Pages panel's menu to
open the Master Options dialog box, offering the same choices
as the New Master dialog box.

Define a Master from an Existing Page or Spread

You can instantly convert any page to a master page simply
by dragging the spread in the Pages panel from the Pages to
the Master section. Anything on the original page or spread
becomes part of the new master. And if the page you define as
a new master itself had a master, the new one is based on the
original page's master.

Suppose you've been working on an annual report and
like the master for the financial data. You like it so much, in
fact, that you want to reuse it in another document. It's easy.
Simply drag the master page or spread you like from the Master
section in the Pages panel and drop it into the other document,
where it's added to the Pages panel (it's also applied to the
active page). Copying a master in this way doesn't link the two
documents.

Import a Master from Another Document

An active document can include imported masters from any other InDesign document. As long as the master pages have different names, those in your current document won't change. Choose Load Master Pages from the Pages panel's menu to display the Open a File dialog box. Locate and select the InDesign document that includes the master pages you want to reuse, and click Open.

In cases where there are duplicate master names, the Load Master Page Alert dialog box appears. If you want to replace the existing master pages, click Replace Master Pages. On the other hand, if you want to keep the existing pages and add the additional ones, click Rename Master Pages. The new masters are added to your document using the letter subsequent to your existing master pages.

Imported masters are linked from the source document to the destination document (the one receiving the imported masters). Updating the master in the source document also updates the master in the destination document when you reload the master files.

Display Visual Page Numbers

Follow these steps to add automatic page numbering:

1. Open the master page where you want to insert the page number, and draw a text frame in the number's location.

2. Choose Type | Insert Special Character | Markers | Current Page Number. You'll see the prefix for the master page as a character in the text frame.

3. Configure the appearance of the text marker as you would for any other text frame.

4. Close the master page. Pages to which the master page is applied now show the page numbers.

Note If you expand a document to a larger-sized publication, such as a technical manual, you often use sections, parts, or chapters. Read about multilevel page numbering in Chapter 9.

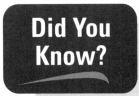

Master Pages Can Have Parents

Although the circumstances get fairly complex, you can base one master on another. Be sure to plan ahead for this process. Suppose you are designing a manual for a product containing several sections. Each component of a section, such as a table of illustrations, index, or procedures, uses its own master structure. When the parent master is updated, all children masters update as well.

Apply and Manage Master Pages

Master pages aren't static. You can manipulate the objects that display on a master page, or *master items,* by applying, hiding, or overriding them.

How to Use a Master

Control masters in the same way as items in most panels. That is, drop an existing master on the trash can icon to delete it; drop an existing master on the New Master icon to duplicate it; or click New Master to create a new blank master.

FIGURE 3-4 Apply a master to an individual page or a spread.

Here are more basics of using masters in your documents:

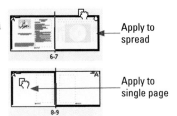

■ Drag a master page icon to a page icon to apply it; if you want to apply a master to a spread, drag it to the edge of the page spread, and drop it when you see the spread framed in black (see Figure 3-4).

■ To apply a master to multiple pages, select the pages in the Pages panel, press ALT/OPTION, and click the master.

■ Would you like to remove the master? No problem. Simply click the None master.

■ If you want to see or print a document without viewing its master page, select the pages, and choose Hide Master Items from the Pages panel's menu. To restore their visibility, select the pages or spreads and choose Show Master Items from the Pages panel's menu.

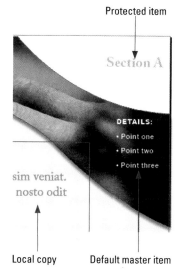

Protected item

Section A

DETAILS:
• Point one
• Point two
• Point three

sim veniat.
nosto odit

Local copy   Default master item

Override a Master Item's Attributes

Suppose you have section introduction pages in a project and want two versions that are nearly the same. You'd like different sections to use different colors and subsections to use fewer objects than the full master displays. One more criterion—you'd like the section numbers to show, regardless of what happens to the master. It's a tall order, but InDesign can handle it.

To override an item's attributes, SHIFT-CLICK to select it on the page, and make the desired changes. You'll see that the bounding box for local copies of master items is solid rather than dotted. Later changes made on the master won't affect the overrides on the local copies, although other modifications are updated on the local copy, shown here.

One other criterion is that the section numbering should always look the same. To make sure you protect it to prevent unintentional changes, select the numbering objects, right-click to display the shortcut menu, and deselect Allow Master Item Overrides. The protected master items don't display a frame edge (like the *Section A* label in the illustration).

Tip Threaded text frames are an all-or-nothing case. If you have a threaded frame that extends over two or more pages, overriding the text frame on one page overrides the entire thread.

You can override a range of items on a master page—enough to create significantly different versions of the same page. Your options include strokes and fills, transformations, lock states, frame contents and corner options, text frame options, and transparency and object effects.

Restore Overridden Items

Fortunately, if you change your mind, you can override your override, so to speak. You can remove overrides for all objects or selected objects on one spread at a time.

- Target the spread in the Pages panel, and choose Remove All Local Overrides in the Pages panel's menu to remove all the overrides.

- Select the object or objects you want to revert, and then target the spread and choose the menu command, shown as Remove Selected Local Overrides.

After removing an override, items assume the master's state again and update in the future as the master updates.

Save and Reopen Documents

InDesign saves much more than what you see on your computer screen. You'll also save links to source files, the current display and zoom level, and your present layout. You can decide whether to include a thumbnail preview, based on where you like to work with your files. These stored parameters are included with the rest of the file's *metadata,* or file information.

Choose a Save Option

InDesign offers different ways to save a file. The option you choose depends on your workflow and what you intend to do with the file later. Choose one of the saving methods described in the following paragraphs.

Save a Document   To save a regular InDesign (INDD) document, choose File | Save. The first time you save the file, you'll see the Save As dialog box. After that, choose File | Save (or use CTRL-S) to save the content since the last time the file was saved. Choose a file format in the Save As dialog box, and click Save to save the file using the chosen name and folder location.

Save a Document Copy   In some workflows, it makes sense to save a copy of a publication at a particular state of development. For example, you may plan two or three versions you'd like to present to a client. As you reach a particular point in the workflow where the content or layout diverges, save a copy. Choose File | Save a Copy to open the Save dialog box. You'll see the filename with *copy* appended by default. Click Save to save the copy as an INDD file and close the dialog box, returning you to the original document.

 Lots of us work with several open files at one time. Save each file in its current location using the CTRL-ALT-SHIFT-S shortcut keys.

Save Backward for Compatibility   You can't open an InDesign CS4 document directly in InDesign CS3. Instead, export the file using InDesign CS3 Interchange (INX) format. Open InDesign CS3, and choose File | Open to convert the file to an InDesign CS3 document. What if you want to go back further than CS3? Once you open the INX file in InDesign CS3, export it again in INX format, which is compatible with InDesign CS2. Each time you export an INX file for an older program version, features exclusive to a newer version are omitted, of course.

Save a Template   Often, you develop publications that are intended for reuse at another time. You may develop a letterhead or a newsletter for monthly distribution, or a sales report that updates weekly. Once you've designed the publication to your satisfaction, choose File | Save As to open the Save As dialog box. Name the file and choose a storage location. Select InDesign CS4 Template (INDT) from the Save as Type drop-down list, and click Save. The next time you start a file using the template, you'll have the desired layout, fonts, text, graphics, and other repeating content at your fingertips, ready to go.

Include Previews

A thumbnail helps you identify your document when you're looking for files in Bridge or Version Cue. InDesign generates the thumbnail preview as a square Joint Photographic Experts Group (JPEG) image each time you save the file. A regular InDesign document produces a thumbnail of the first spread, while a template thumbnail generates images for each page in the template.

Thumbnails add to file size, of course, and aren't necessary if you never look for files via Bridge or Version Cue. On the other hand, if you work with many similarly named, detail-intensive files, you may want an extra-large 1024-pixel preview generated for every file.

■   To include a preview every time you save a document, choose Edit | Preferences | File Handling. Choose the Always Save Preview Images with Documents check box, and choose a thumbnail size from the Preview Size drop-down list. Sizes range from 128 pixels to 1024 pixels. Click OK to close the dialog box and save the preference.

▓ Sometimes it's useful to have thumbnails, particularly if you share files with others and aren't sure of their methods for locating content, or produce templates intended for sharing. In these cases, when you save the file, choose Save Preview in the Save As dialog box in Windows. On Mac, the Always Save Preview Images with Documents setting is selected by default—deselect it to prevent saving a thumbnail. Save the file as usual. The thumbnail generated uses the default size of 256 × 256.

Look Under the Hood

The File Info dialog box contains a great deal of information about your document. Some data is constant and based on external information, such as camera settings. Other data changes according to a file's status, such as the program layout and zoom settings stored each time you save a document in InDesign. Still other types of data let you enter your own information.

FIGURE 3-5 Specify data for the file in the File Info dialog box.

In InDesign, choose File | File Info to open the File Info dialog box (see Figure 3-5).

Many types of data can be stored in a document, ranging from a description to mobile Shockwave Flash (SWF) settings. Scroll through the tabs and lists to find data items.

Several common data categories you'll encounter include:

▓ **Description** Metadata descriptions include information about the file. Here you'll find the document title, author, copyright information, a description of the document, and keywords. Click a field to activate it and enter information.

- **IPTC**   The International Press Telecommunications Council (IPTC) maintains metadata standards for image cataloging in four areas. Describe the visual content of the image in the Content field, list contact details for the author or photographer in the Contact area, provide additional information about the content in the Image section, and show workflow and copyright data in the Status section.

- **Camera Data**   Camera Data describes read-only data captured with the image. Camera Data 1 includes data about the camera and settings used, including the make, model, shutter speed, and f-stop. Camera Data 2 lists read-only file information about the photograph, such as dimensions, resolution, and file format.

If you regularly use eXtensible Metadata Platform (XMP) metadata, check into saving and reusing templates. Templates are a simple way to attach static content, such as copyright and contact information. Your XMP templates work in InDesign, Photoshop, Illustrator—in fact, any program that accepts XMP metadata.

InDesign Has Your Data Covered in Case of Emergency

You're half an hour from a deadline in a thunderstorm, you lose power momentarily, and your new surge protector is safely stored in its packaging on your desk. InDesign stores duplicate data in a temporary file that is separate from your file storage location.

Reopen InDesign and you'll see one of three possibilities:

- If there is recoverable data, the recovered document opens automatically, showing *[Recovered]* after the file's name. Choose File | Save As and save the file with another name to incorporate the data.

- If you've been unfortunate enough to experience a Windows blue screen event, you'll see a dialog box asking if you want to restore the data. Follow the prompts and cross your fingers.

- If the file doesn't open using automatic recovery, sadly, the data is likely corrupt.

By the way, you can change the data storage location by specifying the document recovery data location in the File Handling preferences area.

Open Existing Documents

In many programs, opening a file simply means specifying the file to view. In InDesign CS4, however, there are a few ways to open a file, depending on what you intend to do in the program.

Choose a File

To get started, choose File | Open to display the Open dialog box. Locate and select your file, and select whether to open the file as a Normal, Original, or Copy version of the document. Your options include:

- Choose Normal/Open Normal to open your latest version of a document or template. This is the default, and opens a file in the same state as it was when last saved.

- Choose Original to open the starting version of a document or template. Sometimes, you want to generate variations of a document for similar output.

- Choose Copy to open a copy of the latest version of the document or template. Again, you may want to generate variations, but with modifications from the original.

If you want to use one of the files you've worked with recently, choose File | Open Recent, and select one of the documents.

 Do you rely on the Recent Documents list and wish there were a few more files listed? Change the preference: Choose Edit | Preferences | File Handling in the Preferences dialog box, type a value in the Number Of Recent Items to Display field, click OK, and you're good to go.

Warning!

Your InDesign publication files aren't static, stand-alone entities. In many cases, you're working with associated color profiles, ancillary files, and fonts. When you open a file, InDesign checks for associated content and displays warning messages if there are issues.

Color Profile Mismatch　Color profiles are an important print issue. InDesign lets you choose options in the Color Settings dialog box to display mismatch warnings. You'll receive a warning when the program finds different color settings in the file you're opening from those used in InDesign. Click OK to close the warning, choose an option in the Profile or Policy Mismatch dialog box, and click OK. (Read about color policies in Chapter 14.)

Missing Links   We're not referring to the mythical creature that bridged the ape/man chasm, but links from images or other placed content. InDesign tracks files associated with your document and displays a warning in the Links panel if the linked content is missing or modified, shown here. Click Fix Links Automatically to have the program locate missing links, or click Don't Fix to bypass the location process. (Read about links and restoring them in Chapter 10.)

Missing Fonts   When you open a file using fonts that InDesign can't find on your computer, you'll receive a warning listing the missing fonts. You can click Find Font to locate the missing font or define a substitute, or click OK to let InDesign use a default font. (See Chapter 5 to learn about working with fonts.)

Summary

A fundamental part of learning about any software program is the care and handling of files, the subject of this chapter. Keep in mind that if you perform any sort of repetitive, settings-based activity in InDesign, there's probably a way to save the settings for reuse.

In this chapter, you saw how to choose settings for a new document, how to customize settings, and how to save them for reuse as a document preset. Instead of opening a blank file, you can start from a template, which contains preconfigured items, from master pages to frames, images to text.

To successfully work in InDesign, it's important to understand how pages, spreads, and master pages work, and how to manipulate them on the document window or in the Pages panel. We looked at a variety of ways to control document pages and examined master pages in some depth.

The latter part of the chapter described methods for saving files, including templates and file previews. You had a look at some of the file information content included in the InDesign file. The chapter wound up with discussions on how to open existing documents (not as straightforward as you may have thought!) and how to handle missing items.

Up next, check into more page features. You'll see how to use different methods for navigating a document and features like margins, guides, and grids to help lay out your pages.

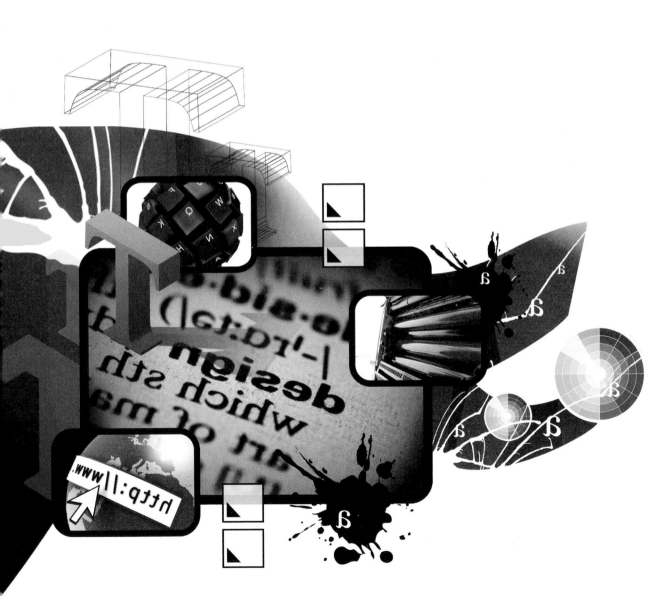

4

Navigate and View
an InDesign Document

How to...

- Navigate within your InDesign documents
- Switch between layers
- Zoom in and out and pan around
- Preview your document
- View your rulers
- Adjust margins and columns
- Use guides, grids, and Smart features

Figuring out how to get around is important—whether you're navigating in your car in a new city or using software that's unfamiliar to you. While InDesign's interface is pretty simple and intuitive, it's also very rich, which means there are a lot of features to work with and understand.

When it comes to navigation, you have many options for moving between pages and documents, as well as moving around within your pages. You also have several options for how you zoom in on your work for those jobs that require getting really close to the page for accuracy and to step back when you need to see the big picture.

Other tools, which help you move around and view different parts of your document, are essential for consistent placement of your document's objects—things like the ruler, the guides, and the grid. These enable you to make precise adjustments to the location and relationships between objects on the page and within the page itself.

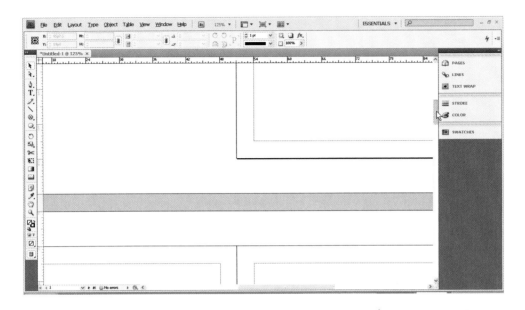

FIGURE 4-1 The scrollbar on the right represents the entirety of your document; you can use it to scroll from beginning to end, stopping on the page you want to see or work on.

Move Between Pages

Imagine you have a ten-page document. Or a 100-page document. And you want to go from page 2 to page 9 (or 99) quickly. What to do? InDesign offers several choices, each useful in its own way, depending on the circumstances.

- Drag the scrollbar on the right side of the workspace until the page you want is in view, as shown in Figure 4-1.

- Choose Layout | Go to Page and enter the desired page number in the dialog box, as shown in Figure 4-2.

- Use the controls in the lower-left corner to select a page from the pop-up list, or use the arrow buttons to move forward and backward, as shown in Figure 4-3.

- Use the Pages panel by double-clicking the icon for the page you want to go to, as shown in Figure 4-4.

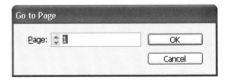

FIGURE 4-2 Can't be more specific than this—type a page number, and click OK.

With all these options, you won't have any trouble moving from page to page. No one way is better than another; each one is convenient, depending on what you're doing, how many pages you have, and, most of all, your preference.

FIGURE **4-3** Select a page by number or move through your pages incrementally.

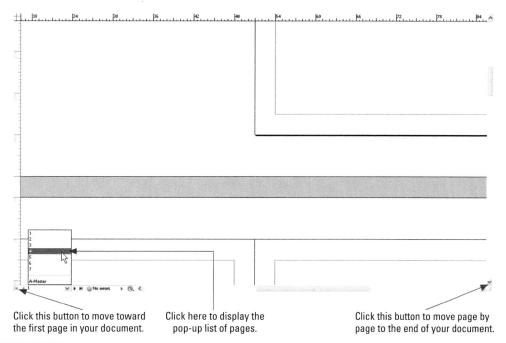

FIGURE **4-3** Select a page by number or move through your pages incrementally.

Click this button to move toward the first page in your document.

Click here to display the pop-up list of pages.

Click this button to move page by page to the end of your document.

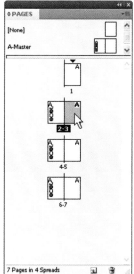

FIGURE **4-4** Go to any page by double-clicking its Pages panel icon.

Maneuver Layers

As Chapter 13 explains, layers are important to your InDesign documents. While you don't have to use layers to separate your objects, it can be convenient and empowering to do so, and if you're using them, it's important to know how to move around between them and display their contents.

First, to move between layers, you need the Layers panel to be displayed (choose Window | Layers if you don't see it in the dock), and then you need to click the layer you want to work with. To hide a layer, as shown in Figure 4-5, you simply click the visibility icon, or "the eye."

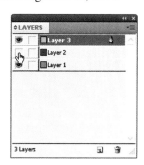

FIGURE **4-5** Hide your layers by clicking the eye.

To redisplay a hidden layer, click the empty box where the eye was, and the eye and your layer return to visibility.

To rearrange layers, simply drag them in the Layers panel. Moving them moves their content in terms of its stacking order, which is typically the reason one moves layers in the first place. As shown in Figure 4-6, to move a layer and bring its content to the top of the stack of any overlapping content on other layers, drag the layer up in the Layers panel.

Of course, as discussed in Chapter 13, to move content from layer to layer, you have several choices: You can cut it (Edit | Cut) from one layer and paste it (Edit | Paste) to another (as long as Paste Remembers Layers is off in the Layers panel menu), or you can create the content with a particular layer selected in the first place.

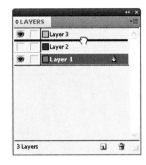

FIGURE 4-6 Restack your layers within the Layers panel.

Zoom and Pan

Zooming and panning are almost as much fun as they sound. Zooming allows you to quickly zoom in on, or get closer to, any object in or area of your document. You can also zoom out, or get farther away from your document, when you need to see everything at once. Panning, of course, is your key to visually moving around in the document, so that even when you're close to the document (zoomed in tight) you can quickly view something on the left side of a spread and then something on the right side—or on the previous or next spread.

Zooming In and Out

Some of your work in InDesign will require that you view an object—or even just part of an object—at a very high magnification, or zoom. If you're repositioning wrap points around an image, for example, or trying to place two objects "just so" relative to each other or to the edge of the page, you'll want to be as close as possible to the objects themselves. To zoom in tight, try any of these methods:

■ Use the Zoom tool, which is activated by pressing the z key or clicking the tool in the Toolbox, shown in Figure 4-7. By default, the tool zooms in with each

FIGURE 4-7 Focus on a particular object by clicking it with the Zoom tool selected.

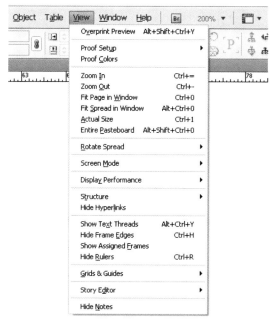

FIGURE 4-8 The View menu offers several ways to get closer to or farther away from your document.

click (or you can drag around an area to focus the zoom on a particular spot), or you can press the ALT key to zoom out with each click.

■ Press the ALT key as you roll the scroll wheel on your mouse. Roll up to zoom in close; roll down to zoom out.

■ Use the View menu, as shown in Figure 4-8. The commands, Zoom In, Zoom Out, Fit Page in Window, Fit Spread in Window, Actual Size, and Entire Pasteboard, are handy when you want to achieve any of those perspectives on your work.

■ Use the keyboard. You've got several keyboard shortcuts (also listed with their companion commands in the View menu) to choose from.

■ Zoom in with CTRL-=.

■ Zoom out with CTRL-–.

■ Fit the page to the window with CTRL-0 (zero).

■ Fit the spread to the window with ALT-CTRL-0 (zero).

■ See your work in actual size with CTRL-1.

■ View the entire pasteboard—the page/s and the space around them—with the long and finger-intensive ALT-SHIFT-CTRL-0 (zero) keyboard combination.

Tip Mac users will use the COMMAND key wherever CTRL is referenced in the previous list and the OPTION key instead of ALT. See the sidebar "How To Interpret Commands for Use on Mac" in Chapter 1 for a complete list of Mac equivalents.

Panning Around

The Hand tool, shown in Figure 4-9, lets you move around in a document by clicking the workspace and dragging your mouse. You can use it at any level of zoom, but it's handiest when you're zoomed in tight and don't want to have to zoom back out to see the next area you need to look at and then zoom back in. Instead, pan from place to place, page to page, until you're looking at what you want to see. As also shown in Figure 4-9, your mouse pointer turns to a hand when the Hand tool is active. Your mouse turns to a fist when you click your mouse to pan around.

FIGURE 4-9 Click the Hand tool (or press the h key) to pan within your document.

When you're using the Hand tool, you can quickly switch to the Selection tool on a temporary basis by pressing the CTRL key. With the key pressed, you can move any object you click, and then return to the Hand tool when you release the key.

New to InDesign CS4 is the Power Zoom feature. Using the Hand tool, press and hold down the mouse button, and the view automatically zooms out to show the current page and the entire surrounding pasteboard. A red box indicating the area that's visible also appears, just before the zoom. Once Power Zoom has occurred, use your scroll wheel at the same time you're holding down the left mouse button, and you can resize the red box and move your mouse to focus on an area you want to zoom in on.

Use Preview Options

In most applications, previewing is a step done just before you print, as in Print Preview, a command typically found in the File menu. InDesign, however, gives you more and better options than that through a variety of view modes that allow you to see your document as close to print quality as possible—or in a more "draft" look, where you're just looking at overall layout and are not concerned with the details or exact appearance of your artwork or text. Of course, options for a compromise between these two ends of the preview spectrum also exist, allowing you to see your document in relatively fine detail, but without the drain on your display speed or system resources that a higher-quality display can create.

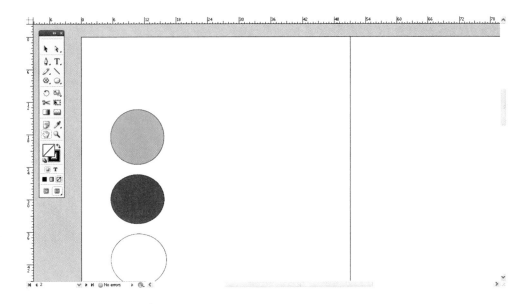

FIGURE 4-10 View your document's bleed area to see what's placed outside the margin.

Like your tools for navigating an InDesign document, your preview options are plentiful, and the ones you choose will be based on the situation you're in at the time. Here are your options:

▨ Use the View | Screen Mode submenu. Choose from Normal, Preview, Bleed, or Slug. Normal view keeps your margin guides onscreen, as well as your frame edges for all or selected objects (press CTRL-H to toggle between seeing all objects' frame edges or just the selected object's frames). Preview hides the margin guides and other nonprinting items, and Bleed and Slug show you those areas—hiding the pasteboard so that you don't confuse items that are simply dragged to that area for later use and those items that are meant to print outside the edges of the page. Figure 4-10 shows the Screen Mode set to Bleed.

▨ Select your display performance. Choose View | Display Performance (see Figure 4-11), and select from Fast, where graphics appear as gray shapes; Typical (for a reasonably good image detail); or High Quality, which shows you your document at near print quality.

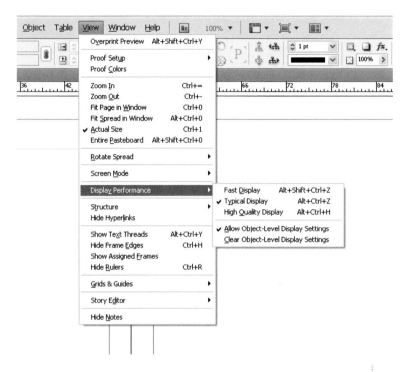

FIGURE 4-11 Pick the quality of your document's display.

This last option does require more system resources, so you won't want to work in it for long. Go back to Typical after you've looked at a page or an object you wanted to check before printing or exporting.

 To change the display performance for the selected object, choose Display Performance from the Object menu.

Set Up the Rulers

Displaying rulers within the InDesign workspace is easy: Just choose View | Show Rulers. If the View menu displays the command Hide Rulers, that means your rulers are already displayed, as shown in Figure 4-12, and choosing this command will remove the rulers from the workspace.

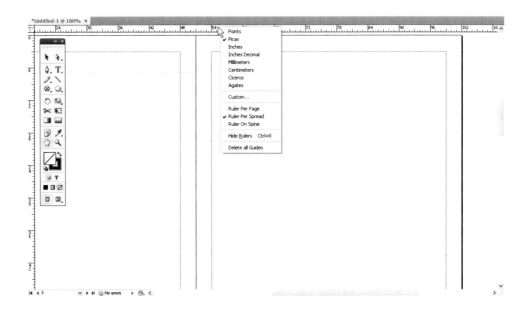

FIGURE 4-12 Right-click the ruler and decide how you want to measure your InDesign document and its objects.

FIGURE 4-13 Set the custom units for the ruler you right-clicked.

Once the rulers are in place, you can edit them, choosing the measurement type they'll display, or even set up your own increments for a completely custom ruler. As shown in Figure 4-12, if you right-click either ruler, you can make your choices from the pop-up menu.

If you choose Custom from the pop-up menu, the Custom Measurement Unit dialog box appears, as shown in Figure 4-13. This dialog box enables you to enter a value that determines the calibrations on your ruler. For example, if you enter 10 points, the ruler will display the currently selected measurement method in increments of 10.

It's important to note that you can set up different measurement methods and units for each of the two rulers. For example, the horizontal ruler can be set to inches and the vertical to picas or any other combination of the available methods. The Custom Measurement Unit dialog box can also be applied to each ruler independently, so you can have different units on each of your rulers.

To set the measurement method for not only the rulers but all other measuring devices—dialog boxes, control panel fields, panels, etc.—you need to access the Preferences submenu by choosing Edit | Preferences (the Preferences command is in the

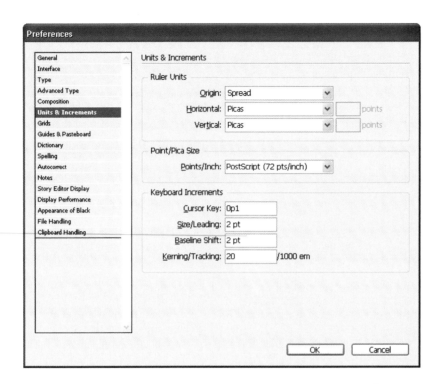

InDesign menu for Mac users). From the Preferences submenu, choose Units & Increments, and the Preferences dialog box appears, shown in Figure 4-14.

Note that you can set not only the ruler units (and for each of your rulers independently), but also set the point/pica size and the keyboard increments for panel fields that allow you to click the up and down arrows to increment and decrement the values for things such as indents, text wrap, and baseline shift.

Once you've set up your rulers' measurement units, you can customize the rulers even further. The Ruler Per Page, Per Spread, and On Spine commands in the pop-up menu (displayed when you right-click either ruler) enable you to choose how the rulers are oriented. If you choose Per Spread (the default) or Per Page, you can also reset the zero point for the rulers by dragging the origin, as shown in Figure 4-15. Drag the origin diagonally from the corner where the two rulers meet, and release your mouse when the vertical and horizontal lines that follow your mouse are on the rulers at the points that you want zero (0) to appear.

FIGURE 4-14 Want to measure in inches rather than picas? Centimeters rather than inches? Make your choices in the Preferences dialog box.

Drag from this point to set your zero points.

Watch these lines to see where your horizontal and vertical rulers' zero points are set.

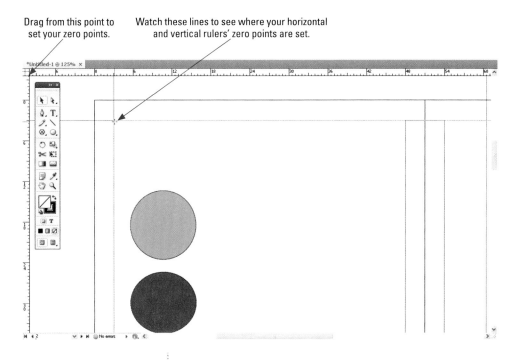

FIGURE 4-15 Measure by the page, spread, or on the document's spine, and set your zero point.

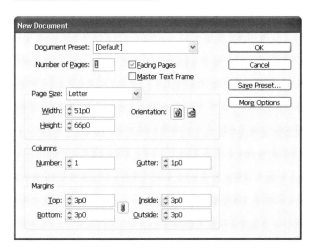

FIGURE 4-16 The New Document dialog box offers options for setting the margins and columns for your document from the start.

Specify Margins and Columns

Typically, you set your margins and columns when you start a new document. The New Document dialog box, shown in Figure 4-16, gives you your first opportunity to establish these key elements for your document's pages. You can set the number of columns and their gutter width, and also set the top, bottom, left, and right margins for the page as a whole. As new pages are added, unless you apply a master with different margin and column settings to them, they'll follow the New Document dialog box.

Of course, you can also change these settings later, for example, when a change in the requirements for a given document are given to you or you alter the plan for the document yourself. How are these after-the-fact changes made? By choosing Layout | Margins and Columns and using the resulting dialog box, shown in Figure 4-17.

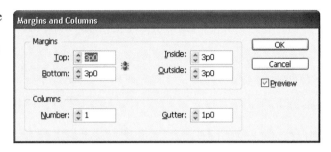

FIGURE 4-17 Make changes to those starting settings through the Margins and Columns dialog box.

Of course, to use this dialog box, you simply enter new values into the fields and click OK. If you want to see what the impact on your document's pages will be, click the Preview check box before confirming anything, and, as needed, move the dialog box aside so you can see the entire document, or at least one of the pages or spreads. The changes take place immediately when you click OK.

Tip If you want to alter the margins and/or columns for a particular page or pages, create a new master and set new margins and columns for that master using the aforementioned Margins and Columns dialog box. Then apply the new master to the pages that should follow these particular settings, and all the other existing pages will continue to follow the current settings applied through the New Document dialog box, or the Margins and Columns dialog box, should changes be made after the document was created. To find out more about creating and working with masters, check out Chapter 3.

Work with Guides and Smart Guides

As the names would indicate—"Guides" and "Smart Guides"—this section is about the onscreen tools that help you position your content. Like guides along a trail through the woods, they keep you on your way and don't let you veer off and get lost. When placing objects in your document, guides keep you from losing the consistency and good composition that's created by lining things up by their sides or midpoints so that your page doesn't look haphazard or thrown together.

So how do you access these guides? It's not like they're standing there waiting for you, providing vertical and horizontal lines by which you can line up your content (that would be the job of the grid, which we'll get to shortly). By default, as you drag objects around in an InDesign document, the Smart Guides appear and tell you when you've got things lined up.

The green guide indicates
the left sides will align.

The blue frame indicates where the red
circle will be once the mouse is released.

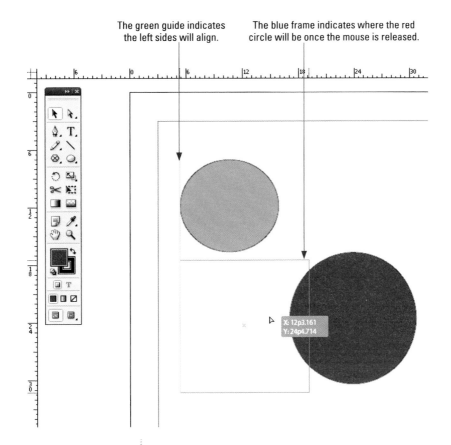

X: 12p3.161
Y: 24p4.714

FIGURE 4-18 Line up objects by their sides, using the guides that appear as you get close to another object on the page.

As shown in Figure 4-18, the guides appear to let us know that the two circles are lined up by their left sides. The guide (the green vertical line) didn't appear until the lower red circle was closer to the left side of the blue circle than to its center or right side. InDesign "guesses" which side of an adjacent object you'd like to line up with and offers guides to tell you when you're in line. If you're centering two objects, a midpoint guide, as shown in Figure 4-19, appears.

Tip   It's possible to have Smart Guides appear on both the left and right sides, as well as the center of the object to which the object you're moving will be aligned. If you're moving something up or down on the page, the Smart Guides can appear on the top and/or bottom (as well as the middle) of the object to which you're aligning.

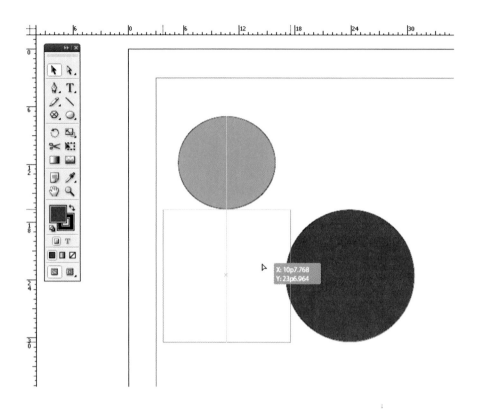

As for Guides, you place these onscreen by dragging from the ruler, as shown in Figure 4-20. Guides you create can be used to line things up manually so you don't have to rely solely on the Smart Guides and so that you can set up a structure for your page and adhere to it more easily. Figure 4-21 shows the guides set up for a newsletter. The guides indicate where the heading graphic will go, the space allocated for a central text frame, and where the page footer can be placed. Putting these guides in place before any content is created or placed allows the designer to map out the document and measure everything, much like an architect's blueprint. The objects can then be drawn or placed within the guides, and assuming Snap to Guides is turned on (View | Grids & Guides | Snap to Guides), it's easy to adhere to them with your mouse as shapes and frames are drawn.

FIGURE 4-19 To center two objects, look for a guide that indicates you're aligned with another object's midpoint.

Tip To move a guide, simply drag it with your mouse using the Selection tool. To delete a guide, click it, also with the Selection tool, and press the DELETE key.

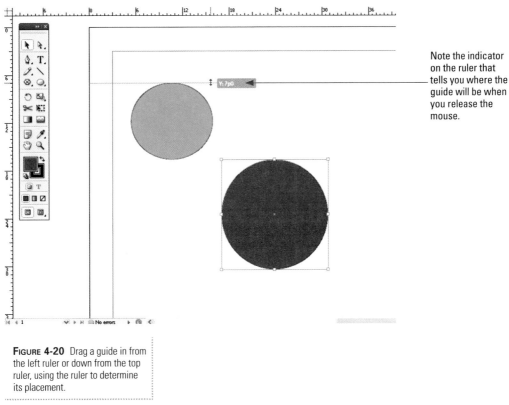

Note the indicator on the ruler that tells you where the guide will be when you release the mouse.

FIGURE 4-20 Drag a guide in from the left ruler or down from the top ruler, using the ruler to determine its placement.

FIGURE 4-21 Set up as many guides as you need to help lay out your document and make sure all of its objects line up easily.

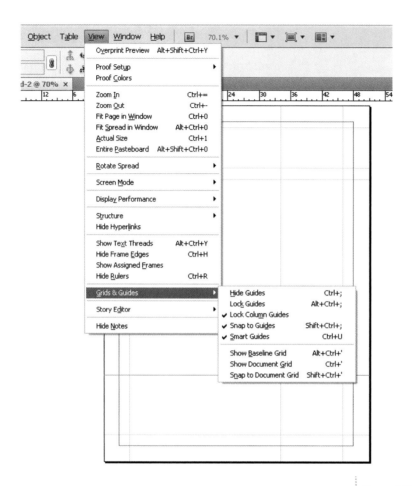

FIGURE 4-22 Decide how guides will be used through the Grids & Guides submenu.

Speaking of that View menu and its Grids & Guides submenu, you'll also find commands for hiding and locking those column guides, as shown in Figure 4-22. The items in the menu that are selected are "on," or in effect. To turn them off, select them again, which removes the check mark.

You'll note that InDesign has chosen colors for your Smart Guides and the guides you create as well. If those colors aren't your favorites, or if the colors in your document make seeing them difficult, you can change them. Choose Edit | Preferences | Guides & Pasteboard, and from the Preferences dialog box (shown in Figure 4-23), choose new colors for the guides, and even for your margins and columns. Just click the colors to the right of each item, and a palette of optional colors appears. Make a choice, and when you're finished selecting new colors for these onscreen features, click OK to apply them.

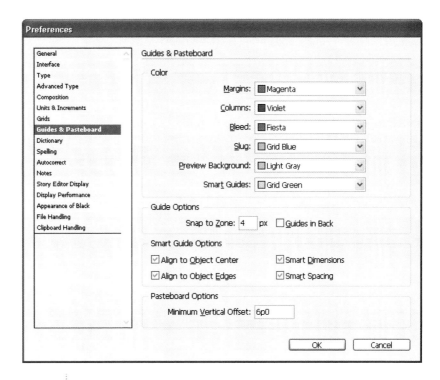

FIGURE 4-23 Choose new colors for guides and other onscreen structural devices through the Preferences dialog box.

 Don't make all your guides and other indicators the same color. It's a good idea to keep some variety in the colors so that you can easily tell these features apart.

Use Smart Object Alignment and Smart Dimensions

Also found in the Preferences dialog box, in the Guides & Pasteboard category, are options for controlling how the Smart Guides work. This includes Smart Dimensions and Smart Spacing, which are also new to CS4—intuitive features that allow you to more easily resize (Smart Dimensions) and distribute (Smart Spacing) objects on the page.

As shown in Figure 4-23, the Smart Guide Options section of the dialog box allows you to turn on these features—or, rather, leave them on, because they're on by default. You can also adjust the Snap to Zone setting (seen just above the Smart Guides Options section), which controls how close you have to get to a guide, lines within the grid, or another object before InDesign will snap to it. The lower the number, the closer you have to get before the snapping feature kicks in.

Once you've made your Smart Guide Options adjustments, click OK to apply them. It's a good idea, of course, to leave them on so you can take full advantage of these helpful features. Smart Dimensions is shown at work in Figure 4-24, where InDesign helps by indicating when the lower circle, which is being resized, is the same width as the circle above it.

FIGURE 4-24 Smart Guides that appear as arrows tell you when a matching width (or height, which would appear as vertical arrows) is achieved.

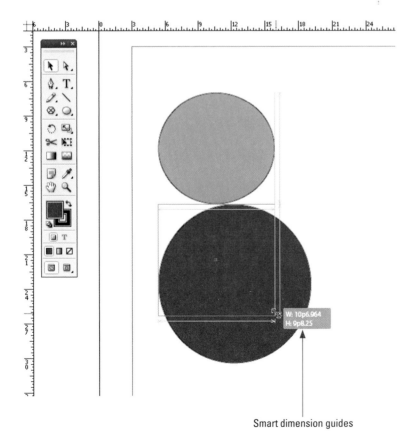

Smart dimension guides

Use Grids

Grids are another way that InDesign helps you line things up on the page. Instead of (or in addition to) the guides you can drag onto the workspace to help you line things up, the grid provides a network of lines that you can choose to snap to so that you have virtually no choice but to line things up in a regimented, linear fashion. The tighter your grid's settings, too, the more regimented that snap will be.

First, to display the grid, choose View | Grids & Guides | Show Document Grid. The result, shown in Figure 4-25, is like a gray sheet of transparent graph paper was placed on your page. The size of the grid is based on the default settings, which you can alter to suit your needs for a tighter or looser grid.

To make the grid more effective, you will want to turn on Snap to Document Grid, which is at the bottom of the Grids & Guides submenu. Once this feature is turned on, as you draw shapes or frames or move objects around, you'll feel your mouse pull toward the grid, making it much easier to line things up horizontally, vertically, and even diagonally.

FIGURE 4-25 The gray grid provides a structure much like graph paper.

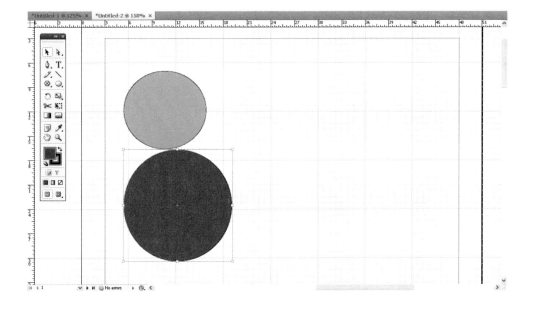

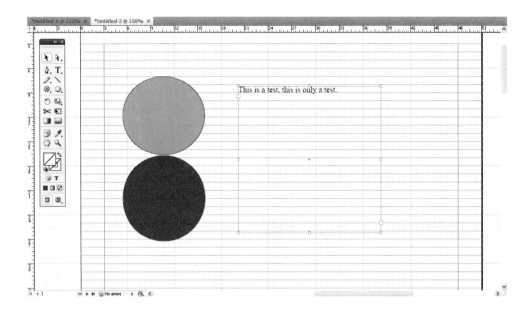

The Baseline Grid, which is also turned on from within the Grids & Guides submenu, applies to text frames and shows the baseline for the lines of text in the frame. This is handy to see if you want to make baseline adjustments, using the Baseline Shift field on the Control panel to raise or lower type relative to the baseline. Figure 4-26 shows the Baseline Grid displayed and text in a text frame seated along that baseline.

Of course, all of these lines can be distracting to look at, so when you're not using them, you can simply reselect them from the Grids & Guides submenu to turn them off. To control their dimensions—the size of the grid and the distance between baselines—you will choose Edit | Preferences | Grids and use the version of the Preferences dialog box shown in Figure 4-27.

Through this dialog box, you can change the color of the grids and control their spacing. Note that the Grids in Back check box is checked, which means objects on the page will not be obscured by the grid.

To adjust the Baseline Grid, you can change its color, where it starts (how far from the top of the page), what it's relative to—Top of Page or Top Margin (if you choose Top Margin, the Start field will measure from that point), how far apart the lines will be (Increment Every), and the view threshold, which controls the magnification below which you can't see the grid.

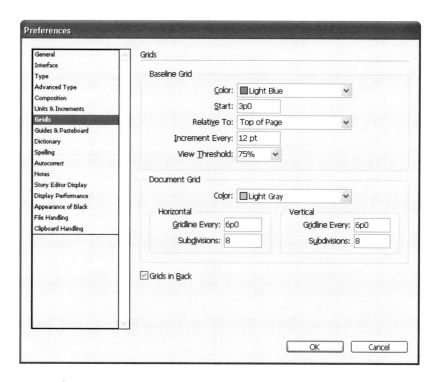

Customize your grids for maximum effectiveness.

You can adjust the color and frequency of the Document Grid using the Gridline Every settings for horizontal and vertical gridlines. The higher the number of subdivisions, the more complex your grid will be.

Tip   Even if you've elected to hide your Document Grid, you can still snap to it. Just leave Snap to Document Grid selected in the Grids & Guides submenu.

Summary

Now that you've completed Chapter 4, you've been introduced to all the ways InDesign provides for moving around in and viewing the various pages of your documents. You can switch between layers, viewing the content on each one (or seeing only certain layers), you can zoom and pan with ease, making it simple to get really close to or far away from your document, and you can preview your document before printing.

You also learned how to add onscreen tools like rulers guides, grids, and the great new "Smart" features that are new in CS4, making your life using InDesign that much easier. In the next chapter, you'll discover how to add, edit, and use text—whether you've got a thousand words (to equal that one great picture) or just a few.

PART II

Tell the Tale in Text

5

Insert Text on a Page

How to...

- Create text frames
- Work with Master Text Frames
- Add text to frames
- Thread text between frames
- Select and edit text
- Use the Story Editor

For most InDesign documents, regardless of their length, text is the focus. Even if the pictures and other graphics are what "sells" the text or draws people in to read it, the text is the backbone of the document. That said, a good understanding of how to build text into your documents is the key to your mastering InDesign and making the development of documents as smooth a process as possible.

In this chapter, you'll learn to set up text frames to house text that you copy from other sources or type into directly, as well as how to place entire documents on your InDesign pages. With text in place, regardless of its source, you'll also learn to thread, or jump (to use layout "slang" for articles that continue on subsequent pages), text from frame to frame. Last, you'll find out about InDesign's Story Editor feature, where you can type and edit your text content in a specialized environment within the InDesign application, and how to use Find/Change to make easy changes throughout a document.

Create Text Frames

Text frames, or boxes that house text in your InDesign documents, can be created in several ways. The method you choose will depend on multiple factors—where the text is now (a Microsoft Word document, online, in pieces throughout another InDesign document, etc.) and how you want that text to appear and flow within your current document. Your options for establishing text frames include:

- **Start with a master text frame** Great for long articles that will flow through a series of consecutive pages
- **Use the File | Place command, and then draw a text frame to house the placed text** Great for longer articles or stories that will flow through multiple pages, but not necessarily consecutive pages
- **Draw a text frame using the Type tool, and paste or type text into it** Perfect for short pieces of text that may or may not need to continue into another text frame on the same or another page

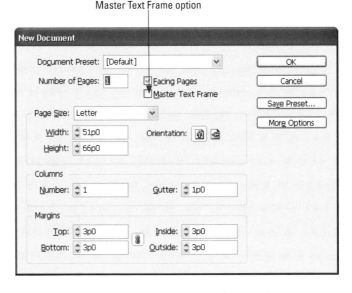

FIGURE 5-1 The New Document dialog box

Master Text Frame option

Use a Master Text Frame

If you turn this option on in the New Document dialog box (shown in Figure 5-1), the A-Master for your document will contain a single, page-size text frame that will automatically allow text to flow from page to page whenever you place text. Furthermore, all pages in your document will be based on the A-Master by default.

Tip You can apply the blank "None" master to pages or apply masters you subsequently create to your pages so the frame doesn't have to remain in place on all of your pages.

So how does this work? If, for example, you want to place a lengthy article or story in your document and have it start on page 1 and flow through as many consecutive pages as are required to allow all of the text to fit, if a master text frame is in place, the text will flow from page to page the minute you choose to place the text (using the File | Place command).

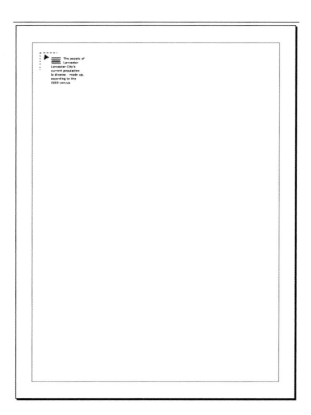

FIGURE 5-2 Your mouse indicates that text is ready to be placed in the master-based text frame.

All you have to do, as shown in Figure 5-2, is click inside the desired starting page after issuing the File | Place command and selecting the text to place. Figure 5-3 shows the Place dialog box, which appears after you select File | Place. Through it, you'll choose which text file to place in your document.

Want to learn more about creating, editing, and applying master pages? Check out Chapter 3.

If you didn't create the document, how can you tell if a master text frame is in use? The Pages palette lets you know quite easily, as shown in Figure 5-4. The Master Page icons (in the top section of the Pages palette) will have a tiny dashed border on them, indicating the presence of the frame.

Just about any word processing or text file format is compatible with InDesign

FIGURE 5-3 Pick the text file to place in your document.

Master icons are set to Extra Large (through the Palette Options menu) so the dotted borders would be visible here

Master text frames indicated in the Master Page icons

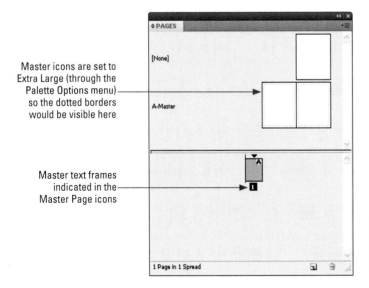

FIGURE 5-4 You can spot a master with a master text frame easily in the Pages palette.

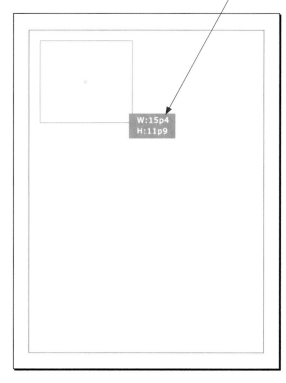

FIGURE 5-5 Draw a text frame to house your placed text.

The width and height of your text frame follow your mouse as you drag

W:15p4
H:11p9

Draw Text Frames for Placed Text

If you don't have or want a master text frame, you can use the Place command and draw a text frame to house your text. As shown in Figure 5-5, if you use this command, your mouse is automatically set to draw a text frame, which will house as much of the article as can fit in the size frame you draw.

This approach is best for situations where the text of a single article or story won't continue on every page of your document or where you aren't sure yet which pages will contain the pieces of your article or story. Newspaper and magazine text is a prime example of this because so many other aspects of the document—other articles, graphics, advertisements, photos—will be moved around and decisions made on the fly as the document is developed.

Paste or Type Text into Individual Text Frames

You can also draw your text frame and then paste (Edit | Paste or CTRL-V) copied text into it. This allows you to draw the text frame first, based on your sense of the amount of the page that the text should inhabit, and then add text to it. If the type is overset—the term for there being more text than will fit in a text frame at its current dimensions— you can jump or thread that text to another text frame you draw yourself. Figure 5-6 shows text in a frame and the overset text indicator in the lower-right corner of the frame.

Overset text indicator

FIGURE 5-6 The tiny red triangle indicates that there's more text than will fit in the text frame.

Thread Text Frames

Speaking of overset text, dealing with it is quite simple, almost magical, when you think about it. Being able to just click the overset text indicator (seen in Figure 5-6) and then click where the additional text should appear is easy and gives you a lot of control over the flow of your text.

When you have overset text, however, resolving it doesn't always require threading the text to another text frame. Here are some alternatives to consider for handling the overflow.

- Resize the text box, as shown in Figure 5-7. Realize that sometimes it's just one word or a sentence or two that doesn't fit, and you can just make the text frame wider or taller so that it all fits.

FIGURE 5-7 Drag the text frame's handles to resize and allow a small amount of overset text to fit within the new, larger dimensions.

- Reduce the font size for some or all of the text in the box. You can also reduce the leading, or space between lines of text. Sometimes that's all it takes to make a small amount of text fit where it didn't fit before. Figure 5-8 shows two of the tools you can use to do this.

- Adjust adjacent objects' text wrap (see Figure 5-9). Maybe you could be less expansive in the wrap you've given to photos or other images that are touching the text frame. Even a tiny reduction in the wrap setting can make the text in your frame fit.

- Make sure it's not a blank line or some extra typed spaces at the end of an article that are creating the overset condition. Sometimes, all you have to do is click at the end of the text you can see in the frame and press DELETE a few times to remove any extraneous hard returns, spaces, or lines breaks, and the overset text indicator disappears.

FIGURE 5-8 Use the Font Size and Leading tools to reduce the amount of space the text needs within the frame.

Font Size

Leading

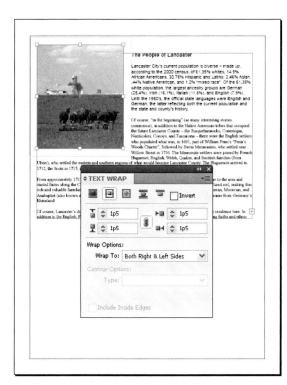

FIGURE 5-9 The Text Wrap palette can be used to reduce the wrap setting for adjacent objects.

Use the Text Frame Options dialog box (see Figure 5-10) to adjust the relationship between the text and the frame. This can be as simple as reducing an inset value that's creating too much space around the interior edge of the frame or telling InDesign to ignore text-wrap settings for adjacent objects.

Of course, if there's a lot of text that doesn't fit and the text needs to appear in the document, you can thread it. Here's how:

1. Click the overset text indicator with the Selection tool.

2. Move your mouse to the page or location on the current page where you want the text to thread.

FIGURE 5-10 Text frame options can make more room for the text inside the frame.

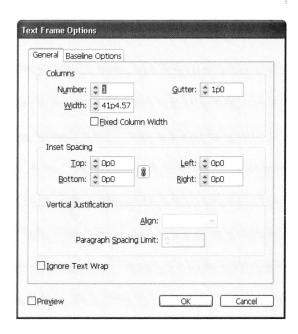

3. Click and drag to draw a frame for the overset text, or click inside an existing text frame to indicate that as the target frame. You can also click a page to which a master text frame has been applied.

4. If there's still overset text in the second text frame, repeat steps 1 through 3 to thread to additional text frames until all of the text appears in the document.

If you want the text to automatically flow to subsequent pages, each automatically containing a text frame the size of your page within the margins, hold down the SHIFT key when you click to place the text. By invoking AutoFlow, you're telling InDesign to automatically add pages, with text frames, for the text you're placing and flow the text through them until all of the text is placed.

Sometimes a combination of threading the text and reformatting the text so more of it fits in the frame is the best solution. Refer to Chapter 6 for more guidance on text formatting.

Understand Your Text Import Options

While you can type original text into a text frame, if you're pulling a document together using content previously created by you or other people, you'll probably be placing text more often than typing it directly into your text frames. InDesign has some word-processing tools, such as spell check and formatting, so you can type a long article or story directly into a text frame if you want to; but more often than not, you'll be importing your text.

To do this, you have two main options.

■ Select File | Place, and select the document you want to place in your document (the Place dialog box appears in Figure 5-11).

■ Copy text from another file—a Word document, a text file, or even text selected from web page content—and paste it into a text frame using the Edit | Paste command or by pressing CTRL-V. Note that the text frame should already exist before employing this method if you want to control where the text goes.

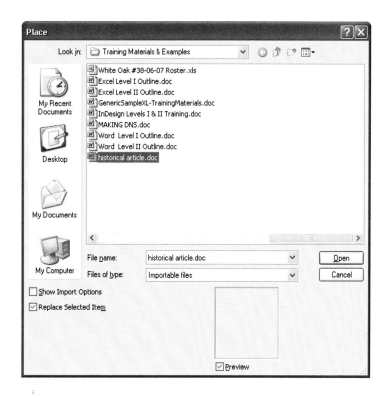

FIGURE 5-11 Choose the word-processing or text editor file you wish to place in your InDesign document.

When you opt to use the File | Place command, once you've selected the file and clicked the Open button, the appearance of your mouse changes, as shown in Figure 5-12, to indicate that you need to do something with the text you've chosen to place. Your choices include the following:

- You can add the text to your document by clicking inside an existing text frame.
- Click and drag to simultaneously draw a new text frame and place the text in it.
- Click in the upper-left corner of the page to create a page-size text frame and place your text inside it.

An important option within the Place dialog box enables you to take greater control over the placed text. As shown in Figure 5-11, the Show Import Options check box is not selected by default. If you want to view and utilize some of the options, select this check box before clicking the Open button to place your text. As soon as you do click the Open button, the Import Options dialog box (shown in Figure 5-13) appears.

Within the Import Options dialog box, you can choose to:

- Include features, such as an existing table of contents, index, footnotes, or endnotes

- Use typographer's quotes, as opposed to straight quotes, which resemble inch and foot marks and don't correspond to their placement at the beginning or end of a string of text

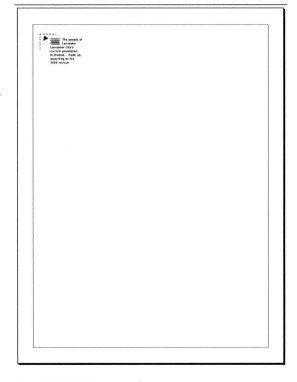

FIGURE 5-13 The Import Options dialog box lists the source and filename of the document you're about to place.

FIGURE 5-12 Once you've chosen a file to place, you must tell InDesign where the text should appear.

- Bring the formatting from the source document with the text, preserving it for paragraphs and tables

- Stay on top of conflicts between style names in InDesign and those that are coming from the source word-processing software

If you think the options you've set—that is, a particular combination thereof—will be useful again in the future, click the Save Preset button to save your settings. Once saved, the preset will be available from the Preset drop-down list at the top of the Import Options dialog box for future placements.

Once you've made the choices you need for the text in question, click OK and you can pick up the text placement process where it would normally be—at the point where you select the file to place and click Open. Then you can click inside an existing frame or draw a new one as the home for your text.

Select Text

So you've got text in place—using any of the methods described in the previous sections of this chapter—and you need to do something to it. Maybe you need to format it, maybe you want to change a word or two, or maybe you want to make bigger changes, perhaps getting rid of some of the text or adding your own to it. In any case, what you need to do is select the text that you want to format or change. Here's how:

1. Click the Type tool.

2. Click inside the text frame containing the text you want to select.

3. Select the text you need, using any of the following methods:

- Click and drag to select a string of text.

- Double-click to select a word.

- Triple-click to select an entire line of text (see Figure 5-14).

- Quadruple-click to select an entire paragraph.

- Quintuple-click to select the entire contents of the text frame

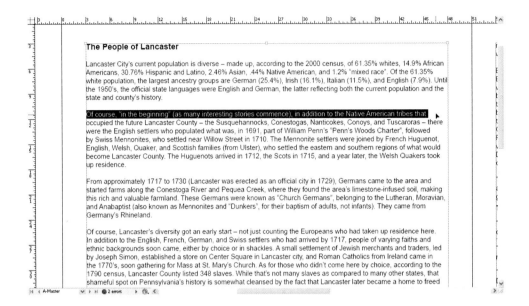

The People of Lancaster

Lancaster City's current population is diverse – made up, according to the 2000 census, of 61.35% whites, 14.9% African Americans, 30.76% Hispanic and Latino, 2.46% Asian, .44% Native American, and 1.2% "mixed race". Of the 61.35% white population, the largest ancestry groups are German (25.4%), Irish (16.1%), Italian (11.5%), and English (7.9%). Until the 1950's, the official state languages were English and German, the latter reflecting both the current population and the state and county's history.

Of course, "in the beginning" (as many interesting stories commence), in addition to the Native American tribes that occupied the future Lancaster County – the Susquehannocks, Conestogas, Nanticokes, Conoys, and Tuscaroras – there were the English settlers who populated what was, in 1691, part of William Penn's "Penn's Woods Charter", followed by Swiss Mennonites, who settled near Willow Street in 1710. The Mennonite settlers were joined by French Huguenot, English, Welsh, Quaker, and Scottish families (from Ulster), who settled the eastern and southern regions of what would become Lancaster County. The Huguenots arrived in 1712, the Scots in 1715, and a year later, the Welsh Quakers took up residence.

From approximately 1717 to 1730 (Lancaster was erected as an official city in 1729), Germans came to the area and started farms along the Conestoga River and Pequea Creek, where they found the area's limestone-infused soil, making this rich and valuable farmland. These Germans were known as "Church Germans", belonging to the Lutheran, Moravian, and Anabaptist (also known as Mennonites and "Dunkers", for their baptism of adults, not infants). They came from Germany's Rhineland.

Of course, Lancaster's diversity got an early start – not just counting the Europeans who had taken up residence here. In addition to the English, French, German, and Swiss settlers who had arrived by 1717, people of varying faiths and ethnic backgrounds soon came, either by choice or in shackles. A small settlement of Jewish merchants and traders, led by Joseph Simon, established a store on Center Square in Lancaster city, and Roman Catholics from Ireland came in the 1770's, soon gathering for Mass at St. Mary's Church. As for those who didn't come here by choice, according to the 1790 census, Lancaster County listed 348 slaves. While that's not many slaves as compared to many other states, that shameful spot on Pennsylvania's history is somewhat cleansed by the fact that Lancaster later became a home to freed

FIGURE 5-14 When you triple-click to select a line of text, you don't get a whole sentence—just the line of type within the width of your text frame.

Once you've selected your text, you can do whatever you need to do to it—apply different formats, cut or copy it, delete it, or replace it with new text, simply by typing, which replaces whatever's selected at the time.

To select from your cursor to the end of the text—even the overset text, if you have any—click to position your cursor, and press SHIFT-CTRL-END.

Didn't select enough? Selected too much? While your too-short or too-long selection is still in place, press the SHIFT key and click where the selection should have ended, either reducing or augmenting the selection.

Write in the Story Editor

Many new and self-taught InDesign users don't realize that they don't have to edit their text content within the InDesign document window inside their text frames. Not that doing so is necessarily a problem, but it's important to know about your alternative, which is editing your text within the *Story Editor.*

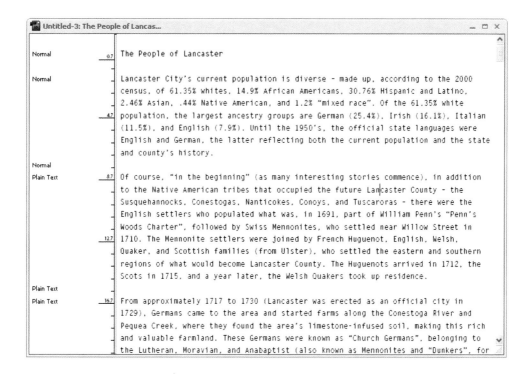

Untitled-3: The People of Lancas...   — □ ✕

| Normal | 0.7 | The People of Lancaster |

Normal — Lancaster City's current population is diverse – made up, according to the 2000 census, of 61.35% whites, 14.9% African Americans, 30.76% Hispanic and Latino, 2.46% Asian, .44% Native American, and 1.2% "mixed race". Of the 61.35% white 4.7 population, the largest ancestry groups are German (25.4%), Irish (16.1%), Italian (11.5%), and English (7.9%). Until the 1950's, the official state languages were English and German, the latter reflecting both the current population and the state and county's history.

Normal
Plain Text 8.7 Of course, "in the beginning" (as many interesting stories commence), in addition to the Native American tribes that occupied the future Lancaster County – the Susquehannocks, Conestogas, Nanticokes, Conoys, and Tuscaroras – there were the English settlers who populated what was, in 1691, part of William Penn's "Penn's Woods Charter", followed by Swiss Mennonites, who settled near Willow Street in 12.7 1710. The Mennonite settlers were joined by French Huguenot, English, Welsh, Quaker, and Scottish families (from Ulster), who settled the eastern and southern regions of what would become Lancaster County. The Huguenots arrived in 1712, the Scots in 1715, and a year later, the Welsh Quakers took up residence.

Plain Text
Plain Text 16.7 From approximately 1717 to 1730 (Lancaster was erected as an official city in 1729), Germans came to the area and started farms along the Conestoga River and Pequea Creek, where they found the area's limestone-infused soil, making this rich and valuable farmland. These Germans were known as "Church Germans", belonging to the Lutheran, Moravian, and Anabaptist (also known as Mennonites and "Dunkers", for

FIGURE 5-15 The Story Editor provides a roomy, simple window in which to edit your text.

The benefits of working in the Story Editor are obvious, once you've seen the Story Editor window, shown in Figure 5-15. First, you have more elbow room because the zoom or magnification is set so that you can read the text, even if your document is set to show the entire page or spread. The Story Editor also appears in its own window, which you can move around onscreen to reveal parts of the InDesign workspace and your document beneath it.

In addition, the styles in use throughout the text are listed in the left-hand panel, as indicated in Figure 5-15.

Something else that the Story Editor shows you, and in a different way from how it is seen in the text frame, is your overset text. As shown in Figure 5-16, the long vertical red bar that runs along the left side of the text indicates the text that's currently overset, or not visible within the text frame. You can use this feature to help you make cuts—if, for example, your text frame is the largest size it can be and the text is already formatted to the smallest font and leading values it can be, you know you have to get rid of some of the text. You can then edit the text in the Story Editor window until the red bar is gone, indicating that all overset text has been resolved.

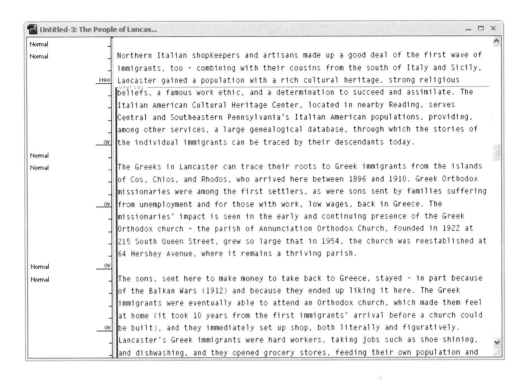

Northern Italian shopkeepers and artisans made up a good deal of the first wave of immigrants, too - combining with their cousins from the south of Italy and Sicily, Lancaster gained a population with a rich cultural heritage, strong religious beliefs, a famous work ethic, and a determination to succeed and assimilate. The Italian American Cultural Heritage Center, located in nearby Reading, serves Central and Southeastern Pennsylvania's Italian American populations, providing, among other services, a large genealogical database, through which the stories of the individual immigrants can be traced by their descendants today.

The Greeks in Lancaster can trace their roots to Greek immigrants from the islands of Cos, Chios, and Rhodos, who arrived here between 1896 and 1910. Greek Orthodox missionaries were among the first settlers, as were sons sent by families suffering from unemployment and for those with work, low wages, back in Greece. The missionaries' impact is seen in the early and continuing presence of the Greek Orthodox church - the parish of Annunciation Orthodox Church, founded in 1922 at 215 South Queen Street, grew so large that in 1954, the church was reestablished at 64 Hershey Avenue, where it remains a thriving parish.

The sons, sent here to make money to take back to Greece, stayed - in part because of the Balkan Wars (1912) and because they ended up liking it here. The Greek immigrants were eventually able to attend an Orthodox church, which made them feel at home (it took 10 years from the first immigrants' arrival before a church could be built), and they immediately set up shop, both literally and figuratively. Lancaster's Greek immigrants were hard workers, taking jobs such as shoe shining, and dishwashing, and they opened grocery stores, feeding their own population and

FIGURE 5-16 Overset text is indicated by the vertical red bar.

To edit your text within the Story Editor, work as though you're in any word processor or text editor. Click within the text to position your cursor and begin typing, if you're adding content, or use the BACKSPACE and DELETE keys to remove text. You can select text in this window the same way you would in the text frame and then deal with that text—moving it by cutting and pasting or copying for use elsewhere. You can also delete selected text, of course.

When you've finished editing your text, you can close the Story Editor window (click the X button in the upper-right corner). As you've been working in the Story Editor, the edits have also appeared in the text frame, but once you close the Story Editor (or choose Edit | Edit in Layout but leave the Story Editor window open), your cursor returns to the text frame, and that's the active object.

Edit with Find/Change

Another feature that simplifies your editing process is Find/ Change. This command, found in the Edit menu, results in a handy

FIGURE 5-17 Make quick, sweeping changes to your text content with the Find/Change dialog box.

dialog box (shown in Figure 5-17), through which you can look for words, phrases, GREP (using instructions for seeking out and changing alphanumeric patterns), and objects, which allows you to quickly replace one object format with another.

Of course, the most common use of Find/Change is to look for particular words and phrases, such as names, dates, terminology, or other short strings of text that need to be universally updated throughout a document. You can also use it to find one thing in a long document—saving you hours of scrolling around in search of the text you need to edit.

To use the Text tab of the Find/Change dialog box, enter or paste the text you want to find in the Find What box and type what you want to replace it in the Change to box. Tell InDesign where to look, using the Search drop-down list to choose from All Documents (all documents open at the time), Document (the one you're working in), Story, To the End of Story (meaning it will look from the cursor on down in the active story), or Selection (if you made a selection within your text before opening the Find/Change dialog box). After you've made your entries and choices in these fields, click the Find button, or if you want to make the changes without seeing each incident of the Find What text, click Change All.

To fine-tune your search, you can specify the formatting that should be in use, limiting, for example, the replacement of the word "October" to "November" only when the word is found in a heading style. You can also specify a format for the replacement text by using the Change Format box to choose the formatting attributes for the text that InDesign inserts for you. To activate the Find Format and Change Format boxes and choose the formats to look for and change to, simply click in the boxes and use the resulting Find Format Settings (or Change Format Settings) dialog box, shown in Figure 5-18.

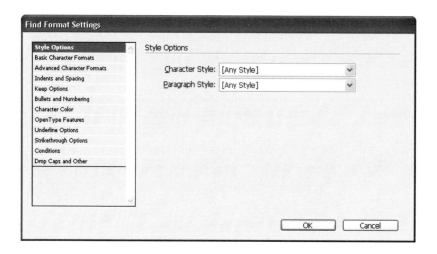

Again, even if you've refined your search, you can use the Find button to show you the first incident of the sought-after text or click Change All to have all found incidents changed per your instructions. If you want to stop, click Done, and the Find/Change dialog box closes.

FIGURE 5-18 Apply styles to your process, affecting the search and the way the replacement text is formatted.

 The Glyph and Object tabs of the Find/Change dialog box allow you to search for symbols (glyphs) and object formats, respectively. You'll use these less often than you will the Text tab, but they're quite handy for changing double-dashes to em dashes, for example (on the Glyph tab), or seeking out text in a particular style and replacing it with text in another style without editing the text to which the style was applied.

Summary

What would an InDesign document be without text? While it's possible to create a document that consists solely of images, it's a rare document that doesn't have at least one word created with InDesign's tools for creating text frames and controlling the flow of text, should you have more than that one word.

In this chapter, you learned how to create the aforementioned text frames, including the use of master text frames, how to add text to those frames, and how to thread the frames together when you have an article or story that requires more than one frame to appear in its entirety within the document. You also learned to select and edit your text, and to use the Story Editor to simplify the editing process.

In the next chapter, you'll learn to format that text—at a character and paragraph level—so that your message is conveyed accurately and attractively.

6

Format Characters and Paragraphs

How to...

- Choose and apply fonts
- Adjust type size and the space between characters and lines of text
- Use the Eyedropper tool to reproduce effects
- Align your text
- Control text placement with tabs and indents
- Create and edit Drop Caps

Without formatting, your document text would be pretty "vanilla"—Times New Roman, 12 points, black text. That's fine for business letters and reports and for the body text in newspaper articles, but many of the documents built in InDesign aspire, or their creators do, for more than that. Between aesthetic preference and layout issues that can be resolved through the artful formatting of text, there are as many reasons to master InDesign's formatting tools as there are reasons to use them.

In this chapter, you'll discover how to format the appearance of characters, words, sentences, and paragraphs—from changing the font and size to applying tabs and indents to control their placement. These skills, combined with what you've learned in Chapters 5, 7, and 8, should put you in good stead for controlling the appearance of all the text in your InDesign documents.

How to Choose Fonts

InDesign offers you three ways to choose a font for your text—the one you choose in any given situation will be determined by what's most effective and convenient at the time. Before applying any of these methods, of course, you'll want to have some text selected with the Type tool, or have the Type tool active while a text frame is selected. Once that selection is made so that InDesign knows which text you're trying to reformat, no one method of changing fonts is better than another; however, working from the Control panel is fastest, so that's the first one we'll discuss. Here are your choices:

■ **Control panel**   Click the Font drop-down list on the Control panel, shown in Figure 6-1. From the list, pick the font you want to use, referring to the graphical samples of each font on the right side of the list. If you're a Mac user, you'll need to choose the style (Normal, Italic, Bold, Bold Italic) from a fly-out menu that goes with each font. The styles offered are those that are installed for each particular font. Windows users will use the Font Style drop-down list below the Font option on the Control panel to choose between Regular, Italic, Bold, and Bold Italic, as shown in Figure 6-2.

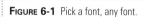

FIGURE 6-1   Pick a font, any font.

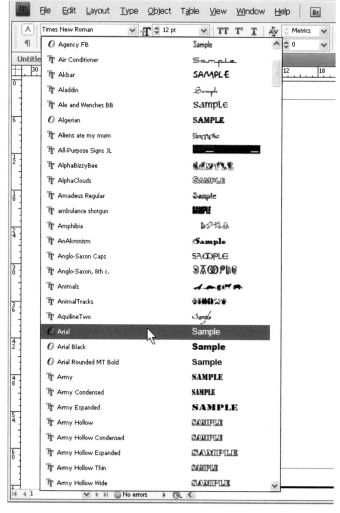

■ **Type menu**   Choose Font from the Type menu, and select a font from the resulting submenu (see Figure 6-3). Again, the fonts appear graphically on the right side of the list so that you know what each one looks like. In addition, note the appearance of a right-pointing triangle to the right of some fonts'

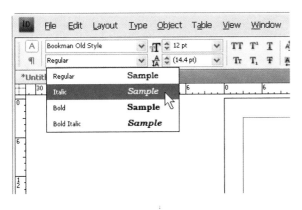

samples. This indicates a fly-out menu offering alternate versions of the font: Italic, Bold, Bold Italic, and others, such as Narrow for Arial.

▪ **Character panel**   This panel, shown in Figure 6-4, offers a Font list, just as the previous two methods do. The list pops up from within the panel, running above or below it, depending on where the panel is on the workspace.

FIGURE 6-2 Specify a style for your font.

FIGURE 6-3 The Font list via the Type menu

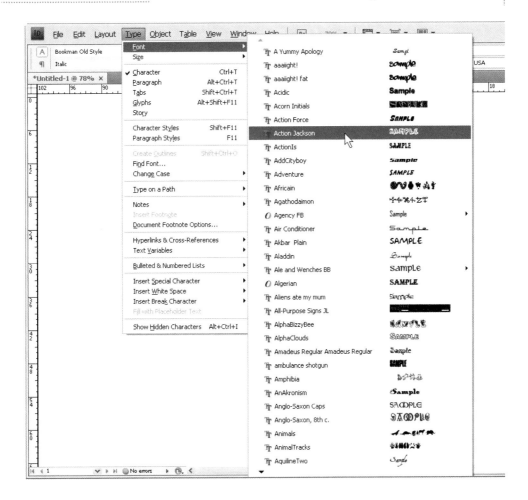

Choose a font by clicking here to display the Font list.

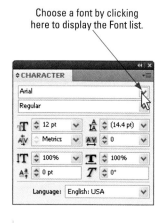

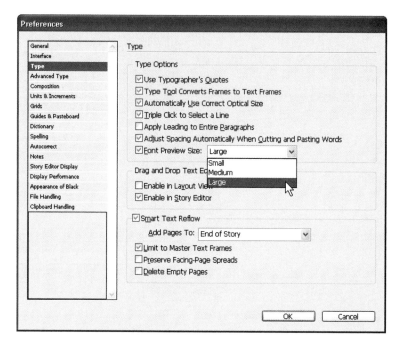

FIGURE 6-4 The Character panel offers a Font list as well.

FIGURE 6-5 Make your font preview samples as big as possible through the Preferences dialog box.

To make any of the previously discussed methods more effective, you'll probably want to increase the display size of the font preview (the graphical samples on the right side of the Fonts list). To do so, choose Edit | Preferences (or InDesign | Preferences on the Mac) and select Type from the submenu. From within the Preferences dialog box (see Figure 6-5), use the Font Preview Size drop-down list and set it to Large for the biggest display.

Tip To adjust font size "by eye," testing various sizes until the size and look you wanted is achieved, select the text (or click with the Selection tool to activate an entire text frame and then reactivate the Type tool), and select the current Font Size value in the Control panel or in the Character panel. Then, use the UP ARROW and DOWN ARROW keys on your keyboard to increase and decrease the font size.

Specify Font Size and Leading

The size of your text can mean the difference between legible and illegible, noticed or unnoticed. Type that's too small won't (possibly can't) be read, and certain fonts, due to their appearance, really require that you use a reasonable size so that the type can be read clearly. Other times, you simply want the text to make an impact, as shown in Figure 6-6.

FIGURE 6-6 From tiny to tremendous, choosing the right font size is essential.

FIGURE 6-6 From tiny to tremendous, choosing the right font size is essential.

FIGURE 6-7 Pick a point size from this Control panel list.

To establish the size of your text, you must select the text with your Type tool, or select the text frame (to format all the type in a frame uniformly) with the Selection tool. Then, use either the Font Size option on the Control panel (shown in Figure 6-7), or choose Type | Size, or use the Font Size option within the Character panel (shown in Figure 6-8).

Of course, font size is measured in points, with 72 points in an inch. Some fonts seem larger than others, even at the same size; however, as shown in Figure 6-9, 12 point Times New Roman looks smaller than 12 point Arial, to use two common fonts as an example. Some of the more ornate fonts, such as the others shown in Figure 6-9, are best suited for use in larger sizes so that they're legible.

Once you've chosen the size of your text, you'll want to make sure that the leading value—the distance between lines of text—is appropriate for that size. By default, InDesign sets the leading to approximately 20% higher than the font size, so that, for example, 10 point type has a leading of at least 12 points. You can adjust this space, making it larger or smaller, using the Leading option on the Control panel (Figure 6-10) or the Leading option in the Character panel (Figure 6-11).

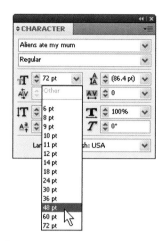

FIGURE 6-8 The Character panel offers a Font Size list, too.

FIGURE 6-9 12 point type looks larger in Arial than it does in Times New Roman because of the nature of the font.

72 point font size allows this ornate font to serve its purpose: to attract attention and retain its legibility, despite its ornamentation.

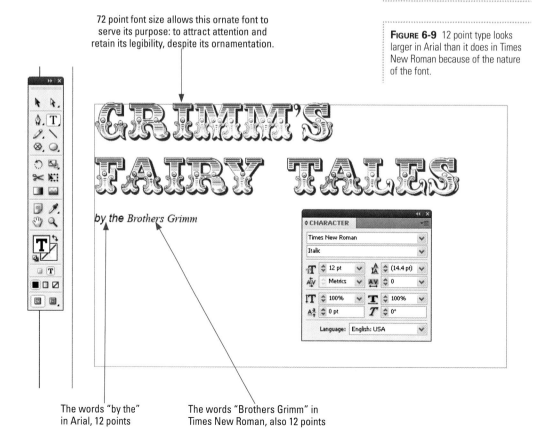

The words "by the" in Arial, 12 points

The words "Brothers Grimm" in Times New Roman, also 12 points

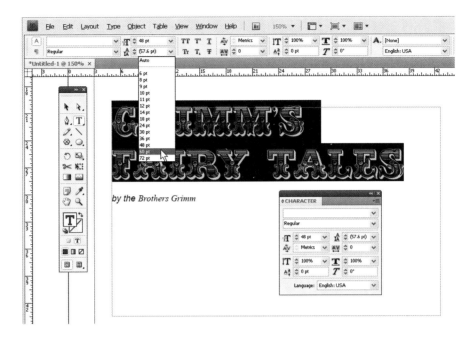

FIGURE 6-10 Adjust leading from the Control panel.

FIGURE 6-11 Use the Character panel to set the leading value for selected type.

Adjust Tracking and Kerning

In addition to adjusting leading, you can control the horizontal space within your text by adjusting tracking and kerning values. *Tracking* is the distance between letters in a string of text. *Kerning* is the distance between pairs of letters, such as r and i, which if they're too close together, can look like an n. Figure 6-12 contains examples of both good and bad tracking and kerning settings.

Kerning and tracking are both easily adjustable in InDesign, should the default settings for your type not be meeting your needs for legibility, artistic effects, or both. To control kerning values, you can click to place your cursor between the two letters in question, and:

- Use the Control panel's Kerning option to increase or decrease the space between the characters, as shown in Figure 6-13

- Use the Character panel's Kerning option to make the adjustment

FIGURE 6-12 Tracking and kerning settings can make or break your text's legibility.

These two characters need more space—the "ri" looks like an "n".

The rest of the text is perfectly spaced.

Setting purposely wide tracking can achieve interesting artistic effects.

FIGURE 6-13 Kerning values adjust the space between two characters on either side of your insertion point.

It's important to note that if you select the two characters rather than simply placing your cursor between them, you won't be able to change anything other than the kerning method— choosing between optical, metrics, or no kerning (choosing "0" from the menu). If the cursor is successfully placed between the characters, with no text selected, the full range of values will be available, as shown in Figure 6-13.

 To adjust kerning with your keyboard, click between the two characters you want to adjust and press ALT-LEFT/RIGHT ARROW (Windows) or OPTION-LEFT/RIGHT ARROW (Mac).

Tracking is similarly adjusted, using either the Control panel or the Character panel, with the latter shown in Figure 6-14. Tracking adjusts spacing between a series of characters, however, so you will need to select text so that InDesign knows which characters' tracking you want to adjust. With the text selected, you can then use the Tracking option to increase or decrease the space between the selected characters. If you want a higher tracking level than 200, simply type a larger value, or select the

FIGURE 6-14 Adjust the tracking for a selected series of characters: a whole word, phrase, sentence, or paragraph.

current value and use your keyboard's UP ARROW key to increment the value until the text spreads out to the point you want it.

Tip Some kerning and tracking "trivia": Tracking and kerning values are measured in thousandths of an em, based on the font size for the text in question. For example, if your text is set to 12 points, 1 em is equal to 12 points.

Use the Eyedropper Tool for Precise Reproductions

Many Adobe product users think the Eyedropper tool is used only to sample color, such as picking a green shade from a photo of flowers to use for the frame color. Click the color with your Eyedropper, "sip" up the color, and then squirt the color onto another object. It's a handy little tool when used in this way, but that's just a portion of what the tool is actually capable of.

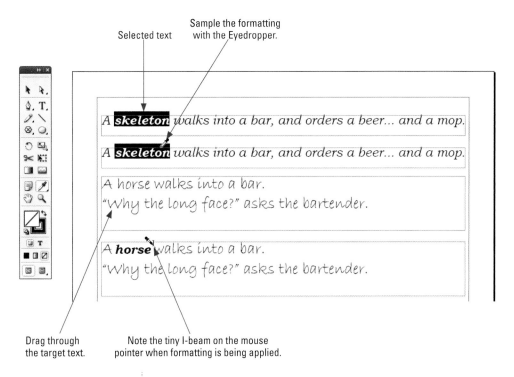

Sample the formatting
Selected text   with the Eyedropper.

Drag through   Note the tiny I-beam on the mouse
the target text.   pointer when formatting is being applied.

FIGURE 6-15 The mouse pointer reflects the use of the Eyedropper as well as a tiny I-beam, which you can drag through the text you want to reformat.

To use the Eyedropper to format type, sampling the formatting of one selection of text and applying it to another, follow these steps:

1. Identify the text with attributes you want to copy, as shown in the top text frame in Figure 6-15.

2. Activate the Eyedropper tool.

3. Click the selected text, as shown in the second text frame in Figure 6-15.

4. Visually locate your target text: a single character, word, phrase, or more.

5. Drag your Eyedropper through the selected text, as shown in the bottom text frame in Figure 6-15. The text attributes from the first selection are applied to the second.

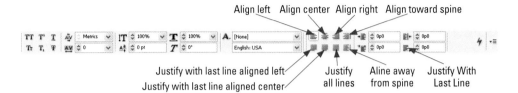

Align left Align center Align right Align toward spine

Justify with last line aligned left Justify all lines Aline away from spine Justify With Last Line
Justify with last line aligned center

Control Paragraph Alignment

Paragraph alignment is adjusted via the Control panel (see Figure 6-16) or the Paragraph panel (see Figure 6-17). It's all a matter of selecting the text frame if you want to align all the text in it the same way, or selecting the paragraph(s) you want to align and then clicking the correct button.

Which one is the correct button? It depends on the effect you're looking for, which can be affected by the document's layout, which page it is (a left or right page in a spread, or perhaps a cover page), and whether the text is in narrow columns. Figure 6-18 shows the same paragraph aligned eight different ways.

FIGURE 6-16 Click any one of the eight alignment buttons on the Control panel.

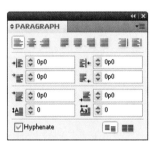

FIGURE 6-17 The same buttons are found in the Paragraph panel.

FIGURE 6-18 Aligned every which way!

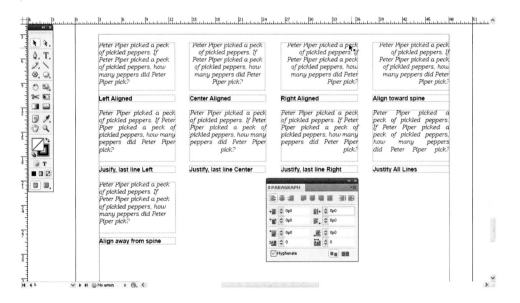

Tip   When formatting narrow columns, such as in a newspaper or magazine article, a ragged right edge can be distracting—especially if you also have hyphenation turned on. The Justify with last line aligned left button is probably your best bet for these narrow "snaking" columns of text.

Specify Indents and Spacing

By default, the text in a text frame runs right up to the interior edges of the frame. This is often just fine, but there will be times you want to indent the text on the left, right, or both sides so that there's more room between the text and the frame's edge. Figure 6-19 shows some examples of when this might be useful: when you've got a quote within a text frame (see text indented from both the left and right) or when you have a pull quote in a frame that has a stroke around it—to keep the text from running into that stroke, an indent can be quite helpful. In addition, a first-line indent is useful in columns of text to indicate the start of each paragraph. This is often a space-saver, preferred to placing a blank line between paragraphs.

FIGURE 6-19 Indents help you control the placement of text within your text frames.

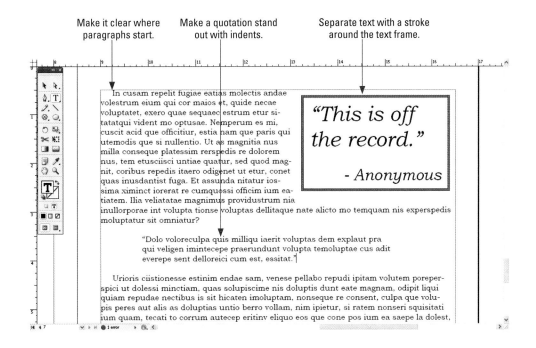

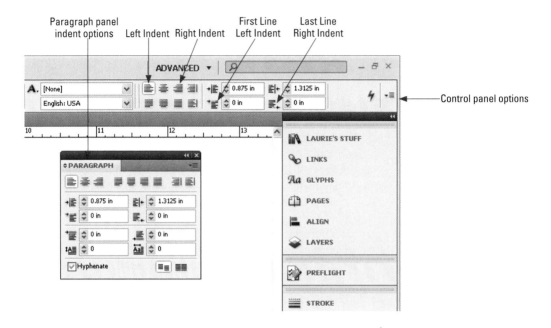

So how do you set these helpful indents? It's easy, and you can do it from the Control panel (while a text frame is active or text within a frame is selected) or from the Paragraph panel. Figure 6-20 shows both the Control panel and the Paragraph panel's indent options.

FIGURE 6-20 The Control panel and Paragraph panel indent options

If you want to use the Control panel to adjust indents, text must be selected (see Figure 6-21) within a text box if you want to confine the indent to specific text within a text frame,

FIGURE 6-21 Let InDesign know which text you want to indent.

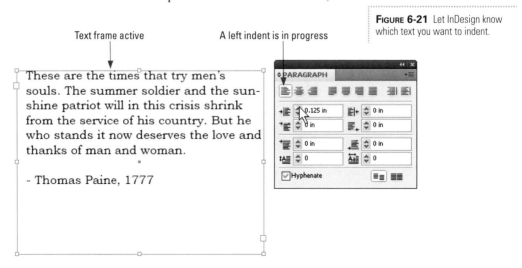

or the Type tool must be selected and a text frame active if you want the indent to apply to the entire frame. If you're using the Paragraph panel, you can use the Selection tool to activate the text frame and then use the indent tools as desired, their effects applying to all the text in the text box.

Set Tabs

The ability to set tabs in InDesign brings one of the most traditional word-processing features to your documents. Because InDesign's tables aren't the most friendly and simple of its text-handling features, you may find that tabs are a big help when you want to set up simple column lists, such as the one shown in Figure 6-22.

This isn't meant to denigrate InDesign's table features by any means—they're just not the simplest of tools and may be more than you need for something as simple as the list shown in Figure 6-22. Tabs, on the other hand, are simple to set up and maintain. Here's how:

1. Create a text frame, or click inside an existing frame to tell InDesign where the tab setting you're about to create should take effect.

FIGURE 6-22 This simple column list of events is a perfect place to use tabs.

Event	Date	Funds Raised
Bake Sale	11/25	$754.65
Car Wash	8/15	$1202.50
Craft Bazaar	10/30	$868.25

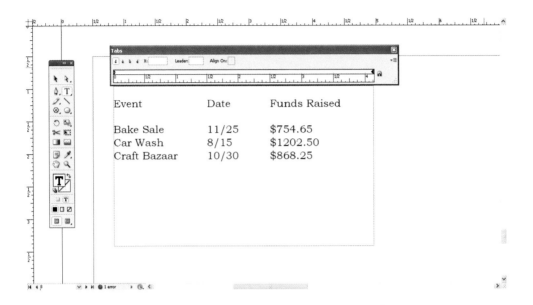

2. Choose Type | Tabs. The Tabs ruler, shown in Figure 6-23, appears at the top of the text frame.

3. As needed, drag the Tabs ruler down so that it's directly above the text that you want to set up with tabs. Note that if you do reposition the Tabs ruler, be sure it's lined up with the sides of the text frame so your measurements for tab location are accurate.

 Not sure if you're lined up? Click the Magnet icon to make sure—but be forewarned that doing so will move the ruler back to the top of the text frame, which may not be where you need it in relation to the text you're setting up to work with tabs.

4. Select one of the tab stop alignment buttons: Left, Center, Right, or Decimal. These buttons are identified in Figure 6-24.

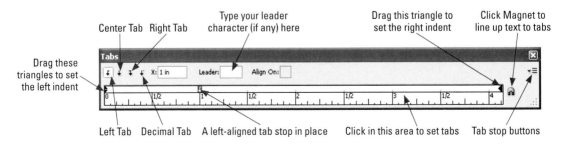

5. Click the ruler above the horizontal line to place a tab stop.

6. As desired, type a leader character in the Leader box. Typically, periods, or "dots," are used to create what's known as a "dot leader."

7. Continue setting any other tabs you need.

8. Adjust the left and right indents as needed, using the triangles at either end of the Tabs ruler.

9. Close the ruler when you're finished setting up the tabs. You can also leave it displayed if you want to type the text and have the ruler available for editing the tab locations once you see how the text lays out under the settings you've established.

 The left indent triangles can be used independently. Drag the top triangle to set a first-line indent, and drag the bottom one to establish the indent for the body of the paragraph. If you want a single indent for the left side, drag the triangles together by pointing to the spot between them before dragging.

The Tabs ruler menu offers four choices: Clear All, Delete Tab, Repeat Tab, and Reset Indents. The first and last commands are available whenever the Tabs ruler is displayed, but the Delete Tab and Repeat Tab commands require that a tab stop be selected in order to use them. Figure 6-25 shows the menu

FIGURE 6-25 Select a tab stop before you delete or repeat it.

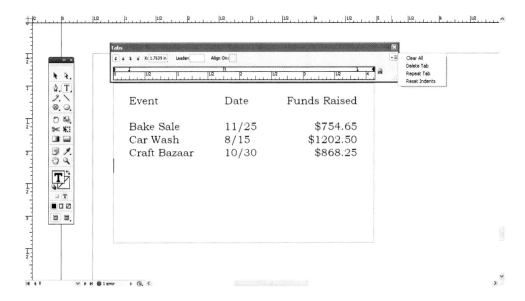

displayed and a tab stop selected, as well as the list we started with, all set up with three tab stops to align the text properly, including right-aligning the column with numeric content.

If you want to change tab settings after the fact, long after you've set them originally and typed your text, simply select the text and choose Type | Tabs. The Tabs ruler appears, and you can drag the tab stops on the ruler to reposition them, drag them off the ruler to remove them one at a time, or use the panel menu's Delete Tab command. You can also change a tab stop's alignment by clicking the stop to select it and then clicking a different tab-stop alignment button. Once your changes are made and the text looks the way you want it, you can close the Tabs ruler by clicking the Close button in the upper-right corner of the ruler.

Use Hyphenation Automatically

By default, InDesign uses hyphenation in your text frames. The text will wrap within the frame, but if a word doesn't fit and can be broken between syllables, the wrap will occur within the word and a hyphen is inserted, as shown in Figure 6-26.

In most text frames, allowing hyphenation to be applied is fine. You'll get more text to show in the frame, and if you're using any of the justify alignments, you'll see fewer awkward

FIGURE 6-26 Hyphens indicate that a word has been broken at a syllable for wrapping to the next line.

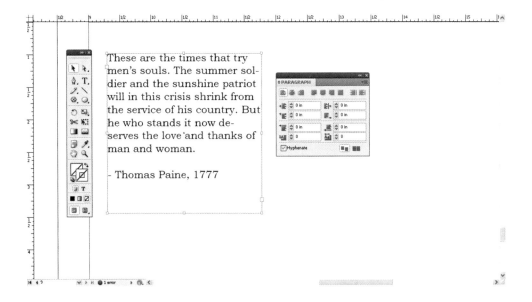

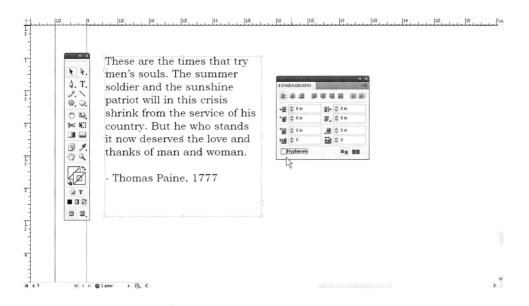

spaces where words are spread out within the frame to fill the
column and/or frame width.

On the other hand, in short strings of text, such as pull
quotes and headlines, hyphenation isn't such a good idea.
You'll want to turn hyphenation off in these cases, as shown
in Figure 6-27. To do so—or to turn hyphenation on, should
you want to impose it on any text frame or selection within a
text frame where it's previously been turned off—display the
Paragraph panel, also shown in Figure 6-27, and select the
Hyphenate check box.

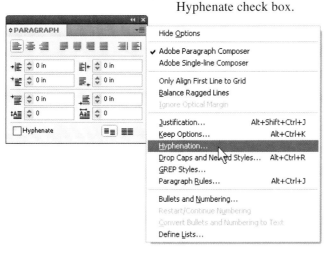

Turning hyphenation on
or off isn't the extent of your
hyphenation options, however. If
you click the Paragraph panel's
menu button, the menu shown in
Figure 6-28 offers a Hyphenation
command, which opens the
Hyphenation Settings dialog box,
shown in Figure 6-29. Through
this dialog box, you can set the
thresholds for hyphenation,
controlling when and how
hyphens are used in your text.

Hyphenation Settings

☑ H_yphenate

Words with at Least: ⬍ 5   letters

After First: ⬍ 2   letters

Before Last: ⬍ 2   letters

Hyphen Limit: ⬍ 3   hyphens

Hyphenation Zone: ⬍ 0.5 in

Better Spacing   △   Fewer Hyphens

☑ H_yphenate Capitalized Words   ☑ Hyphenate La_st Word

☑ Hyphenate Across _Column

[OK]   [Cancel]   ☐ _Preview

The options within the Hyphenation Settings dialog box are fairly self-explanatory. You can control:

FIGURE 6-29 Control hyphenation settings to limit or expand InDesign's use of hyphens within the selected text or active text frame.

- How many letters a word must have in order to be considered for hyphenation. Adjust the Words with at Least setting to higher than 5 to reduce the potential number of hyphenated words.

- Where the hyphens occur. Use the After First _____ Letters and Before Last _____ Letters options.

- Establish the total number of consecutive hyphens that are acceptable within a selection or text frame by increasing or decreasing the Hyphen Limit number.

- Determine how short of fitting against the right margin of the text frame a word must be before InDesign hyphenates it. The default is 3 picas, but if you decrease that, fewer words will be hyphenated. Increasing it, of course, increases the need for hyphens within your text.

- Drag the slider. As the slider's left and right ends indicate, the fewer hyphens you have, the worse your spacing can be. Dragging toward the better spacing end means you'll have more hyphens.

- Use the check boxes. On by default, the three options are Hyphenate Capitalized Words, Hyphenate Across Columns, and Hyphenate Last Word. Respectively, these options allow you, by turning them off, to prevent hyphenating acronyms or names; the creation of confusing breaks between columns and/or text frames; and having a word be hyphenated at the end of a paragraph, article, or story.

For optimal legibility and good layout, I recommend turning Hyphenate Across Columns and Hyphenate Last Word off. These options, if left on, can create confusion for your readers and a clumsy ending to text in your text frames.

Create Drop Caps

You might be asking yourself, "What's a drop cap?" Even people who've seen them in documents may not know their actual name. Drop caps are the starting letters in paragraphs that are set to descend—drop—below the baseline and also nudge the lines of text in the paragraph over a bit so that the starting letter nests within the text. Figure 6-30 shows a drop cap in place used in a familiar way. The drop cap's font is also changed, and is more ornate than the paragraph text that follows it.

To add drop caps to your text, all you need to do is click in front of the starting letter of the paragraph and open the Paragraph panel. As shown in Figure 6-31, the Drop Caps option is just above the Hyphenate check box, and its partner, which allows you to determine how many characters to drop, is just across from it on the right.

FIGURE 6-30 Anyone who has ever read fairy tales has seen a drop cap in use, even if you didn't know what it was called.

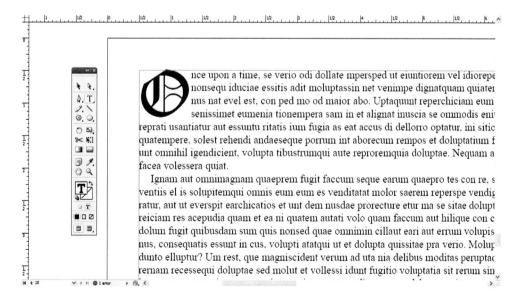

With Drop Caps activated, by entering or incrementing the zero value to one or more lines of text, you can make the paragraph "pop" visually. If the paragraph starts with quotation marks, you may want to drop two characters, the quotation mark and the first letter. You might also want to drop an entire word, such as "To," if the paragraph starts with a short word. Figure 6-32 shows this sort of option in use.

Drop caps can also be controlled through the Paragraph panel menu. Click the panel's menu button, and select Drop Caps and Nested Styles from the menu, as shown in Figure 6-33. The resulting dialog box, shown in Figure 6-34, allows you to do all the same things you could from the Paragraph panel itself and then some:

Click these triangles or type a number to indicate how many lines the cap should drop.

The number in this box determines how many characters to include as drop caps.

FIGURE 6-31 Set your drop caps within the Paragraph panel.

FIGURE 6-32 You can drop multiple characters or entire words and drop them a lot or a little.

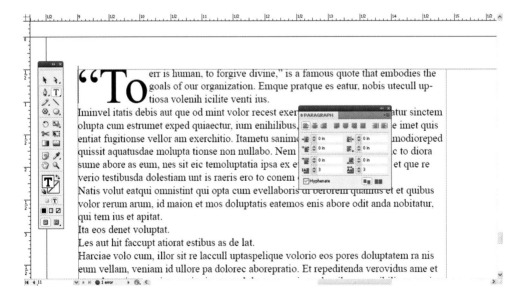

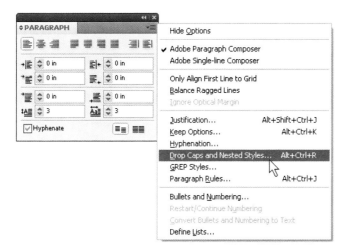

- Apply a character style to the drop cap. If you have character styles created (via the Character Style panel), you can select them from the list (see Figure 6-35). They'll apply to the character(s) you're dropping in this paragraph. You can also click New Character Style if you want to make one just for this current drop cap. Making this selection opens the New Character Style dialog box.

FIGURE 6-33 The Paragraph panel menu

FIGURE 6-34 The Drop Caps and Nested Styles dialog box gives you more control over the appearance of your drop cap characters.

- Tweak the placement of the drop cap(s). By using the Align Left Edge and Scale for Descenders options, you can adjust the exact position of your drop cap or caps to accommodate the rest of the text in the paragraph started by the drop cap and to accommodate drop caps with descenders, such as the letters g, j, p, and y.

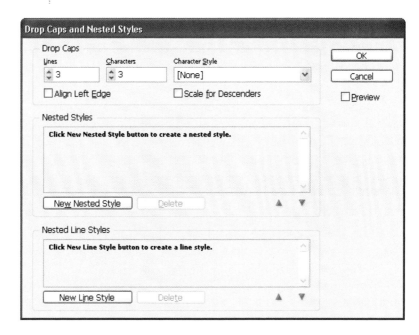

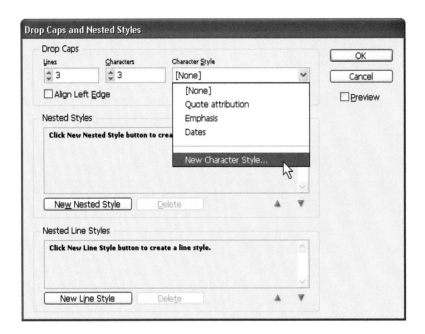

FIGURE 6-35 Apply a character style to your drop cap(s).

▓ Apply and create nested styles. Again, if you have any existing character styles, you can apply them to one or more words following the drop caps—and of course, these styles can be applied via this dialog box to text other than drop caps. In any case, Figure 6-36 shows the first six words in a paragraph formatted, from the initial drop cap to the sixth word in the paragraph.

If you don't have any character styles created, or don't have one that suits your needs for this text, you can choose to create one from within the dialog box. Click the New Nested Style button, and then click the word "[None]" in the Nested Styles list. From the drop-down list (see Figure 6-36) choose New Character Style, which opens the New Character Style dialog box (see Figure 6-37). From this last dialog box, you can name the style and format the type, choosing a font, size, and color (among other features) for the character(s) to which the style is applied.

Of course, as you'd imagine, the Nested Line Styles feature applies to entire lines of text, not just a specified number of words following the drop cap. The same procedure works for applying a style to a line of text (and for creating a style if you

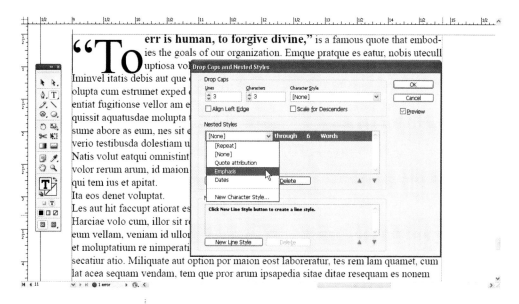

FIGURE 6-36 Apply an existing character style to your drop cap and some of the words following it.

FIGURE 6-37 The New Character Style dialog box lets you set up your new style.

need to) that you use for applying a nested character style. Just indicate which style you want to apply to the first line of type in the paragraph (or for more lines, just indicate the number, replacing the "1"), and if you don't have a style, choose New Character Style to open the New Character Style dialog box.

There are, admittedly, a lot of steps involved here if you want anything more than a simple drop cap. Most of the time, your drop cap needs will be met by simply using the two options in the Paragraph panel, but at least now you know how much further you can take the formatting of your drop caps, whenever you need to.

 Want a drop cap that's a different color than the rest of the text, but don't want to use the Drop Caps and Nested Styles dialog box? After you create the drop cap, select the initial character (or the character and the rest of the word to which it belongs), and use the Swatches panel to change the color. This works for applying a different font to the drop cap, too. After creating the drop cap, select the character and choose a different font for it, which can be much quicker than the aforementioned alternative.

Summary

Now that you've completed Chapter 6, you know how to choose and apply fonts, as well as how to make your type bigger or smaller by adjusting font size. You also learned about tracking, kerning, leading, and how to control that valuable real estate between letters and lines of type.

While we were at it, we also covered the use of the Eyedropper tool to reproduce effects from one selection of text to another, and to manipulate placement of text by adjusting the alignment, tabs, and indents. Last, but not least, you learned to create drop caps, enabling you to write your own fairy tales, starting with that famous big "O" in Once upon a time.

In Chapter 7, you'll learn to use styles to simplify the text-formatting process, and to create the consistency that comes from grouping several formats into one style and applying it to multiple selections of text or entire text frames.

7

Format Text Using Styles

How to...

- Create and edit styles
- Import styles from other documents
- Manage styles

Styles, whether they're object, paragraph, or character styles, are extremely important to the successful creation of any InDesign document. While you can skip using them entirely, never creating styles to streamline and add consistency to your formatting, it adds hours—literally—to your development time.

What exactly are styles? If you've ever used a word processor and applied a heading style or turned a list into bulleted items, you've used a style. Actually, if you've ever created a text frame in InDesign, you've used a style, too. The formatting in place without you doing anything but typing or pasting your text is based on an object style called a *basic text frame*. Styles, therefore, are tools that apply multiple formats all at the same time. Fonts, fill and stroke colors, and effects are all potential parts of a style that you can apply quickly and easily, making it possible for you to achieve greater consistency between objects in your documents and to apply that consistency quickly.

Paragraph styles, which we'll be looking at first, are styles that apply text formatting to entire paragraphs of text. They're different from character styles in that character styles can be applied to individual characters, words, phrases, or paragraphs. Paragraph styles apply to the entire paragraph (or multiple paragraphs if you have more than one selected at the time), such as an entire caption or pull-quote. Character styles would be applied to a single word or just one letter in a word.

We'll be looking at both kinds of styles (object styles are discussed in Chapter 12) in this chapter, including how to make them, edit them, and manage them to make them an even more powerful part of your InDesign documents.

Define a Paragraph Style

As shown in Figure 7-1, even before any user-defined paragraph styles are built, there's a basic style in use for paragraphs, dictating the default font, size, color, leading, and tracking (among others) for any new text frame you create. You can view what makes up that basic paragraph style by double-clicking it in the Paragraph Styles panel, which opens the Paragraph Style Options dialog box, shown in Figure 7-2.

To create a paragraph style of your own, you need to give InDesign an example of the formatting you want the new style to apply. This means taking existing text and applying formatting and effects as desired until the text looks the way you want any text to which the style is applied to look. Once the text is formatted—including font, size, leading, kerning, tracking, vertical scale, baseline shift, horizontal scale, skew, any character style you want to incorporate (making it part of

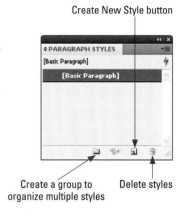

Create New Style button

Create a group to organize multiple styles

Delete styles

FIGURE 7-1 Basic Paragraph is the style on which your new text frames' paragraphs are based—until you create and apply your own paragraph styles, that is.

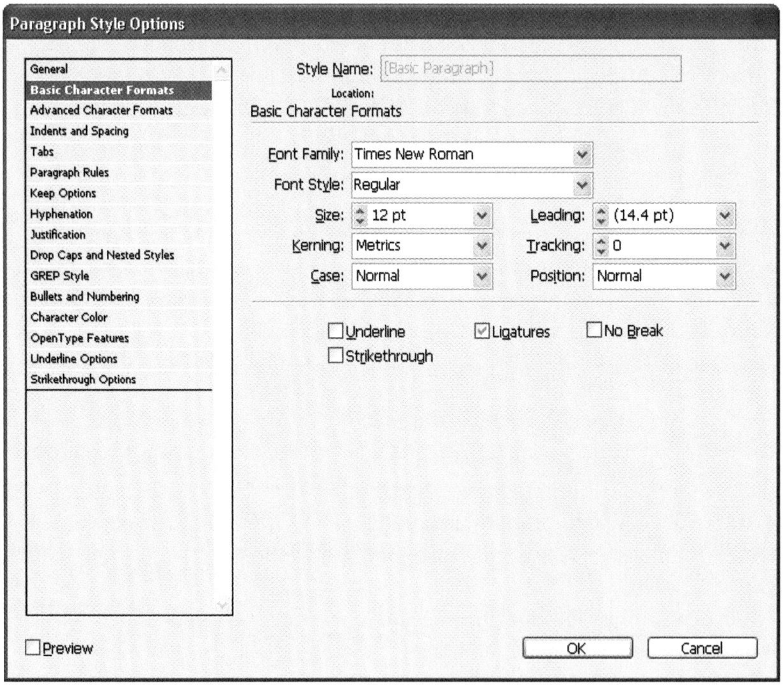

FIGURE 7-2 View the Basic Character Formats settings for the Basic Paragraph style.

the paragraph style), alignment, indents, and color—you're ready to click the Create New Style button in the Paragraph Styles panel. And that's all it takes—one click of that button, and your new style is created.

Modify a Paragraph Style

Of course, the new style has a generic name, which you'll want to change. "Paragraph Style 1" isn't going to be very useful tomorrow or next week or next month, when you can't remember what formatting that style was set up to apply. This is especially important once you have more than one of your own styles in the panel. You'll want to be able to tell them apart at a glance.

To rename a style and to make other changes, which you'll invariably want to do, all you need to do is double-click the style in the Paragraph Styles panel. This opens the Paragraph Style Options dialog box, shown in Figure 7-2 and again in Figure 7-3. The default view of the dialog box gives you the

FIGURE 7-3 The General view of the Paragraph Style Options dialog box

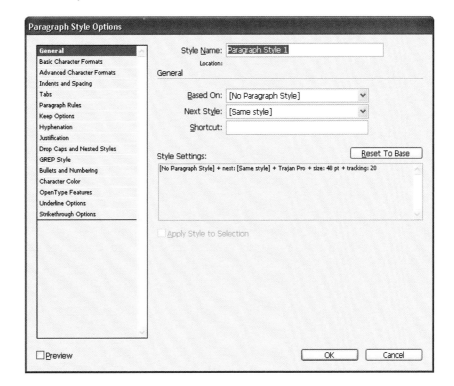

opportunity to change the style name and choose its general settings: the style on which the new style is based (Based On), the style that will apply automatically to the next text typed after any paragraph to which the style is applied (Next Style), and a keyboard shortcut to invoke the style. A list of the style's attributes also appears in the Style Settings box.

You can use the list on the left to view and change any other aspect of the style, from character formats, to tabs, to bullets and numbering. Each category displays a different set of options, which you can view to remind yourself what you set up when the style was created, or you can change them to alter the formats applied by the style.

When you've made all the changes you need, click OK to close the dialog box and return to your document. To use the style, select some text and then click the style's name, or place your cursor within a paragraph and click the style in the Paragraph Styles panel. It's that simple!

Once you've got your own styles created, be they paragraph or character styles, you can use the Options dialog box to make new styles simply by dragging an existing style to the Create New Style button (thus making a duplicate of the style), double-clicking the style copy (the word "Copy" appears in its name), and then using the Options dialog box to tweak the style's attributes and give it a new name.

Define and Modify a Character Style

To create your own character style, you'll follow the same procedure as you would to create a paragraph style. Format the text the way you want to be able to format other text in the future, and then click the Create New Style button in the Character Styles panel (shown in Figure 7-4). A new Character Style 1 appears in the panel, which you can rename and modify as desired by double-clicking the style in the panel. The Character Style Options dialog box, shown in Figure 7-5, provides all the tools you need to change the way the style will affect your text and, of course, to rename it to something relevant and descriptive.

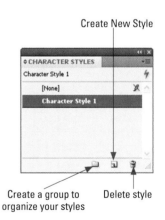

Create New Style

Create a group to organize your styles

Delete style

FIGURE 7-4 The Character Styles panel with a new generically named style in place

Click to view
settings in these
categories.

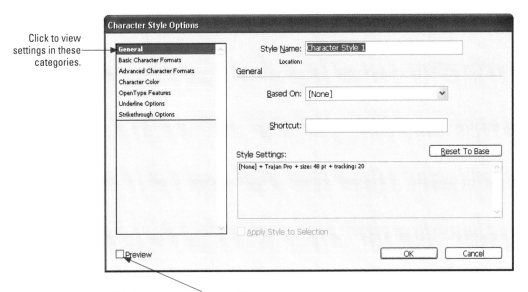

Click Preview to see the style within your
document while the dialog box is still open.

FIGURE 7-5 View and change
the formatting your style applies
to text.

What's OpenType? This category in the Character Style Options dialog box allows you to
implement specialized character and typesetting attributes in your text when OpenType
fonts are in use. Each of the check boxes and lists in this area of the dialog box allow you to
completely customize how InDesign displays your OpenType fonts. To find out more about these fonts
and their options, visit www.adobe.com/type/opentype.

Import Styles

Thankfully, you can take styles from one InDesign document
to another, eliminating the need to re-create styles in different
documents. The process of sharing them between documents is
simple.

1. Display the Character Styles or Paragraph Styles panel
(for whichever kind of style you want to import).

2. Click to display the Panel menu, as shown in Figure 7-6,
and choose Load Character Styles (or Load Paragraph
Styles). You can alternatively choose Load All Text
Styles to import all text styles at once.

FIGURE 7-6 Display the Panel menu and choose if you want to load one particular style or all of the styles in another InDesign document.

FIGURE 7-7 Pick the InDesign document bearing the style(s) you want to import.

3. From within the Open a File dialog box, shown in Figure 7-7, double-click the InDesign document with the styles you want to import.

4. In the resulting Load Styles dialog box (shown in Figure 7-8), select the styles you want to import by clicking the check box next to each one you want, and then click OK.

FIGURE 7-8 Select the check boxes for those styles you want to import.

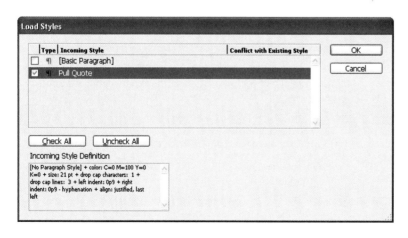

If you try to import a style that has the same name as a style you already have in your target document, you'll want to have selected either the Auto Rename or Use Incoming Style Definition check box. Their names are rather self-explanatory, but suffice to say you're choosing whether to override your existing styles with the new ones (if they have the same name) or to create a new style with a new name when a naming conflict arises.

Manage a Set of Styles

As simple as styles are to create, apply, and edit, if you have a lot of them, you may want to organize them—placing them in groups that help keep styles with different jobs or purposes separate from the rest. As shown in Figure 7-9, grouping styles also makes for a shorter, simpler display in the panel, be it the Paragraph or Character Styles panel. If you have a lot of styles, placing them in groups will make life easier in many ways.

To create a group for your styles, click the Create New Style Group button, identified in Figure 7-9. Style Group 1 (or 2, if it's your second group) appears in the panel, and you can rename it as desired. Just double-click it, and use the resulting Style Group Options dialog box (shown in Figure 7-10) to give it a name that will help describe the styles that are part of the group.

Speaking of which, how do you place styles in a group? It couldn't be easier. Just drag them into the group, as shown in Figure 7-11. A small box follows your mouse pointer; when the target group is highlighted, release your mouse.

Expanded group shows the styles within it.

Styles inside a group are indented.

Collapsed groups don't show their styles until you want to see them.

Create New Style Group

FIGURE 7-9 Organizing your styles into groups makes for a simpler display of your styles and makes choosing them easier, too.

Style Group Options

Name: Headlines

OK

Cancel

FIGURE 7-10 Name your style group so that it's clear which styles you'll find within it.

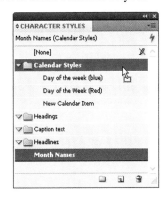

FIGURE 7-11 Drag a style to the group to which it belongs.

You can also create groups within groups for even more organization. If, for example, you have styles for formatting different parts of a calendar, you could break them down into groups called Monthly Calendar Styles, Weekly Calendar Styles, and Daily Calendar Styles, all of which could be inside a main group called Calendar Styles. To create groups within groups, simply select the parent group—the group the new one will live within—and then click the Create New Style Group button.

 Want to get rid of a style? Drag the style to the trash can icon in the Paragraph or Character Styles panel. If you've applied the style to any text within your document, a prompt appears to ask if you really want to delete the style and if you want the formatting to remain in place for the text to which the soon-to-be-deleted style was applied. Groups can also be deleted by dragging them to the Delete Style/Group button.

Summary

In this chapter, you learned about styles—how to create them, how to edit them, how to bring styles into one document from another by importing them, and how to manage your styles so that you can always find and use them whenever you need them.

From which formats can be included in a style, how the styles are applied, and which naming conventions are most convenient and logical, you learned just about everything there is to know about styles as they relate to text. And once you've created them, you now know how to store them in sets for quick access.

In Chapter 8, you'll be moving further into the topic of text—namely, how to create lists and tables to store text in structures of your own design.

8

Design a Layout with Lists and Tables

How to...

- Design bulleted and numbered lists
- Add tables to a document
- Format table structures
- Create table and cell styles

Readability is an integral element of a well-crafted page. You'll often see similar elements grouped within a unifying structure, such as bulleted and numbered lists. Where your information contains several pieces of data for each element, the simplest way to present it is laid out in a table. In this chapter, read how InDesign tackles lists, tabs, and tables.

Organize Contents with Bullets and Numbers

Bullets and numbers identify collections of similar concepts. Items in a bulleted list are in no particular order, while a numbered list obviously has an order. Bullet characters are stored in the document's metadata just as other styles are.

Order Content Using Bullets

Bullets are a straightforward method for listing content. Display a bulleted or numbered list using the automatic options in the Control panel, or design and apply a paragraph style. Bullets and numbers inherit text formatting from the first character of the paragraph to which they're attached. For example, bold applied to text assigns bold to the character as well.

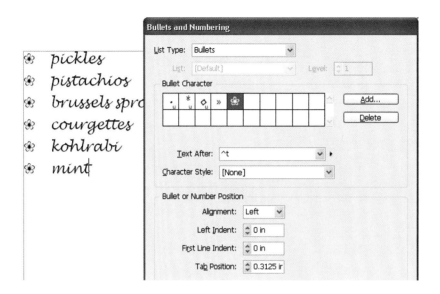

You won't want one or two characters standing out from the rest of the list. In that case, design and use a character style for the bullet or number (check out styles in Chapter 7).

FIGURE 8-1 Configure the appearance of a formatted bullet.

Format a Bulleted List

If you aren't using any different first characters in the list, select the list paragraphs with the Text tool and press ALT as you click Bullets on the Control panel to open the dialog box (see Figure 8-1). Choose Bullets from the List Type dropdown box, and select one of the default bullets from the dialog box, or click Add to open a dialog box where you can select a custom bullet. Select the settings you want for indents, and click OK to close the dialog box and apply the bullets.

Note   Some bullets listed in Figure 8-1 show a "u" below their icons, identifying them as bullets stored with the Unicode value only, rather than the font family and style as well as the Unicode value.

Bullet Behavior

InDesign manages the appearance of the bullet, number, or separator using a format you can control, although the characters don't function like normal text. That is:

- You don't select bullets or numbers on the page.

- InDesign updates numbers automatically; you can't change them manually.

Create Running Captions

You often see running captions for sequentially numbered figures or tables. To complete a running caption, choose basic numbering features, including the numbers list type, a defined list, and a numbering style.

Configure the appearance in the Number box by adding text, spacing, and other metacharacters. For example, if you want your items to use sequential numbers labeled as *Figure-space-number-.tab* and then the text, enter this string:

```
Figure ^#.^t
```

Tip Use the Table Of Contents feature described in Chapter 9 to produce a list of figures or tables. Read about designing paragraph styles in Chapter 7.

- Automatically generated characters aren't inserted in the text, so you can't locate them by a text search.
- You don't see the characters in the Story Editor either, with the exception of a display in the Paragraph Style column.

Work with Numbered Lists

For a simple numbered list, click Numbered List on the Control panel to apply numbers, or press ALT-CLICK Numbered List to open the dialog box and choose from default settings, such as the number's appearance and spacing characters.

Numbers are usually more complex than bullets, and can be used in multiple configurations. Before you can add several list levels, such as numbered lists with a set of lettered sublists, you need to define the lists. A *defined list* is the key to more complex bullet and numbering features, letting you interrupt one list with another list or other content—producing a layout like this book. By defining multiple lists, you can interrupt one list with another and maintain number sequences in each list.

To define a list, choose Type | Bulleted and Numbered Lists | Define Lists to open the dialog box. Click New in the Define Lists dialog box to open the New List dialog box, and type a name for the list.

Two criteria are selected by default. Select whether to continue numbers across stories and/or to continue numbers from previous documents, specify if you're working in a book format, and click OK to close the dialog box. Click OK again to close the Define Lists dialog box.

Tip A numbered list imported from Microsoft Word automatically defines a list.

Apply Numbering to a List

To number a list, select the text and press ALT as you click the Numbered List button on the Control panel to open the Bullets and Numbering dialog box (see Figure 8-2).

Follow these guidelines to choose number settings:

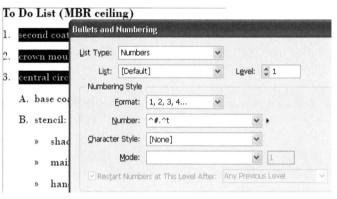

FIGURE 8-2 Specify settings for number types and styles.

1. Specify the list type and select a list name. The initial numbering level can use the Default list.

2. Choose styling for the number. The Mode options define where to start numbering (refer to the next section for details).

3. Specify number position using the same options as those shown in Figure 8-1 for configuring bullets.

4. Click OK to close the dialog box and apply the numbering.

Restart or Continue Numbering for a List

Whether a single or multilevel list, you can revise numbering at any time, or you can continue numbering a list following insertion of other sorts of content. Place the Text tool insertion point where you want to make a change, and choose the relevant command from the shortcut menu.

■ **Restart Numbering** Choose this command to renumber the list from 1 or A in a regular list or from the first lower-level number in a multilevel list, as shown here.

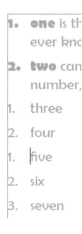

■ **Continue Numbering**   Choose this command to continue numbering a list after inserting other types of content. Use a variation on this command to number a list across stories. In the Bulleted and Numbered Lists dialog box, choose the list to use from the Define Lists drop-down list, and click Edit. Then choose Continue Numbers Across Stories.

You can't use the Default list since it won't run across stories.

To Do List (MBR ceiling)

1. second coat outside ring - persimmon

2. crown moulding - ivory

3. central circle

    A. base coat - sheer persimmon

    B. stencil:

        » shadow layer - semisheer copper

        » main stencil - persimmon/pearlized

        » handpaint highlights - pearl/persimmon tint

    C. blend coat - sheer copper tint

    D. top coat - sheer persimmon

4. ring to edge - 5″ border, persimmon/pearl/copper

    braid (handpaint 1/2 strength)

Create Multilevel Lists

Use a multilevel list to produce an outline of your content in a ranked hierarchy. Number formats are assigned to each level, up to a possible nine levels. In order to display a ranked hierarchy on your document, each level requires its own paragraph style. When designing the styles, use the same defined list. To define a style's position in the hierarchy, type a number in the Level box in the Paragraph Style Options dialog box.

In the example shown here, the numbered items use the Default list, the lettered items use a defined list, and the bullets are a separate list.

Display Content in Tables

InDesign uses tables as a text-based structure enclosed within a text frame. You configure the table's contents like any other text, viewable in the Story Editor. Tables flow like inline graphics in a set of threaded frames. Unlike ordinary text frames, however, you can't use a frame containing a table with text on a path.

Rows and columns make up a table's structure, with each intersecting space defined as a cell. Cells function like individual text frames for holding text, graphics, or even other tables.

A table is simply a tabbed layout with visible borders. In the old days, tabs were set manually on typewriters using the *Tabulator* key to lay out a table structure. Read more about tabs in Chapter 6.

Build a Table

There are several ways to build a table, depending on your requirements and available resources. For example, if you have a Microsoft Excel spreadsheet, import it into an InDesign table rather than starting again, or copy and paste text from a page into InDesign and create a table from it. To reuse an existing table as part of another one, simply insert it into a cell on your new table.

Create a Table from Scratch

You can easily start a table from scratch in InDesign. First, draw a text frame to the width you want for the table, as the table uses the frame's width as a default.

Follow these steps to create a table:

1. Double-click the frame at the location where you want to insert the table. InDesign uses the location of the Type tool's insertion marker as the table's upper-left corner.

2. Choose Table | Insert Table to open the Insert Table dialog box.

3. Choose the number of rows and columns for the table.

4. Specify the header and footer rows. You can use one or more of each, which display for every element of your table if it extends over multiple columns or frames.

5. Click OK to close the dialog box and insert the table.

Row height is based on a table style, paragraph style, or default slug using the default leading value.

Place a Table

Tables imported from Word or Excel are embedded by default. The contents remain editable in a Word document or an Excel spreadsheet you place in a document, if you use the Place command and choose a file handling preference. To set the preference, choose Edit | Preferences | File Handling, and choose Create Links When Placing Text and Spreadsheet Files.

Choose File | Place to open the Place dialog box, and click Show Import Options. Then, locate and select the file containing the table, and click Open. The Place dialog box closes, and the Import Options dialog box appears.

Specify the characteristics for the table, which vary according to the type of file you're placing. For example, an Excel spreadsheet offers options to select the sheet, cell range, and cell alignment. Specify the table's format in several ways, ranging from a formatted table to unformatted, tabbed text. Click OK to close the dialog box and import the content.

Convert Text to a Table

Use existing or added characters to define separators that let you easily convert text into a table. InDesign recognizes numerous characters for defining rows or columns. To take advantage of a regular page structure, it's simplest to use commas or tabs for column separators and paragraph returns for row separators.

Select the text using the Type tool; then choose Table | Convert to Text to open the dialog box. Choose the character for both the column separator and row separator, or type a custom character. Click OK to close the dialog box and create the table. The table matrix uses a uniform cell structure and inserts blank cells if you're missing content in a row.

If you use the same character for both separator types, you have to specify the number of columns in the table. If you use another character as a separator, the next time you use the feature, you'll find your custom character on the list.

Work with Table and Cell Contents

Although a table displays a specific layout, you can use many of the same features as for a regular text frame, with the exception of footnotes. In fact, each cell in a table works like an independent frame. Not only can a cell use text, you can also insert graphics and place external files.

Selection	How to Make the Selection
Text in a cell	Drag over text with the Text tool.
Cell	Click inside the cell and choose Table	Select	Cell.
Row	Move pointer over left edge of row; click when arrow displays.
Column	Move pointer over upper edge of column; click when arrow displays.
Table	Move pointer over upper-left corner; click when angled arrow displays.
Similar content	Click inside cell, right-click, and choose Select to open a submenu; choose Header Rows, Body Rows, or Footer Rows.

TABLE 8-1   Selection Methods to Identify Different Table Elements

Select Table Elements

Be careful when selecting table contents, since different commands apply to different elements. Selecting the text in a cell isn't the same as selecting the cell itself. Different selection options are shown here and described in Table 8-1.

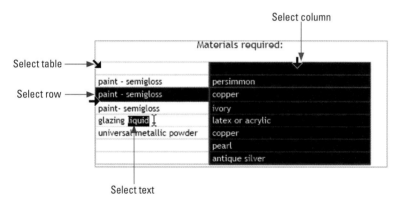

Insert Content into a Table

To insert text in a table cell, activate the cell with the Text tool, and start typing. Press ENTER to insert a new paragraph in the same cell. Press TAB to move to the next cell, type the contents, and so on.

Along with typing text, you can copy and paste from another source, or choose File | Place to insert a file into the cell. For a text file, edit it as required. If you place a graphic file, be aware that the cell height increases to fit the graphic (with a fixed cell height), but the cell width doesn't change (see Figure 8-3).

Take Care of Cell Oversets

Depending on the cell's contents, you may have overset content, as shown in Figure 8-3. To select contents, click in the cell, press ESC to select the hidden content, and decrease font sizes.

For images that extend beyond the cell borders, select the cell and choose Cell Options | Text from the shortcut menu. In the dialog box, select Clip Contents to Cell, and click OK to resize the image.

Too wide for cell   Appropriate size

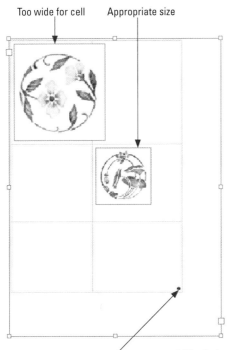

Exceeds cell height (overset)

FIGURE 8-3 Graphics may need modification before adding to a table cell.

If your graphic is larger than the cell width, or if the row has a fixed height causing an overset, it's best to paste the graphic on the pasteboard, resize it or crop it as necessary, and then insert it into the table. You can't drag a graphic from one cell to another. Instead, cut and paste it into the desired location.

Adjust a Table's Layout and Appearance

The simplest way to design a table is to start with a basic layout and then customize as required. Table appearance depends on the element specified. For example, the text frame holding the table may influence the overall appearance and layout. Selecting the table lets you apply features such as alternating row colors; selecting cells offers other choices; while selecting characters offers still more choices.

Work in the Panels

There are myriad ways to perform most layout actions: using keystrokes, panel settings, Control panel options, menu commands, shortcut menu commands, Table Options and Cell Options panels, or Table panel commands (see Figure 8-4).

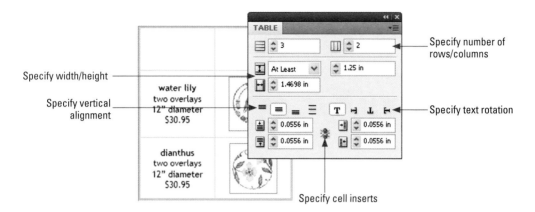

Specify number of rows/columns

Specify width/height

Specify vertical alignment

Specify text rotation

Specify cell inserts

FIGURE 8-4 Find many configuration settings in the Table panel.

Layout Shortcuts

Instead of using panels, use the following shortcuts working directly on the page:

- **Insert rows or columns** Move your mouse over a column or row border to show the double-arrow icon. Click and hold the mouse, and then press ALT and drag downward to add another row, or drag right to add another column.

You can't drag to insert rows or columns at the left or top of a table. Instead, you'll select the rows or columns. Also, be sure to click the mouse before pressing the keys or you'll display the Hand tool instead.

- **Delete rows or columns** Move the mouse over the right or bottom edge of a table to show the double-ended arrow. Press ALT and drag up to remove the bottom row, or drag left to remove the right column.

- **Resize columns and rows** Move the mouse over the edge of a column or row to show the double-ended arrow, and drag left/right to change a column width, or drag up/down to change a row width. If you press SHIFT, the other rows and columns aren't affected.

- **Distribute columns and rows** To make columns proportional, press SHIFT and drag the right table edge to resize all columns proportionally, or drag the bottom table edge to resize all rows proportionally.

- **Merge cells**   Customize the layout of a table by merging cells, such as you'd use for a title. To merge, select the cells with the Type tool, and choose Merge Cells from the shortcut menu. To unmerge, select the cell with the Type tool, and choose Unmerge Cells from the shortcut menu.

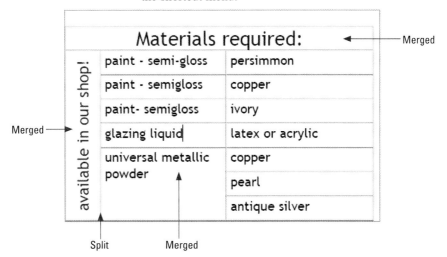

- **Split cells**   Customize a table by splitting cells vertically or horizontally. Click in the cell you want to split, or select a range of cells. Right-click to open the shortcut menu, and choose Split Cells Vertically or Split Cells Horizontally.

Long Tables Can Use Headers and Footers

When you create a long table, the table often spans more than one column, frame, or page. You can use headers or footers to repeat the information at the top or bottom of each divided portion of the table. Insert a header or footer as part of the table creation process, or convert existing rows in the table.

Select the row or rows, and choose Table | Convert Rows | To Header or To Footer to open the dialog box. Specify how often you want to use the header or footer on the page, and click OK to close the dialog box (Windows). On Mac, simply select the row or rows, and choose Convert to Header Rows from the shortcut menu (if you chose rows at the top of the table) or Convert to Footer Rows (if you chose rows at the bottom of the table).

Options	Common Choices
Table Setup	On this tab, you'll find settings for body rows, columns, header/footer rows, borders, and the amount of space inserted before and after the table in a text frame.
Row Strokes	Specify whether to use alternating patterns of row strokes, useful in complex alphanumeric tables.
Column Strokes	Choose the same features as row strokes to color alternating columns.
Fills	Choose whether to use alternating patterns applied to the fills of rows.
Headers/Footers	Define the numbers of header and/or footer rows and their repeat.

TABLE 8-2 Features for Customizing Your Table's Appearance

The Formatting Order

InDesign recognizes table and cell styles as separate from paragraph or character styles, although you can use them all in a table. Whether you format and save styles or not, each document includes the *[Basic Table]* style to apply to tables and the *[None]* style for removing styles assigned to cells. Formatting applies to cells in order, starting with header/footer cells, then left column/right columns, and finally body rows.

Adjust Table Options

The Table Options dialog box brings together settings from a variety of panels and menus used to modify the appearance of your entire table. Select a cell, row, column, or the entire table, and choose Table Options | Table Setup from the shortcut menu to display the five-tabbed Table Options dialog box, described in Table 8-2.

FIGURE 8-5 Be sure to preserve local formatting to maintain your table's appearance.

It's common to include alternating stroke and fill settings for segments of your table. Keep in mind that table options override cell stroke and fill formatting. Be sure to select the Preserve Local Formatting options in the appropriate tabs in the Table Options dialog box. In this table, local formatting, table settings, and styles combine to fill and stroke the table (see Figure 8-5).

Materials required:

	Item	Color or Shade	GO
available in our shop!	paint - semi-gloss	persimmon	...
	paint - semigloss	copper	...
	paint- semigloss	ivory	...
	glazing liquid	latex or acrylic	...
	universal metallic powder	copper	...
		pearl	...
		antique silver	...

Options	Common Choices
Text	Specify the insets (internal border) as well as vertical justification. You'll find clipping, text rotation, and first baseline settings here as well.
Strokes and Fills	Choose cell stroke configurations. Choose a gap color for gapped strokes. Select a fill color for the selected cells. All colors include tint options.
Rows and Columns	Define row heights, either as absolutes or as the minimum. Define the width for a selected column. Choose Keep Options, such as where to start a new row, and Keep with Next to prevent widows and orphans.
Diagonal Lines	Specify diagonal stroke appearances and whether to draw content or stroke in front.

TABLE 8-3   Specific Cell Features You Can Configure

Adjust Cell Appearances

Like the table options, InDesign offers configuration choices for cells. Select the cell or group of cells, and choose Cell Options | Text from the shortcut menu to display the four-tabbed Cell Options dialog box. An overview of the choices is listed in Table 8-3.

Store Table and Cell Styles

Rather than repeatedly formatting your table items, save and apply styles. A table style applies to the entire table, such as borders or alternating fills. A cell style lets you save and reuse settings for insets, paragraph styles, strokes, and fills. A table's style can contain specific cell styles, such as headers or footers.

To design a style, select content in your table, and then choose Create New Style from the Table Styles or Cell Styles panels' toolbars to open their respective dialog boxes. You'll

Cells Can Use Tabs

Sometimes, you want to use an indent within a cell, especially if you're designing a complex table or one with a number of user instructions. Place the Type tool's insertion point where you want to insert the tab, and then right-click and choose Insert Special Character | Other | Tab from the shortcut menu. If you need to make changes, select the columns or cells, and choose Type | Tabs to open the panel and adjust the settings.

find a subset of the same settings tabs as those described previously for the table options (listed in Table 8-2) and the cell options (listed in Table 8-3).

In the General tab, name the style, and choose whether to base it on another style and whether to include a paragraph style. Click Preview at the lower corner of the dialog box to view changes in the table as you work on the style's options. Click OK to close the dialog box and complete the style. To apply the style, select the content on the table, and click the style's name, as you see here.

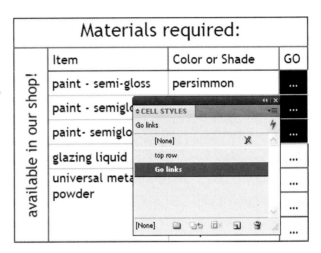

Summary

This chapter looked at a variety of features you can use to organize content in InDesign. Although there are multiple ways to perform the same functions, the discussion was limited to basic menu features and a shortcut or two. There simply isn't the space for an exhaustive description!

Use the bullet and numbering features in InDesign to order and display similar content on a page, from a simple bulleted list to multilevel lists that span an entire book and numerous hierarchy levels. We looked at ways to start a table from scratch or using external content, and how to format, design, and style a table in InDesign.

Up next, see how to craft a book file. InDesign refers to a *book* as a specific structure that controls multiple documents and master pages.

9

Work with Long Documents

How to...

- Define a book
- Maintain consistency across book files
- Control numbers across chapters and pages
- Work with a table of contents
- Construct an index for a book

InDesign Creative Suite 4 (CS4) is many things to many people. Where some use it for ad layouts or other short documents, many use it for laying out longer projects, ranging from annual reports to magazine issues to books.

In this chapter, go between the covers for the scoop on constructing a document that combines multiple files into an InDesign book. You'll see how to number pages and control text across several publications. Then, turn to the tools InDesign conveniently offers for creating tables of contents and indexes.

Create a Book Publication

Regardless of the project breakdown, a book structure keeps file sizes small, allows multiple people to work on the project simultaneously, and includes features for standardizing appearances and numbering.

Not only that, you also can export, package, or print components of the book from the Book panel without even having the files open. Working with different page sizes and orientations in the same publication requires an external plug-in—or you can simply include the various components in a single book.

Start a Book Project

You don't need to have all of the component documents ready to start a book file. As you'll read later in the chapter, it's easy to add more documents to a book. The first step is to create the structure for the book itself.

It's a good idea to create a project folder to store the book's file, the component documents, and support files such as templates, fonts, libraries, and so on.

Build the Book Framework

InDesign stores all the content for a book project in an .indb file. One book file can have up to 9,999 document pages. If you need to use more pages, break it into several documents, and use the Book feature to synchronize master pages, styles, and pagination.

Follow these steps to get a book started:

1. Choose File | New | Book to display the New Book dialog box.

2. Type a name for the book in the File Name field. The Save As Type (Save on Mac) field defaults to a *book*, using the .indb file format.

3. Locate and select the folder where you want to store the book. Click Save to close the dialog box and display the Book panel showing your book name in the panel's tab.

Import the Content

At the start of the project, the Book panel is empty. Choose Add Document from the Book panel's menu to open the Add Documents dialog box. Locate and select the files you want to use for the book, and click Open to close the dialog box and load the files into the book file. Then, choose Save Book from the Book panel's menu.

During your work sessions, you may see different icons, depending on the status of your files (see Figure 9-1). For example, if you delete or rename a document formerly included in

FIGURE 9-1 The Book panel shows a number of indicators.

a book file, you'll see a red "missing" icon. If you make document changes independently of the book file by opening the document directly, the book file shows a "modification" icon. A document opened by someone else shows a lock icon; a closed file doesn't show an indicator.

Change and Replace Content

There are a few options for changing content in a book file.

- To swap a component, select the item's name on the Book panel, and then choose Replace Document from the Book panel's menu.

- To delete a component, select its name on the Book panel, and choose Remove Document from the Book panel's menu, or click the Remove Document (–) icon at the bottom of the panel.

- Reorder the contents in the Book panel by dragging an item up or down in the panel.

Work with a Book File

The key to understanding where to find a particular command depends on the task. For example, the Book panel includes commands for saving the book, while you can save component files using program menu commands and shortcuts.

Handle a Book File

The book file is a separate entity from its component files. You don't need the book file open in InDesign in order to work on the documents included in the book. When you next open the book file, you'll see an icon indicating the file has changed.

You can open a book file just like any other InDesign file. That is, double-click its icon or name from its storage location, or open it from within InDesign from the File menu's list of recent documents. The Welcome screen doesn't include the book file on the list of recent documents.

Handling the Book panel is much like using any other panel in InDesign, although it isn't a default program panel. Display the Book panel like any other panel—collapse it, tear it from the panel dock, add it to a group, and so on.

Add Navigation Elements

The most common navigation element in any book or document is a page number (described in Chapter 3). In a multisegment document, you'll also find content on the pages identifying a section or chapter. InDesign provides an easy-to-use process for generating a table of contents for quick orientation to a book's contents. Use the indexing feature InDesign provides if you're designing a book where your intended readers need to search for particular terms or phrases.

Control Page Numbering

Specify page numbering across a book's files from the Book panel's menu. Select Book Page Numbering Options to open the dialog box, where you'll find five options. Make your choices, and click OK to close the dialog box.

 Before configuring pages in a book, make sure each document uses automatic page numbering and that each document starts on page 1.

Here's the best way to use the options:

- Choose Continue from previous document if you're working on a single-sided document. For example, if DocA ends on page 20, DocB starts on page 21.

- Choose Continue on next odd page if you're working on a book where new chapters generally start on the right (odd) page. For example, if Chapter 1 ends on page 17, Chapter 2 then starts on page 19.

- Choose Continue on next even page if you're working on a magazine, periodical, or brochures such as seasonal tours, where new content often starts on the left (even) page. For example, if Barbados Hotels ends on page 17, Jamaica Hotels starts on page 18.

- Select the Insert Blank Page check box if you want blank pages inserted automatically when you've specified starting a new unit on either an odd or even page. In the recipe book example, InDesign adds a blank page at the end of Chapter 1 to maintain the pagination, shown here. You have to assign a master page to the blank pages manually.

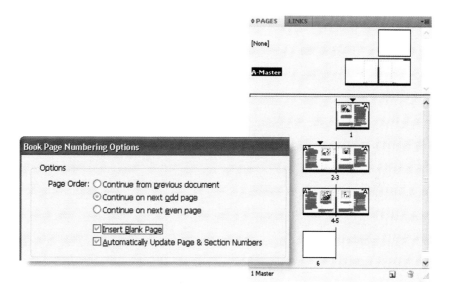

Select the Automatically Update Page & Section Numbers check box to repaginate as you work. Use this option when multiple components are missing from the book. If you prefer, deselect the check box and choose Update Numbering from the Book panel's menu whenever you want an update.

There's More to Pagination than Page Numbers

You may think missing content is the biggest issue for incomplete pagination. It makes sense, and it *is* an issue—along with two additional important issues. Be sure to apply styles to the component files, and make sure the fonts intended for the book are available. Unless these two requirements are met, InDesign can't calculate accurate text flow.

Show Chapter Numbers

In many documents—both books and other types of publications—you see text that changes according to the page where it displays. The most common example you'll see in a book is a chapter number. In InDesign, chapter numbers are assigned by the book containing the documents.

Follow these steps to add chapter numbers using a text variable inserted on the master page of any document:

1. Click to place the cursor in a text field where you want to display the variable, and choose Type | Text Variables | Define to open the Text Variables dialog box. Click New to display the New Text Variable dialog box (see Figure 9-2).

2. Type a name for the variable, such as **ChNo** (Chapter Number) in the example, and then click the Type drop-down arrow and choose the variable type, such as Chapter Number in the example.

3. Add text or symbols before or after the number according to your layout. For example, type **Chapter** in the Text Before field to preface each instance of the text variable with the word. Click the arrow to open a list of symbols and spaces, and choose an option if desired, such as an em space in the example, shown as the metacharacters ^m in the Text Before field.

4. Click the Style drop-down arrow, and choose a number or character option for the number's style.

5. Watch the configuration in the Preview area at the bottom of the dialog box. When you're finished, click OK to close the dialog box and return to the Text Variables dialog box, where you'll see the new variable listed. If the cursor is in the desired location for the variable, click Insert, and then click Done. Otherwise, click Done to close the dialog box.

6. To add the variable to another page, choose Type | Text Variables | Insert Variable | ChNo (or your custom

FIGURE 9-2 Define new text variables for items like chapter numbers.

variable's name) to apply an instance of the variable. As you see, the variable displays the content defined in the Text Variable dialog box and uses whatever style you assign to the text.

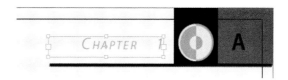

 Note The structure for the ChNo object defining the text makes up the *text variable*. Each occurrence of the variable on the page shows as an *instance* of that variable.

Synchronize and Update Content

Imagine how time-consuming it would be to manually update page numbering, table of contents, indexes, and so on each time

 **How to...** **Use Other Text Variables**

Other variables you often see in a book project define a running header or footer showing different content on the left and right pages, such as a section name on the left and a topic or subject on the right.

Write a running header or footer variable on your master page. In the document, InDesign pulls the text using the style defined in the variable and inserts it into the header or footer. Suppose your page contains three headings using the *head3* style, the style defined in the variable. By default, the text from the first heading also displays as the header or footer. If you prefer, specify the text from the third heading instead.

For a running head based either on a paragraph or character style, use the same method as described earlier for chapter numbers to define headers for your project.

 Note Other types of text variables include creation date, filename, modification date, output date, and so on.

you made changes! Fortunately, one of the strengths of a book project is maintaining an up-to-date status.

1. InDesign offers a method for synchronizing a book's component files. First, click the box to the left of a component file to define an exemplar called a *style source*. You'll see an indicator in the box, as shown in Figure 9-1.

2. Choose Synchronize Options from the Book panel's menu to open the dialog box, listing features to copy from the style source to your other files. Select and deselect options as necessary (see Figure 9-3).

3. Select the Smart Match Style Groups check box to prevent duplication of uniquely named styles moved into or out of style groups.

Read about styles and style groups in Chapter 7.

4. Click OK to close the dialog box, or click Synchronize from the dialog box.

5. If you're back in the program window, click Synchronize at the bottom of the Book panel. InDesign tests content in the other files to that of the style source and modifies it accordingly.

FIGURE 9-3 Specify the items and styles for synchronizing.

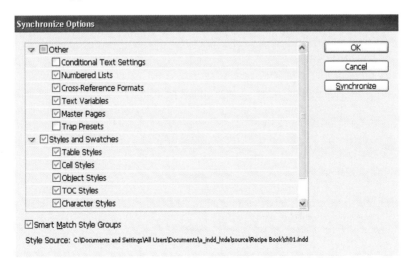

You'll see a dialog box indicating that some files may be changed—click Do Not Show Again in the lower-left of the dialog box to save a mouse click each time you synchronize your book.

Generate a Table of Contents

Traditionally, we think of a table of contents as a list of headings in a book's chapters, although any content that can be identified and referenced on a page—such as illustrations, references, images, or tables—can make up a table of contents.

A table of contents isn't complete until the contents are complete. As you change headings or subheadings, for example, the table of contents updates. Fortunately, InDesign automates the process of creating a table of contents using paragraph styles.

Learn about designing and applying styles in Chapter 7.

Follow these steps to produce the table of contents:

1. Open the book file, and double-click the component for the table, such as the *FM* (Front Matter) document in the example.

2. Choose Layout | Table of Contents to open the Table of Contents dialog box shown here.

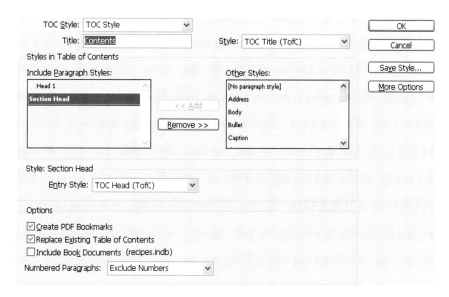

The TOC Style shows as *[Default]* at the top of the dialog box, but changes to *[Custom]* when you modify the style choices.

3. Type your title and choose a style from the Style drop-down list.

4. In the Include Paragraph Styles column, select a style to use for the table of contents from the Other Styles column, and click Add; select a style name, and click Remove to delete it from the list.

5. Select each style in the Include Paragraph Styles column, and choose a style to apply from the Entry Style drop-down list.

6. Select Include Book Documents to create the table of contents from your entire book. Select options such as defining Portable Document Format (PDF) bookmarks or handling paragraph numbers.

7. Click OK to close the dialog box and generate the table of contents.

Click Save Style to save the settings as a style to reuse in another project.

8. Click the loaded cursor on the page. The table of contents displays on the page, as you see in Figure 9-4.

Produce an Index

InDesign offers indexing capabilities that let you create any type of index using markers added to a publication. Indexes range from a simple keyword index to a cross-referenced, multilevel detailed guide.

An index entry includes a topic and a reference to a location where the topic is located (or a cross-reference to another topic).

Mark Content for Indexing

The design and construction of a complex index could be the topic of its own book! Indexing references content in a number of ways, from a term and its page location (a keyword index), to a selection of paragraphs, to a number of pages.

FIGURE 9-4 The table of contents uses the defined styles.

Contents

Appetizers 1

Candied Pecans   2
Baked Artichoke Dip   3
Oyster Spread   4
Creamy Bacon Bits   5
Spinach Rolls   6

Breakfast 9

Green & White Scrambled Eggs   10
Breakfast Queso   11
Breakfast Pudding   12
Cream Cheese and Jam Breakfast Spread   13

Follow these steps to select content for a keyword index using default settings:

1. Choose Window | Type & Tables | Index to open the panel, displaying the Reference list. Select Book to view entries from open documents in a book file.

2. Open the documents you want to index, such as the ch_01 and ch_02 documents in the sample project.

3. Choose Type | Show Hidden Characters to display the index markers as you add them.

4. To insert an index marker to identify the destinations for your index entries, click the location where you want the marker, or select the word or phrase with the Type tool. You can work in either the Layout or Story view. Press SHIFT-ALT-CTRL-[(Windows) or SHIFT-OPTION-COMMAND-[(Mac) to add the marker character at the cursor location or start of a selection. Notice how much easier it is to view the markers in Story view.

 Tip   Select a phrase, such as *green onion,* and substitute the [with] in the shortcut to index the term using the last word in the selection first, such as *onion, green.*

5. Continue adding markers for all documents in your book.

6. Once you've completed adding entries, read through the topics. InDesign offers tools for using consistent capitalization, plurals, designing subentries (such as *Yogurt, vanilla*), and adding cross-references, such as *see also: Vanilla yogurt* added to the *Yogurt* listing (see Figure 9-5).

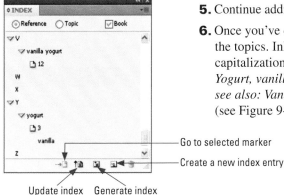

FIGURE 9-5 Check through the index references.

Generate the Index

When you've finished checking the contents, follow these steps from the Index panel to produce your index:

1. Click Generate Index from the Index panel's toolbar or the panel's menu to open the Generate Index dialog box.

2. Choose settings for the index, named *Index* by default. Click the Title Style drop-down arrow, and choose a style for the index; select Include Book Documents to index the entire book. Choose Include Entries on Hidden Layers to add markers from hidden layers.

 Tip   Click More Options on the dialog box to open additional choices for selecting more features, such as level and index styles and nested entries.

3. Click OK to close the dialog box and generate the index. The index content is loaded on to your cursor.

4. Flow the generated story into a text frame. As you see here, you can control the index's appearance like any other text, such as using columns and column breaks.

Index

A
  artichokes 3
B
  bacon 5
  bacon bits 6
  breakfast sausage 11
C
  Candied Pecans 2
  cream cheese 5, 10, 11
E
  eggs 10
M
  maple syrup 2
O
  orange juice 12
P
  Parmesan cheese 3
  prunes 12

R
  refrigerated crescent dinner rolls 5
  rotel 11
S
  scallions 10
  Scrambled Eggs 10
  smoked oysters 4
  sour cream 6
  spinach 6
T
  tofu 3
  tortilla 6
  Triscuit crackers 4
Y
  yogurt 3
  yogurt, vanilla 12

Summary

The old adage "You can't judge a book by its cover" certainly applies to a book in InDesign. As you've seen in this chapter, a book is a type of InDesign file, a separate panel, and a collection of content management features.

Several items make up the concept of a "book." Minimally, a book needs page navigation, such as page numbers, and a visual hierarchy, such as heading styles. Although it isn't necessary to include all of the features, you can incorporate a table of contents, other tables such as figures or references (or tables!), parts or sections, and an index.

Up next, read about working with images in Part III.

PART III

A Picture Is Worth a Thousand Words

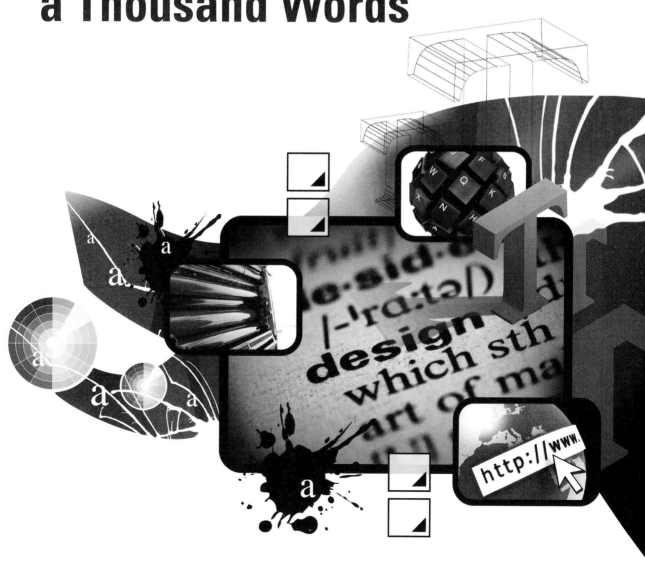

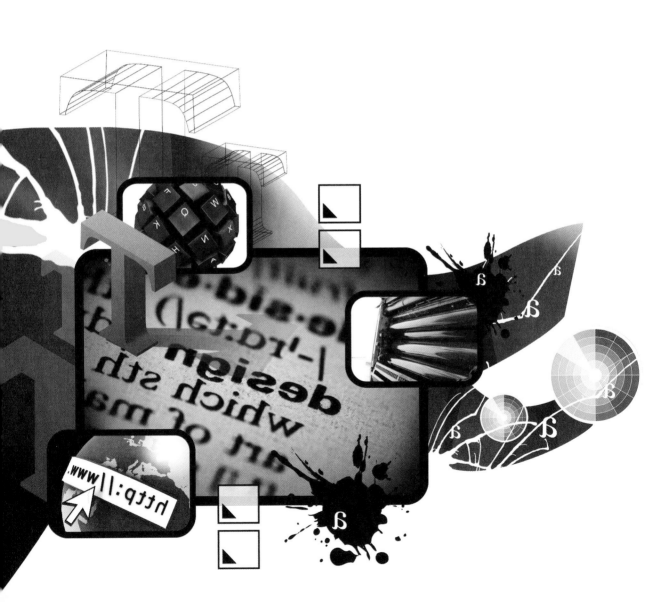

10

Place Images and Graphics

How to...

- Place image files
- Select image features
- Specify placement options
- Use specialized layout techniques

How much of your daily communication is based on images of one type or another? Designing and working in our increasingly visual world demands more efficient tools and workflows. Fortunately, InDesign CS4 is equipped to handle the demand.

In this part, read about different aspects of working with images, graphics, and objects. We start off looking at how to place images and graphics in InDesign in this chapter. Aside from the obvious method of pasting an image on to a page, InDesign offers a number of features to make concise and artistic placements.

Chapter 11 continues with other types of files, including InDesign files. Managing content is an important design aspect, and you'll see how to work with linked and embedded content. You'll see how InDesign offers different methods for saving and reusing your content to streamline your work.

Next, in Chapter 12, discover the drawing and transformation tools in InDesign. For those with experience in other CS4 programs, such as Adobe Illustrator, you'll find the tools familiar. Aside from constructing and modifying shapes, learn how to use them for defining text wraps and text on a path. Finally, see how to capture and reuse your customizations using object styles.

Chapter 13 rounds out the section with a description of layers and effects. Use layers to organize and manage content in a document, and add some final effects for interest and excitement.

It's probably easier to ask how many InDesign projects *don't* contain images or graphics than to ask how many *do*. The ability to handle visual content in InDesign continues to expand with each new version. Along with basic image placement on the page, InDesign offers the option to select layers from some file types for placement.

Once the image reaches the page, choose from a number of ways to configure the placement. For example, you can work with an image's frame and its contents to produce a modified version of your original artwork. Paste an image into a frame to display a variable portion of the image, or use a clipping path—either imported or drawn in InDesign—to customize the layout further.

To Place, to Drop, or to Paste— That Is the Question

Bring graphics into InDesign using the Place command, using drag-and-drop, or using various copy and paste actions. Each method is useful for different reasons. The Place command offers the most control of your assets, including resolution, color, and components such as pages or layers. Placed content offers links to its source files. Dropped content, while linked to your source files, doesn't offer import options.

If you don't need to control functional aspects of the image or graphics, copy and paste lets you easily embed a file into your project. A pasted image isn't linked to the source file, so updating the original file has no bearing on the pasted copy.

Obey the Import Rules

InDesign uses many types of graphic formats, including a number of bitmap and vector formats. Read short descriptions and when to use different file types in Table 10-1.

Place a Graphic File

Various file types offer different import choices, described in upcoming sections. You can control or override different aspects of the imported files, such as layers or color profiles, without affecting the original content.

Regardless of the type of file you're importing, the method for placing an image file or a file from Illustrator, Photoshop, or Acrobat follows several basic steps:

1. Choose File | Place to open the Place dialog box. Locate and select the file you want to work with.

File Format	Description and Common Uses
Bitmap (.bmp)	Standard Windows bitmap image format; doesn't support cyan-magenta-yellow-black (CMYK), and supports only up to 24-bit color. Use for low-resolution printer or non-PostScript printing.
Encapsulated PostScript (.eps)	Good for online publishing in Portable Document Format (PDF), but poor print output to non-PostScript printers. Prepress-quality resolution, precision, and color. InDesign can use clipping paths in EPS files exported from Photoshop. Imported EPS files automatically insert spot colors into the InDesign Swatches panel.
Graphics Interchange Format (.gif)	Standard for online graphics, uses lossless compression, and maximum of 256 colors. Poor image display; efficient for solid-color illustrations, such as symbols or logos.
Joint Photographic Experts Group (.jpg)	CMYK, red-green-blue (RGB), and grayscale color support. Uses lossy compression. InDesign supports clipping paths in JPEG files generated by Photoshop. Best for continuous-tone images online, but can be used for commercial printing.
Macintosh PICT (.pict)	Widely used for Mac graphics and transferring files. Best for compressing images with large color patches, such as illustrations and logos. InDesign supports PICT files in both Windows and Mac versions, as well as RGB PICT and embedded QuickTime images. PICT graphics aren't intended for commercial printing, can't be color-separated, and are device-dependent.
PCX (.pcx)	Common format in Windows. Supports RGB, indexed-color, grayscale, and bitmap color. Can use some types of lossless compression. No alpha channel support. Not for commercial printing.
Portable Network Graphics (.png)	Alternative to GIF for online use. Uses adjustable, lossless compression. Can display 24-bit images online. Supports transparency in both alpha channel and a designated color. RGB bitmapped PNG images print as composites, not as color separations.
Tagged Image File Format (.tif)	Widely supported bitmap image format in CMYK, RGB, grayscale, Lab, and indexed-color modes. InDesign supports clipping paths, alpha channels, and spot color channels in TIFF images.
Windows/Enhanced Metafile Formats (.wmf)/(.emf)	Windows file formats used for vectors. WMF can contain raster image data. Not for commercial printing or online use; best for sharing content among applications.

TABLE 10-1   Image Formats Based on Features and Uses

2. Select Show Import Options, and click Open to display the Import Options dialog box, the contents of which varies according to the type of file being imported.

3. Choose your settings, and click OK to close the dialog boxes and load the cursor in InDesign.

4. Click the desired location to place the file.

Place Illustrator Files

How you save and export the artwork from Illustrator, as well as how you bring it into InDesign, affects what you can do with the artwork. Place an Illustrator file created in Illustrator 8 or newer in an InDesign publication.

Plan a Workflow

Plan ahead when designing illustrations for your InDesign projects. For example, you may find it useful to designate different artboards or review your layer structures before ending an Illustrator session.

Keep the following concepts in mind as you work:

- If you want to work with objects in InDesign, copy them in Illustrator, and then paste them on to your InDesign document. The pasted structures remain editable, so you can use transformation tools, effects, color, and so on, as desired.

- Illustrator CS4 offers multiple artboards that function like separate pages. If you want to use a specific artboard, use the Place command, and specify which artboard to import in the Place dialog box.

- Place an Illustrator file when you need to select layers. A placed file behaves as a single object and doesn't offer editable paths, objects, or text. For editing, select the object and choose Edit | Edit Original to open the graphic in Illustrator. If you intend to use variable layer options in Illustrator, don't use nested layer sets, as InDesign can't work with them.

Specify the Placement Options

During the import process, you'll see the Place dialog box label shows the file as a PDF import of the selected Illustrator file. For example, the Place dialog box for the file dots.ai is named Place PDF (dots.ai). As you place the Illustrator file, choose import option settings (described in Step 2 previously) from two tabs in the Place dialog box.

Your choices, shown in Figure 10-1, include:

- **General tab**   Here you'll find options to select and preview pages, designate the background as transparent, and choose the Crop option.

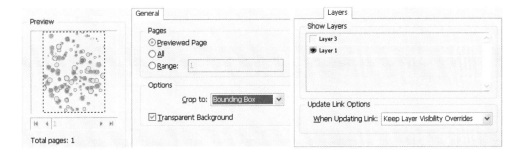

- **Layers tab**   On the Layers tab, select and deselect the layers to import. Also, define how links should update. If you've deselected layers, you can specify that overrides be maintained, or use the host PDF file's layer visibility.

Place Photoshop Files

Use content created in Photoshop 4 or newer in your InDesign projects, including layer comps. Follow the steps outlined in the earlier section, "Place a Graphic File," and specify options in the Image Import Options dialog box. Options chosen in InDesign don't affect the original Photoshop image.

Choose features from the following three tabs in the dialog box:

- Choose settings on the Image Options tab to use a path, mask, or alpha channel from your Photoshop file in InDesign to define text wraps or remove backgrounds. On the Image tab, select Apply Photoshop Clipping Path to use the object from the Photoshop file in InDesign as a transparent object. Select the Alpha Transparency option from the Alpha Channel drop-down list on the Image tab.

- On the Color tab, define whether InDesign uses color management using an embedded International Color Consortium (ICC) color management profile stored in the Photoshop file. Leave the profile as is, override it in the Import Options dialog box, or assign a color profile to the graphic in InDesign.

■ On the Layers tab, adjust the visibility of the top-level layers in InDesign, as well as view different layer comps. If the image contains layer comps, choose the layer comp you want to display from the Layer Comp drop-down menu.

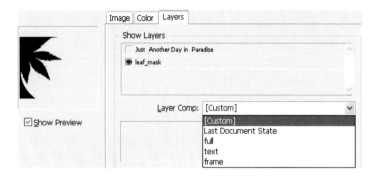

Place PDF Files

Import PDF files as single pages, a page range, or an entire multipage (or multiartboard) file into InDesign, although you can't import links, buttons, movies, or sound content from a PDF file into InDesign. Once you select a PDF file in the Place dialog box, you'll see the same Place dialog box and options as in Figure 10-1.

PDF pages behave as individual objects, and their contents behave in different ways according to page and document characteristics. Managing linked PDF files differs from many other file types due to security and PDF page structures. Read more in Chapter 11.

Look for these chameleon-like features:

■ The PDF content changes resolution according to the page scale and screen resolution.

■ PDF content placed in an InDesign document prints at the device resolution just as other content when printed to a PostScript printer.

■ When printed on a non-PostScript printer, vector objects on a placed PDF page print at the same resolution as the other vector objects in the document.

■ Bitmap objects print at the best resolution defined in the PDF file.

Place InDesign Files

InDesign lets you place one or all pages from one document as objects into another document. Choose File | Place, and select the file. In the Show Import Options dialog box, choose the pages to use, and then specify the page crop setting and layer visibility for the page or pages.

 If you want to import different layers on various pages, import as-is and then delete content from the pages, or repeat the place process for each different arrangement you want to place.

InDesign loads the pages in the graphics icon. Click to import and place a page. The next page in sequence loads the graphics icon; click again to import and place the second page, and so on. InDesign treats each placed page as a single object, listed in the Links panel. If your placed pages themselves contained placed content, the placed items are shown as a sublist for the page in the Links panel.

You Can Set Layer Visibility in InDesign

If you choose the wrong layers or decide to make some changes after an image file comes into InDesign, don't worry. You can choose layer visibility options after the fact. Select the file in your InDesign document, and choose Object | Object Layer Options to display the dialog box. Select or deselect layers as desired. If you have a Photoshop file containing layer comps, select the comp to display. You can also specify whether to maintain the selected visibility or restore the original file's settings when you update the link. Click OK to close the dialog box, and you're set.

Place Multiple Files

Suppose you've assembled all the material for a project into a single folder to get started. Rather than bringing one file at a time into your document, place them all at once. InDesign lets you drop content into existing frames, create new ones, or assemble them into a grid.

Select and Preview the Files

Choose File | Place, and select the files. You can use a mixture of graphics, InDesign, text, PDF, and other files. Click Open to close the dialog box and return to InDesign. You'll see the loaded cursor, showing a thumbnail of the first file selected. In the Links panel, the filenames show with *LP* (loaded in place) for their location.

If you don't want to see the thumbnails, open the Preferences dialog box. On the Interface panel, deselect Show Thumbnails On Place.

Place the Items in Frames or a Grid

You can work with existing frames or draw frames as you place the content.

- ▣ Click to place the file into an existing frame, or press ALT/OPTION-CLICK an existing frame to replace its contents.

- ▣ Click on the page to place the upper-left edge of a frame and the file, or click-and-drag to place the file and define a frame size.

The next time you want to use a number of graphics on a page, use this method for dropping multiples into a grid:

1. Select the files as usual, and move the loaded cursor over the page as usual.

2. Press CTRL-SHIFT (Windows) or COMMAND-SHIFT (Mac), and drag.

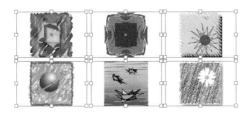

FIGURE 10-2 Drop several items from a loaded cursor on to the page in a grid layout.

3. While you're pressing keys with one hand and manipulating the mouse with the other hand, define the layout of the grid using more keys:

■ Press the UP ARROW and DOWN ARROW keys to change the number of rows.

■ Press the LEFT ARROW and RIGHT ARROW keys to change the number of columns.

■ Press the PAGE UP and PAGE DOWN keys to change spacing between grid frames.

4. Release the mouse to lay out the grid and images (see Figure 10-2).

Tip Unless you have a third hand or trained monkey at your disposal, for a right-handed person, press the modifier keys at the right of the keyboard (in the vicinity of the arrow and other keys) with your left hand, and use your mouse as usual with your right hand. Once you start dragging out the bounding box, you can let go of the modifier keys.

Drag or Paste Graphics

InDesign treats and uses content you copy and paste differently from that you drag-and-drop on a page, depending on the type of file you're using. In general, copy and paste actions are affected by the clipboard settings, while drag-and-drop bypasses the clipboard. Drag-and-drop usually adds the item to the Links panel, while copy and paste actions don't.

Not only does the type of action influence what you can do with the image after it's on your InDesign page, the type of file and its source also play a part.

Use Illustrator Graphics

Illustrator behaves differently from a file you may drag into an open InDesign document from your Finder or Windows Explorer. Whether you copy and paste or drag-and-drop an Illustrator object, you can select and edit the graphic's paths, as you see here.

Once your Illustrator graphic is in InDesign, any attributes imported with the file or applied in InDesign are preserved if you copy and paste or drag a graphic between two InDesign documents or pages. The link information travels along with the graphic (learn more in Chapter 11).

Drag-and-Drop Images

Drag a graphic from Illustrator, Bridge, Windows Explorer, the Mac Finder, or your desktop, and drop it on an InDesign page. Like the Place action, the content you drag-and-drop is listed in the Links panel, except for Illustrator files. However, you don't have import option choices, as with the Place command.

To save time, you can select multiple files to drag-and-drop. Click the loaded graphic icon in InDesign to drop the files on your pages. If you drag a file and change your mind mid-drag, drop it on a panel title bar to cancel the process.

When you copy a graphic from another document, it may be modified by the system clipboard before the paste action. If you paste an item and notice the image or print quality seems affected, try to drag-and-drop instead, or use the Place command for the most control.

Display Images on a Page

Getting content into your InDesign document doesn't stop when the image or graphic shows up on your page. Take advantage of the many ways you can show and control graphic content in your layouts.

InDesign includes several ways to change the size of an image, including letting the frame control the content's size. Try some special pasting methods to take advantage of masking parts of a graphic you don't want to use on the page.

Rather than using a basic frame for displaying an image, control what you see using clipping paths, either drawn in InDesign or imported with your file, for added interest.

Change the Scale

Resizing images is a task you'll do in InDesign over and over. However, for more control in certain types of images, you can scale your images instead.

The difference may seem subtle, and sometimes it is. To resize an image, you change its width and height. To scale an image, you specify a percentage value related to the original scale. Looking at a stroked object and one with linear contents like text is the simplest way to see the two techniques in action.

Sized   Original   Scaled

FIGURE 10-3 Resizing (left) and rescaling (right) a frame have different results.

Here's an example: The center text frame in Figure 10-3 measures 1.5 inches square. The left text frame is resized to 3 inches square. The frame is larger, but the text size and stroke remain as originally drawn. Now look at the right frame. This frame, scaled to 200 percent, also has a size of 3 inches square, but the text and frame contents increase in scale as well.

You can modify dimensions and scale of a frame and/or its contents, depending on the tool you use for selection.

■ InDesign lets you scale both the frame and its contents at once. Select the frame with the Selection tool. In the Control panel, change the values in the Scale X Percentage and Scale Y Percentage fields.

■ Use the Direct Selection tool to select the frame content to adjust it independently of its frame. Once selected, change the values in the Width and Height fields in the Control panel to rescale it. Or, change the values in the Scale X Percentage and Scale Y Percentage fields to rescale.

Tip You don't have to do the math to scale a frame or its contents. Regardless of the active measurement system in your object, you can specify a value in percentage, and InDesign does the calculation. The same works for other measurements.

Fit an Object to Its Frame

You can use the frame surrounding any image you paste or place on a page to manipulate the image's size and proportions. InDesign offers several fitting commands to do the work for you. Fitting options apply directly to images only, but you can use them with nested text frames.

An object placed or pasted into a frame aligns with the upper-left frame corner by default; the outer edge of the content aligns with the center of the frame's stroke (check out Chapter 12 to learn about strokes). To manipulate the frame and its contents, select the frame on the page, and right-click to display the shortcut menu. Choose Fitting and the specific option (see Figure 10-4).

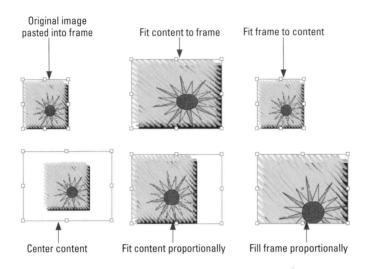

Original image
pasted into frame

Fit content to frame

Fit frame to content

Center content

Fit content proportionally

Fill frame proportionally

FIGURE 10-4 InDesign offers several methods to control graphics and their frames.

Choose from the options listed in Table 10-2 to manipulate the frame/image display on the page.

Tip Double-click any corner handle on the frame to resize it automatically; double-click a side handle to resize the frame on either the X or Y axis.

Fit Option	Changes Made
Fit Content to Frame	Content resizes when you choose this option and doesn't maintain image proportions. The frame is unaffected.
Fit Frame to Content	Resizes a frame to fit its content. The frame's proportions are altered to match the content proportions, if necessary. This is useful for resetting a graphics frame that you accidentally altered.
Center Content	Center the content within the frame. The proportions and sizes of the frame and contents aren't changed. Use this feature when you want to place an image against a colored background within the frame.
Fit Content Proportionally	Maintain your image's proportions and resize the image to fit the frame. If the image and frame have different proportions, you'll have some empty space, either horizontally or vertically, within the frame.
Fill Frame Proportionally	Maintain an image's proportions. The content changes its size, while the frame's dimensions remain static. If the content and the frame have different proportions, the frame crops the content.

TABLE 10-2 Options for Coordinating Images and Their Frames

Control an Image Using Its Frame

Every graphic has a frame. You can manipulate the content separately from the frame and use the frame itself to manipulate the content. InDesign allows you to use the frame to *crop,* or block out, parts of the image by resizing either the frame or the contents. You can also *mask* an image, which works the same as cropping, except that masks generally are shaped rather than linear.

Add or Remove Frame Contents

One frame holds one object, but you can group objects and then drop them into a frame. Follow these steps to combine two items—in this case, a text block and its background shape.

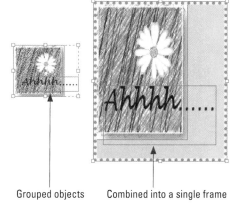

Grouped objects   Combined into a single frame

1. Select the objects' frames on the page using the Selection tool.

2. Right-click and choose Group. You'll see the separate bounding boxes replaced with a dashed box indicating the grouped object's edges.

3. Choose Edit | Cut to remove the content from the page and store it on the clipboard.

4. Draw a blank frame the desired size on the page. Choose Edit | Paste Into. Now the two objects are in a single frame and can be sized or scaled as you like.

Use the same method for pasting a single graphic into a frame, omitting the grouping step, of course.

If you want to take content out of a frame, select the object using the Direct Selection tool; select text with the Type tool. Press DELETE or BACKSPACE to remove the content. If you want to use it elsewhere, cut the content, select the frame to receive the object, and paste the content into the new frame.

Pan Frame Contents

By default, moving a frame with the Selection tool also moves the contents. You can move the frame and contents separately to show only a specific part of your image.

To pan content within the frame, click the image with the Direct Selection tool. You'll see the cursor change to a hand if the image is an imported graphic; otherwise, the cursor retains the tool's cursor when selecting text or graphics drawn in InDesign.

For easier visibility, hold the mouse down to activate the dynamic graphics preview before you start to drag to reposition the image. The preview shows a ghosted version of the image outside of the graphic frame's area and the normal image view inside the frame. As you drag, the nonghosted image area changes within the frame (see Figure 10-5).

Move the Frame over the Contents

If you need to reposition the frame on the page, you can do so without moving the contents, as shown in Figure 10-5. Click the frame with the Direct Selection tool, and then click the center point. When you see solid anchor points instead of the default hollow anchor points, drag the frame.

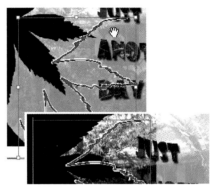

FIGURE 10-5 Move the contents within a frame (top), or move the frame over the contents (bottom).

Crop Objects

Crop off unnecessary graphic content using graphic frames. You can work with a graphic's frame in several ways. Here are your options:

- To trim off an edge from an image or graphic in a frame, select the object with the Selection tool, and drag a resize handle on the bounding box. Like many other actions involving proportions, press SHIFT as you drag to maintain the aspect ratio.

- Use one frame to crop another frame's contents. Select an object you want to crop and copy it. Then, draw or select an empty frame or path smaller than the copied object, and choose Edit | Paste Into to insert the object cropped to the new frame's dimensions.

- Set up a frame before adding its contents. Draw the placeholder frame, and then choose Fitting | Frame Fitting Options from the shortcut menu to open the dialog box. Specify the crop amount for any side, and click OK to close the dialog box.

Control Visibility with Clipping Paths

Suppose you're working on an article about fruit trees. Don't settle for a tired old layout with your images shown in tidy (but boring) rectangles. Add some fruity goodness by showing just the striking fall leaves against the backdrop of your page.

Distinguish the Path from the Frame

Have you wondered where clipping paths get their colors from and how they relate to the graphics you're drawing them on? Wonder no more.

Draw a graphics frame on your page, and it shows the color of its assigned layer. Now work on a clipping path within the frame, and you'll see a totally different color. InDesign uses the inverse color of the layer to show the clipping path, useful if your clipped path runs along some of the graphics' frame edges. For example, a red layer shows a cyan clipping path, a purple path shows a light green clipping path, and so on.

If you change your mind about a clipping path, and realize you should have used a frame, simply choose Object | Clipping Path | Convert Clipping Path to Frame. Of course, the separate clipping path disappears.

A clipping path defines what part of the underlying artwork shows on the page, but is separate from the frame, unless you include the frame as part of the path. There are a number of ways to produce a clipping path, including:

- Use an alpha channel or path included with some types of imported images.

- Approximate a clipping path using the Detect Edges option in the Clipping Path dialog box.

- Draw a path from scratch using InDesign's drawing tools, and insert the graphic into the frame using the Paste Into command. If you draw a path, insert a graphic, and then move that graphic, the "clipping" of the graphic is lost. (Read about drawing in Chapter 12.)

Use an Image's Path or Alpha Channel

Take advantage of paths or alpha channels imported with an EPS, TIFF, or Photoshop Document (PSD) image since the graphic automatically maintains its transparency.

If you aren't a whiz with the InDesign drawing tools, plan ahead and work with tools and features in your image's source program. For example, the default transparency in a Photoshop image converts to an alpha channel in InDesign automatically. If you don't have a transparent background, either erase the background or define an alpha channel in the Channels panel or using a layer mask.

To use an alpha channel in InDesign, follow these steps:

1. Select the content in the image, and choose Object |
   Clipping Path | Options to open the dialog box.

2. Click the Type drop-down arrow, and choose Alpha
   Channel from the list.

3. Specify any adjustments you
   want to make to the path,
   and click OK to close the
   dialog box.

Automatic Clipping Paths

Do you ever use clipart that shows
an object against a solid white or
black background and would like
to use it sans background, but don't
have a clipping path?

InDesign has you covered with
the Detect Edges feature, available
in the Clipping Path dialog box.
Select your image content using
the Direct Selection tool, and
choose Object | Clipping Path |
Options to open the dialog box
(see Figure 10-6). From the Type
drop-down list, choose Detect
Edges. You'll see the lightest
tones affected. Choose additional
clipping path options, and click
OK to close the dialog box and
clip the image.

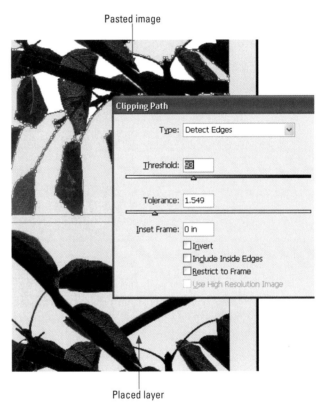

Pasted image

Placed layer

FIGURE 10-6 Create a clipping
path using the image's edges.

Specify How Clipping Paths Function

You usually need to modify the settings for the clipping path
from image to image for the best results. Some of the settings
work together, so you'll have to tweak them for the perfect
clipping path.

Specify the Darkest Pixel Value   Threshold defines the darkest
pixel value used for the clipping path. The higher the threshold
value, the greater the range of transparent pixels. Drop the value
down if you lose light-colored pixels.

Define Lightness Limits   Tolerance works in conjunction with the Threshold value by specifying how close a pixel's value can be to the defined threshold before it joins the clipping path. Generally, a higher tolerance level produces a smoother clipping path with fewer anchor points as more pixels are absorbed into the threshold. A lower tolerance creates a tighter clipping path with more anchor points. Adjust the tolerance level according to the characteristics of your image. For example, an egg image can use a high tolerance, while a palm frond image likely looks better with a low tolerance for more content definition.

Shrink the Frame   Often, clipping an image using threshold and tolerance settings results in extra space, sometimes containing scattered darker pixels if you're trying to clip a patterned background. Adjust the Inset Frame value slightly to hide those nasty pixels. If you'd like to use some space around a clipped image, specify a negative value for the Inset Frame value to expand the clipping path.

Swap Clipping Tones   If your image has a dark background, select Invert to start the clipping path with the darkest tones and then add lighter ones by adjusting threshold and tolerance.

Poke Through the Holes   For an amateurish clipping job, clip the outer edges of a graphic with the Clipping Path command and place it on a colored background, leaving internal areas of the image with the original background color (shown in the upper image in Figure 10-6). On the other hand, show your InDesign smarts by using the Include Inside Edges feature to remove those errant bits of background. Where there are similar areas of brightness you want to remove and maintain, you'll have to adjust threshold, tolerance, and inset frame values.

Stop at the Frame   For interesting and sometimes simpler clipping paths, use the Restrict to Frame option. Your path may then combine some interesting curves along with straight lines.

Precision Clipping   InDesign can calculate the transparent areas of an image for clipping using either the screen resolution or the actual file resolution. Choose Use High Resolution Image to generate precise clipping (which may be noticeable in a print file), or deselect to clip based on the screen resolution, which is fine for online or onscreen use.

You can't choose the clipping precision for an alpha channel, as InDesign only uses the actual resolution of an alpha channel.

Summary

I'm sure you've realized that InDesign offers much more than a convenient way to paste an image on to a page. As you'd expect from such a well-rounded piece of software, you can tailor the placement and appearance of an image in multiple ways.

Import images from a variety of programs, and specify the layers to import. You can use a variety of tools and features to scale and fit images on the page, as well as inserting them into objects like frames and paths.

Coming up, more on working with files, images and otherwise. See how to use InDesign files and how to manage imported content. You'll also learn about ways to save and reuse content for convenience.

11

Manage Files and Content

How to...

- Manage linked content in the Links panel
- Handle linked PDF files
- Save content as snippets
- Store, save, and reuse library contents

A long with designing and creating layouts on your document pages, InDesign offers a variety of tools to use for managing your content. Maintain links to content to save on file size and provide updated images as they occur. Define reusable content as snippets for quick reuse, or formalize the reusable content in a library.

Manage Linked Content

Inserting a few high-resolution graphic files in an InDesign page would likely slow your computer down significantly. To avoid the slowdown, InDesign displays lower-resolution graphics on the page. The graphic may be linked or embedded in your document.

Linked artwork doesn't bloat an InDesign document's size. Multiple copies of the same file, or layers from the file, can be placed in a document without multiplying the size, unlike using embedded artwork. Embedded files are stored in your InDesign document at their full resolution, and each copy you add increases the file size accordingly.

On the other hand, linked artwork maintains its connection to the source file and requires updating each time you modify the source file's contents. An embedded file functions independently of its source file, allowing you to make modifications at will.

In InDesign, you control characteristics of your images in the Links panel.

If your bitmap file is 48 kilobytes (KB) or less, InDesign transparently embeds a full-resolution image instead of using a screen resolution. You'll see the link information listed in the Links panel and can modify or update the image as the source file changes, unlike a file you embed manually.

Get Around the Links Panel

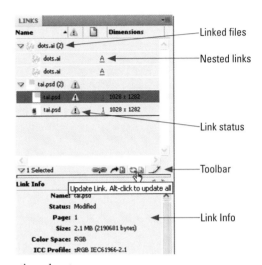

FIGURE 11-1 View linked file information in the Links panel.

All InDesign workspaces, except the Typography workspace, show the Links panel as part of their arrangements. In the Links panel, you'll find every linked file and all embedded files listed by name.

Sometimes, you'll find a nested link, indicated by a drop-down arrow to the left of its name. Click the arrow to view the subordinate links. Nested links occur when you use more than one copy of a particular file, or if you're using InDesign or Encapsulated PostScript (EPS) files that themselves contain links (see Figure 11-1).

Use the Links panel to locate and gather information about your files. In the example shown in Figure 11-1, finding a file isn't a big deal. In a file like a catalog chapter, the Links panel might easily contain many dozen links.

If you aren't sure where a particular graphic or file is located in your document, click the page link to show the file centered on the document window.

 Like all things InDesign, there are several ways to display the file. Along with double-clicking the link mentioned here, you can select the file and click Go to Link on the Link panel's toolbar, right-click the selected file and choose Go to Link from the shortcut menu, or choose Go to Link from the Link panel's menu.

Review File Status

All files placed in a document are listed in the Links panel. These include both local (on disk) files and assets that are managed on a server.

 There is one exception—files copied and pasted from a web site via Internet Explorer aren't listed in the Links panel.

When the same graphic appears several times in the document, the links are combined under a disclosure triangle in the Links panel. When a linked EPS graphic or InDesign document contains links, the links are also combined under a disclosure triangle.

A linked file can appear in the Links panel in several ways. A file without an icon is current. The modified icon means the source file is newer than the document version. The missing icon means the source file can't be located (it's been renamed, moved, or deleted). Finally, the embedded icon means the InDesign file contains the image data and the image is no longer linked to the original source file.

You'll know where your linked objects are, even if you don't have them on a publication page. Single letters refer to master pages, *OV* refers to overset text, and linked objects on the pasteboard are denoted by *PB*.

Learn About Your Links

The Link Info section at the bottom of the Links panel shows metadata about the file. In the panel, you can read the data and change what types of information display, but you can't change the data or add or remove it from the file's metadata.

Double-click a link, or select a link and click the Show/Hide Link Information icon to toggle the panel open.

Select a file in the Links panel, and choose Utilities I XMP File Info from the panel menu. Depending on the type of file you're using, you'll find information ranging from camera data to mobile Shockwave Flash (SWF), Illustrator document profiles to the raw data.

Read about changing and using metadata in Chapter 2.

Modify the Links Panel's Display

You aren't restricted to the sets of categories shown in the Links list and Link Info area of the Links panel. Add or remove additional categories according to your needs.

Change the Information Listings

Both the categories at the top of the Links panel and the headings in the Link Info section are defined in the same dialog box.

Follow these steps to change the information shown in the Links panel:

1. Choose Panel Options from the Links panel's menu to open the dialog box.

2. Select and deselect check boxes for the Show Column list to define the contents at the top of the Links panel.

3. Repeat the choices for the Show In Link Info list to define information shown at the bottom of the Links panel.

4. Click OK to close the dialog box and modify the panel, shown here.

Sort the View

The categories in the list at the top of the Links panel are dynamic, in that you can reposition them and sort using any column. Click a category heading to sort by that category, such as Date; click again to change from ascending to descending order.

How to...

Embed Linked Files or Link Embedded Files

You don't have to maintain a linked file as a link. For convenience, and if you're sure you won't need to update the file or send it to a print shop, embed it instead. Just be aware that embedding files increases your document's size.

Select the file, and choose Embed All Instances Of [file] from the Links panel's menu. The link icon changes to the embedded file icon, shown here in the first two listings.

Note Linked text is an exception—once you unlink the text, it disappears from the panel.

You can go in reverse, too, by linking embedded files. Select the file and any instances you want to link, and choose Unembed Link or Relink from the Links panel's menu. You're prompted to link the file to your original or to a new folder. If you choose to start a new folder, InDesign asks for a location and name for the folder, and creates new graphics using the information embedded with the file.

If you're working on a project where you don't need information, such as the Date category, move the column out of your way. Click to select the heading. As you drag it horizontally, you'll see an indicator move with a closed hand icon at the divider line between two columns. Drop the heading when you've moved it to an appropriate location.

Manage the Links

Fortunately, just as there are many ways to add and link files to an InDesign document, there are also many ways to manage the links. Some seem obvious, such as relinking a file, while others are designed to streamline your workflow and save time.

This section describes the ways in which you can handle links along with examples and some preferences you need to set to use the features.

Update Links

A link requiring updating shows a caution triangle, as you see here. You can update the links in several ways, depending on your project requirements. If you choose Preserve Image Dimensions When Relinking in the File Handling preferences, any transformations applied to the original file are reused automatically.

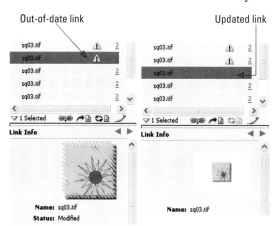

Out-of-date link

Updated link

Your choices include:

- Select the link's listing in the panel and click Update Link on the panel's toolbar.

- To update all modified links at once, ALT-CLICK Update Link on the toolbar.

- To update one instance of a graphic inserted multiple times, select it from the sublist and click Update Link. Use this option if you want to use slightly different versions of the same image without having to relink content or use different files.

Take Care of Missing Links

Select a link showing the red missing link icon, and click Relink to open the Relink dialog box. Locate and double-click a file to bring the link up-to-date.

Restore multiple missing links with one action if you have the content in a single folder. In the Relink dialog box, select the Search For Missing Links In This Folder check box at the lower-left corner of the dialog box. Any other missing links are relinked, provided the files are in the same folder. If you find that you have a missing link or two for some reason, choose Utilities | Search For Missing Links from the Links panel's menu.

Two file handling preferences affect how links are managed, including:

- **Check Links Before Opening Document** InDesign checks links as your document opens by default. When deselected, your document opens without testing the links in your file. Also, the Find Missing Links Before Opening Document preference is disabled.

- **Find Missing Links Before Opening Document** When active, your document opens immediately and InDesign attempts to locate the missing link source files. If you turn off this option, InDesign does not attempt to resolve the missing links.

Link to a New File

Rather than updating or relinking an existing file, change a link to a different file, which is handy if you make changes to content and use different filenames. Select the file in the Links panel, and click Relink to open the Relink dialog box. Select Show Import Options if you want to review the replacement file's features. Locate and select your replacement file, and click Open to replace it in the document.

Manage Linked Files' Folders

If you aren't bound by any corporate or organization file naming system, take some time to set up a consistent file management system. Once you've collected a few thousand assets, you'll be glad you did! Along with naming, get in the habit of defining folder locations. You have three options, depending on your workflow.

Specify a Default Relink Folder Here's another file handling preference option. From the Default Relink Folder menu, leave the default option, Most Recent Relink Folder, selected to display the last folder used for relinking. If you prefer, select Original Relink Folder to have InDesign track back to where the file was located when first integrated into your project.

Copy Links to a Different Folder   If you aren't sure what files you'll end up using in a project and want an easy way to keep track and sort them, here's an option. As you finalize your project contents, select the links in the Links panel, and choose Utilities | Copy Link(s) To from the Links panel's menu to open the Select a Folder dialog box. Open or create the folder where you want to store your project assets, and click Select/Choose. The links aren't removed from the original locations, however. You need to choose Relink to Folder in the Links panel's toolbar to update the links to the new folder.

 Copying the links isn't the same as packaging a file for printing. See how that's done in Chapter 19.

Relink to a Different Folder   Here's another slick trick: If you're constructing a publication for print with numerous high-resolution images, make a set of low-resolution copies to use for your layout. As you come to the end of your project, relink your assets to a folder containing the high-resolution content. Select the links and choose Relink to Folder from the Links panel's menu to open the Select a Folder dialog box. Locate and select the folder. If your high-resolution images use the same names, select Match Same Filename But This Extension and type the extension. Click Select/Choose to close the dialog box and replace the images.

PDF Links

Links to Portable Document Format (PDF) files are a bit different from other file types, in that there are a few more ways to break the links. As if there weren't already enough link-breaking, headache-making, thoughts-of-career-changing things you could do!

A placed PDF page in your InDesign file is a preview linked to a specific page in the PDF file. Because of this particular type of link:

- If you add, delete, or reorder the pages in your original file, the PDF preview may be different from your original. If that's the case, place the page again.

■ If the security status of the original PDF file changes, such as adding password protection, you won't be able to update your links unless you have access to the file's password (see Figure 11-2).

Reuse File Contents

Many times, you need to reuse content. Maybe you've designed a great layout for a graphic and some associated text, but only need to use it a couple of times—not worth the effort of creating and using a template. Other times, you might be working on a publication that draws from the same pool of items, such as text, graphic elements, logos, and so on. In either case, InDesign has a solution. For casual reuse, build a snippet; for ongoing projects, store your assets in a shareable library.

FIGURE 11-2 Insert the password to open a protected PDF file.

Save Content as Snippets

Save time with snippets—files containing bits and pieces you can reuse in another document. The quickest way to make a snippet is to select one or more objects on your page and drag the selection to the desktop. Name the file, and you're finished—the content and any layer information are ready for reuse.

Add Snippets to a Document

You place snippets like other files and can use both InDesign XML Snippet (IDMS) and InDesign Snippet (INDS) files in InDesign CS4.

Note Previous versions of InDesign used the INDS extension; InDesign CS4 uses the IDMS file format. But beware—InDesign CS4 snippets aren't usable in older versions of the program.

Specify Where a Snippet Displays

Choose or override the program preferences for handling snippets, based on your usual work practice. Choose Edit | Preferences | File Handling to open the panel. You can choose Position At Original Location if you want the objects in a snippet to automatically display at the same positions as the original. Otherwise, choose Position At Cursor Location to place snippets where you click the page.

Remember which setting you choose for future use, as you can override it. If you generally want a snippet to land at the same location as the original, press ALT if you need a snippet at the cursor location, and vice versa.

Choose File | Place and select one or multiple snippet files (of either file format). Click the loaded cursor where you want to place the upper-left edge of the file. You'll see the snippet contents selected on the page so you can drag to reposition if necessary. Move to the location for subsequent snippets, if you've chosen multiples, and click to place each of them. If you place a snippet inside a text frame, it becomes an anchored object.

To use a snippet saved on your desktop, drag it into InDesign, click to define its upper-left corner, and drop it into place.

Create Your Own Library

As your InDesign expertise increases, you look for ways to save time and increase efficiency. Object libraries are a perfect method to achieve both those worthy goals. You can build your own library or import and share libraries with others. A library can contain different sorts of items, including graphics, text, entire pages, guides, objects drawn in InDesign, and so on.

Build Your Library

To create a new library, choose File | New | Library. In the dialog box, name the file and select its storage location. Click Save. The new library opens as a dialog box in the InDesign window.

To add one or more objects, or even an entire page, to your library, select and drag the object or objects into the panel. Press ALT as you add content to see the Item Information dialog box, shown in Figure 11-3. You can also select an object or objects in your document and then click Add Item in the Library panel's menu.

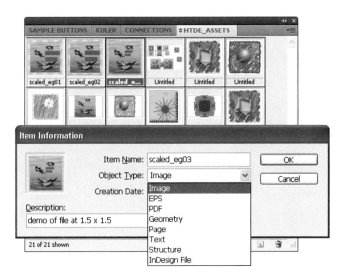

For more control over how the objects integrate into your library, make sure the page containing the objects is active in InDesign. Open the Object Library panel's menu and choose Add Items On Page [x] As Separate Objects to add multiple items, or include the page layout and content as a single object by choosing Add Items On Page [x].

FIGURE 11-3 Add information and descriptions about your library items.

Open and Use Library Contents

Choose File | Open to locate and select your library file or files. InDesign checks the library format, converting older library files to new formats that you'll need to save with new names. Each library file opens as a panel you can tab through and use like other program panels.

Library files use the INDL extension.

When it's time to use your library contents, drag an object from the panel to your page. To replicate the original page location, select the object, open the Object Library panel's menu, and choose Place Item(s).

If you're having trouble finding items in a large library, use search or sort options.

■ Choose Sort Items from the Library panel's menu and choose an option. You can sort by name, type, or relative age of the file.

▧ Choose Show Subset from the Library panel's menu to open the dialog box shown here. Search for items by name, date, keywords, or sort by file types. When you're finished, click OK to close the dialog box and show the subset items.

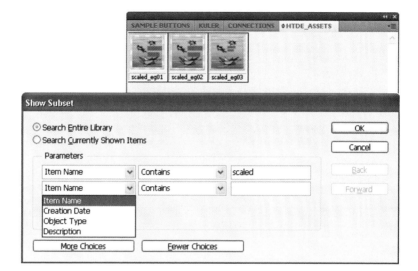

▧ When you're finished with the subset, choose Show All from the Library panel's menu to remove the filter and show your complete list of assets.

Even InDesign Libraries Have Rules!

You don't have to speak in whispers around InDesign, and scribbling isn't an issue, but there are a few rules for working with library files.

Keep these concepts in mind as you develop your library collection:

▧ You can share library files, but only one person can have a specific library file open at one time. If you run into scheduling issues, simply make a copy of the file. If the library includes text, provide copies of fonts used, if the font's reuse rights allow.

- Content added to a library maintains its respective page, text, or image attributes. Grouped items remain grouped, and text maintains its formatting.

- Library items may or may not retain their paragraph, character, or object styles. If you insert a library item using the same names as existing styles, the library item takes on the document's styles; other styles are added to the document.

- Images and graphics added to a library duplicate the original content and link information. Updating the original graphic updates the thumbnail for the library copy. Deleting or moving the original doesn't delete the copy, but you'll see a missing link notice the next time you use the library item.

 In multilayered objects, the original layers are preserved if you choose the Paste Remembers Layers setting in the Layers panel's menu.

Summary

There's nothing like scrambling for a missing file a few minutes before a deadline—well, except perhaps scrambling for a missing file, not finding it, and rebuilding it in a panic, only to find it the next morning. Once that chill running down your back has gone, let's review. Managing assets may not be the most exciting aspect of working with any program, especially a visually interesting one like InDesign. However, we all know how important it is, as you saw in this chapter.

The second part of the chapter looked at reusing assets stored as snippets for informal or quick work, or stored in a library for larger and shared projects.

In the next chapter, get up close and personal with the drawing tools in InDesign. You'll see many ways to build your own graphics, masks, and so on, right in your document.

12

Draw and Use Objects in InDesign

How to...

- Create shapes and frames
- Use the Pen tool
- Align and distribute objects
- Adjust text wrap settings
- Create and use object styles

Every item on the page in your InDesign document is an object. This includes your text frames; shapes; and rectangular, elliptical, and polygonal frames. Chapter 5 showed you how text frames are created and managed. In this chapter, we'll focus on the other types of objects—shapes, geometric frames, and paths—and how they work together, both with text and as parts of an overall document.

Another thing you'll learn in this chapter is how the use of object styles can speed up the process of formatting your objects and allow you to achieve consistency throughout your documents. You'll find out how to create and edit object styles and apply them to any object in your InDesign creations.

Create Shapes and Frames

Note that this section is entitled "Create Shapes and Frames," the "and" telling us that these are two different things. We point this out because they're often thought to be the same thing, and some users mistakenly create them for interchangeable purposes—but they're separate entities with separate functions.

First, shapes are just that—geometric shapes that can be filled with color and given a stroke, or outline. You draw them to add graphical content to your pages, as shown in Figure 12-1. They can be part of individual pages or applied to your page masters, if they need to appear on every page. They can also house text, as shown in Figure 12-2, allowing you to place text inside of shapes other than standard text frame boxes.

FIGURE 12-1 Shapes serve a multitude of graphical uses in an InDesign document.

FIGURE 12-2 Turn a shape into a text frame by clicking inside it with the Type tool.

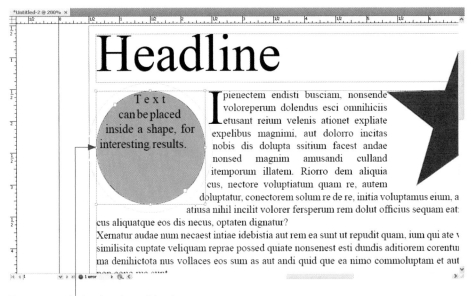

Text wraps to the interior edges of the shape

Using the Direct Selection tool, you can drag
the image around, choosing which parts show
through the confines of the frame.

FIGURE 12-3 The frame, which
has not been given any color fill or
stroke, will not print, but its shape
and dimensions affect the visible
portions of the photo.

Geometric frames—rectangular, elliptical, and polygonal
frames—on the other hand, are meant to house graphics, such
as photos or clipart. They cannot house text. As shown in
Figure 12-3, the shape of the frame can be used to control how
much of a photo appears on the page.

Learn about moving an image inside a frame in Chapter 10.

Draw Shapes

So now that you know what shapes are, let's create them. It's a
simple process, allowing you to take one of two paths: one where
you click and drag and draw a shape, or one where you enter the
values for the shape-to-be and let InDesign create the shape for
you, based on your input. Let's take the click and drag method first:

1. Click and hold your mouse down on the Shape tool to
select the shape you want to draw: a rectangle, ellipse,
or polygon. Figure 12-4 shows the options displayed in
a fly-out menu.

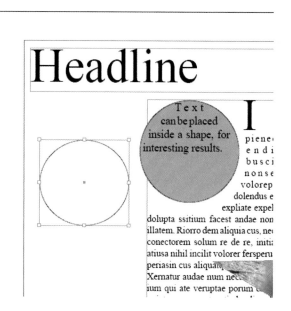

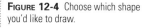

FIGURE 12-4 Choose which shape you'd like to draw.

FIGURE 12-5 The shape has no fill or stroke, but is revealed because Show Frame Edges is the default setting.

2. With the shape you want to draw represented on the Toolbox, move your mouse onto the workspace (the document or the pasteboard, if you don't know where you want to put the shape just yet).

3. Click and drag diagonally away from your starting point. Hold the SHIFT key down as you drag if you want to constrain the shape to one with equal width and height. Be sure that you don't release the key until after you've released the mouse, or the shape will snap to the nonconstrained dimensions it would have been had you never pressed the key.

As shown in Figure 12-5, the resulting shape has no fill or stroke by default—it just has a bounding box to show you the dimensions of what you've drawn. You can then use the Swatches panel to apply a colored fill and/or stroke.

Tip Don't want to see your shape's edges? Choose View | Hide Frame Edges. The keyboard shortcut to toggle between showing and hiding these edges is CTRL-H. On the Mac, you'll press COMMAND-H.

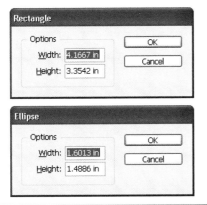

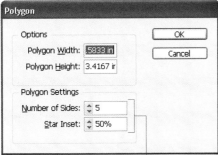

To create a traditional five-pointed star, for example, set the sides to 5 and the inset to 50%.

FIGURE **12-6** You can use the Rectangle, Ellipse, or Polygon dialog box to tell InDesign the exact size, and in the case of the Polygon dialog box, the number of sides and their inset, you want for your shape.

If you want to draw a shape that's a specific size, or in the case of the Polygon tool, with a specific number of sides, follow this procedure instead:

1. Choose the shape tool you want to use: Rectangle, Ellipse, or Polygon.

2. Move your mouse onto the workspace, and click. Don't drag, just click. A dialog box appears, named to match the tool you're using. Figure 12-6 shows the three possible dialog boxes that appear.

3. After entering the values you want, click OK. InDesign draws the shape, as shown in Figure 12-7.

Create Frames

The process of drawing a rectangular, elliptical, or polygonal frame is similar to the process of drawing a shape—identical, in fact, except for the tool you use (see Figure 12-8 for your choices) and what you end up with when you've finished drawing it.

FIGURE **12-7** Instant shape! Tell InDesign what you want, and it appears.

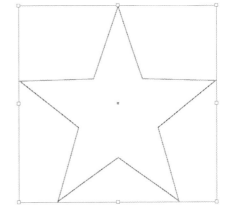

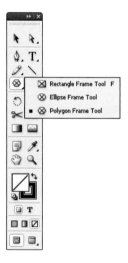

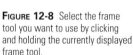

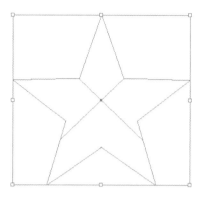

FIGURE 12-8 Select the frame tool you want to use by clicking and holding the currently displayed frame tool.

FIGURE 12-9 The result of drawing a five-pointed star polygon with the Polygon Frame tool and the Polygon dialog box.

You can draw geometric frames with the previously described click and drag method, or by clicking once and using the resulting dialog box. The dialog boxes look the same—it's just the resulting object that's different, in that it's a frame and not a shape. Figure 12-9 shows a five-pointed star frame drawn with the Polygon Frame tool.

Once you've got a geometric frame drawn, you can select it and use the File | Place command to insert an image inside it. Figure 12-10 shows an image inside an elliptical frame. The frame is a perfect circle because the SHIFT key was held as it was drawn, using the click and drag method.

If Replace Selected Item is selected in the Place dialog box, you won't have to click inside the frame to place the image in it; it will just appear inside the selected frame.

Transform Shapes and Frames

There will be times when after you've drawn a frame or shape you will wish it were different—taller or wider—or that it was

FIGURE **12-10** Create a softer edge within your document by placing an image inside an elliptical frame.

bigger or smaller, without changing its aspect ratio (its ratio of width to height). If you need to make these changes, here are your options:

FIGURE **12-11** Drag from a corner handle to resize the shape or frame.

- To keep the aspect ratio intact and just scale the frame or shape, press and hold the CTRL and SHIFT keys as you drag from a corner handle. Figure 12-11 shows a rectangle being resized.

- Enter new values into the Control panel while the shape or frame is selected. Figure 12-12 shows the W (width) and H (height) values being edited for another rectangle. The chain icon indicates that the aspect ratio will be maintained when the changes are made, meaning you can edit the width and the height will automatically adjust, or vice versa.

  You can also scale your shape or frame using the Scale X Percentage and Scale Y Percentage fields on the Control panel.

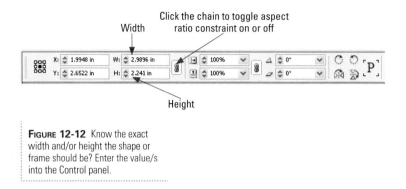

Width

Click the chain to toggle aspect ratio constraint on or off

Height

FIGURE 12-12 Know the exact width and/or height the shape or frame should be? Enter the value/s into the Control panel.

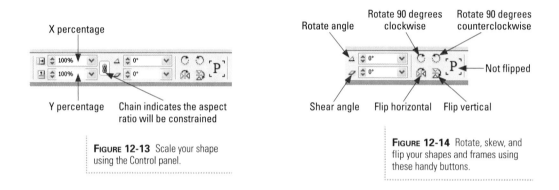

X percentage

Y percentage   Chain indicates the aspect ratio will be constrained

FIGURE 12-13 Scale your shape using the Control panel.

Rotate angle   Rotate 90 degrees clockwise   Rotate 90 degrees counterclockwise

Not flipped

Shear angle   Flip horizontal   Flip vertical

FIGURE 12-14 Rotate, skew, and flip your shapes and frames using these handy buttons.

As shown in Figure 12-13, these settings allow you to enter a percentage value to increase or decrease the size of the shape or frame horizontally (X) or vertically (Y).

In addition to resizing your shapes and frames, let's look at some of the other transformative things we can do to your shapes and frames using the Control panel. The panel is shown in Figure 12-14, with each of its options identified.

For each of these options in the Control panel, you can enter a value, click a triangle (to adjust the current value up or down), or just click a button to make the transformation happen.

Tip You can also use some keyboard shortcuts to speed things up or avoid having to use the Control panel when you want to make a quick change. Press R to rotate your selected frame or shape. Once the R key has been pressed, your mouse pointer turns to a crosshair, and you can drag the shape by dragging your mouse in the direction you want the selected frame or shape to turn. Press V to return to the Selection tool.

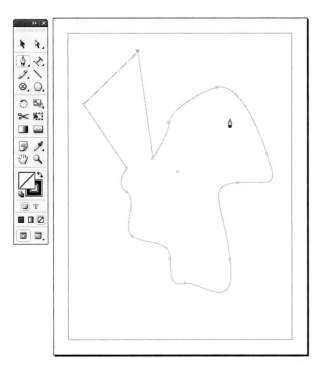

FIGURE 12-15 A combination of straight sides and curves, this shape is completely freeform.

Draw Shapes with the Pen Tool

While it would seem that you can create just about any shape with the Rectangle, Ellipse, and Polygon tools, they're just the tip of the shape-drawing iceberg in InDesign. If you need to create more random or unusual shapes, the Pen tool will help you draw them—with straight sides, curves, or both. You can also just draw paths, or lines, that are curved, straight, or combinations of the two. As shown in Figure 12-15, you can draw any kind of shape, the only limitations being imposed by your imagination and, potentially, your eye-hand coordination in using the mouse.

How does the Pen tool work? It's simple to use. To begin, click the Pen tool (there are three other buttons sharing the Pen's spot in the Toolbox, so check to see that it's the Pen tool that's displayed, as shown in Figure 12-16), and move your mouse onto the document.

After that, you can use these steps to draw a freeform shape with straight sides:

1. Click and move the mouse; then click again to draw the first straight side in your shape.

2. Continue clicking and moving the mouse to draw additional sides. Figure 12-17 shows a freeform shape drawn with straight sides.

3. Come back to the beginning, and look for the tiny circle that appears on your mouse pointer (also shown in Figure 12-17) when you're ready to close the shape.

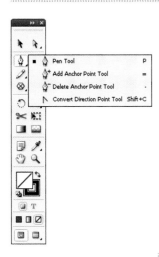

FIGURE 12-16 The Pen tool and its three optional shape and path creation tools.

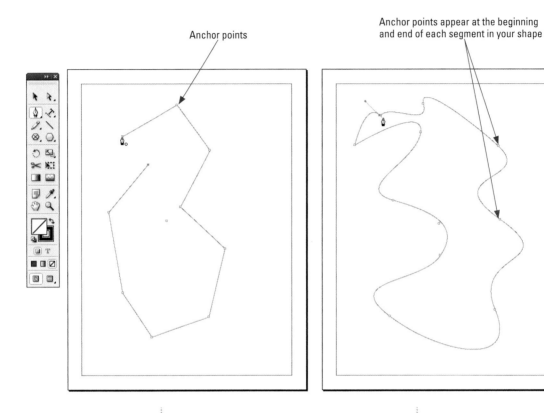

Anchor points

Anchor points appear at the beginning and end of each segment in your shape

FIGURE 12-17 Each segment has its own anchor points, which can later be used to reshape the shape.

FIGURE 12-18 Click and drag to draw curves.

If you want to draw curves in your shape along with straight sides, or draw a shape that's entirely curves, follow these steps:

1. Activate the Pen tool.

2. Move your mouse onto the document, and click and drag to draw the first curve. Figure 12-18 shows a curve in progress. Two handles append to your curve, which you can later use to change the direction of the curve, turning it, for example, from an arc to an "s" curve.

3. Click and drag again, drawing the next curved segment. Again, the distance you drag from the point where you clicked determines the length of your curve, and the direction you drag determines the nature of the curve itself.

4. Continue clicking and dragging to draw curved segments, and when you return to the beginning, indicated by the circle added to your mouse pointer, you can click one final time to close the shape.

When you draw with the Pen tool, your shapes can have loops and segments created by overlapping the sides. Samples of this effect are shown in Figure 12-19, where curves and straight sides overlap, creating closed shapes within the overall shape. When a fill is applied, the effect is more obvious (see shape on the right).

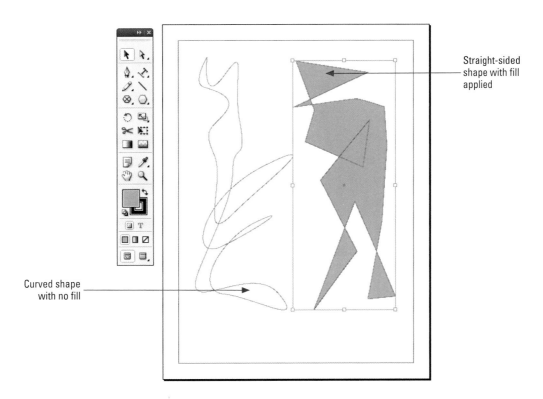

Straight-sided shape with fill applied

Curved shape with no fill

FIGURE 12-19 Loops and closed straight-sided segments can be added as you click and drag to draw your Pen-based shapes.

Of course, to fill your shape—whether it's drawn with the Pen tool or using the shape or frame tools—you simply go to the Swatches panel and choose a color for the fill. If you want to select a color from elsewhere, such as from within a photo or other object in your document, use the Eyedropper tool to "sip" up the color. To do this, select the shape with your selection tool, and then switch to the Eyedropper. Click the color you want applied, and the color you sampled fills the shape.

Define and Edit Paths

Once a shape or frame is drawn, regardless of the tool used to draw it, you can edit its path. Every shape and frame is made from a path, from the starting point to the end. As shown in Figure 12-20, a star drawn with the Polygon tool has the same anchor points that a Pen-drawn shape has—and the anchor points can be used to reshape the star.

 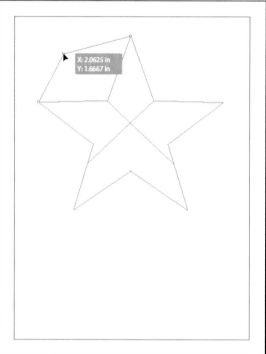

As indicated in Figure 12-20, the reshaping process requires use of the Direct Selection tool. You can use this tool to drag the anchor points that were already part of your shape and to drag those that you add to the shape. To add anchor points, click the Add Anchor Point tool (one of the Pen tool's alternates), and click along the perimeter of the shape. Look for a plus sign (+) on your mouse pointer, so you know you're adding an anchor point and not starting a new path.

To remove anchor points, you'll use the Delete Anchor Point tool. Click the tool to activate it, and then click existing anchor points in the selected path. A minus sign (–) appears, as shown in Figure 12-21.

The last of the Pen tool's alternates, the Convert Direction Point tool, allows you to change the nature of your anchor points. This means that you can turn an anchor point on a straight segment to a curve, or vice versa. Figure 12-22 shows a conversion occurring and a straight side being turned to a curve by dragging the mouse after converting the anchor point.

FIGURE 12-20 Drag the anchor points with your Direct Selection tool and reshape the star.

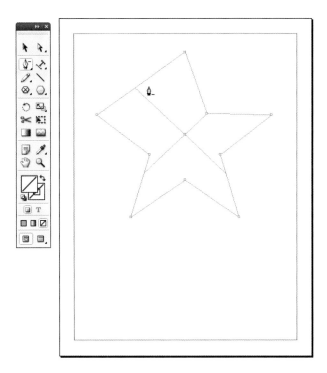

FIGURE 12-21 Remove an unwanted anchor point.

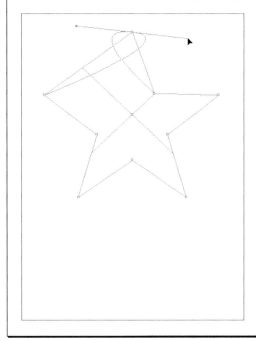

FIGURE 12-22 Convert your anchor points from straight to curved, and then drag to edit the path.

Place Text on a Path

As shown in Figure 12-23, text doesn't have to appear in boxes or run horizontally or vertically on the page. While you can rotate a text box, that's not exactly a lot of creative freedom, so the ability to type around the edge of a shape or along a path is the key to using type in really interesting ways.

To create text on a path, you first need a path. As stated, that path can be one that you drew with the Pen tool, a path around the edges of a shape or geometric frame, or around the edges of a photo. Once you have that path in place, the key to connecting the type to the path is using the Type on a Path tool, shown in Figure 12-24, in a Toolbox fly-out menu. The button, as you'd expect, shares a spot with the regular Type tool.

With your path in place—it needn't be selected—just point to the spot on the path where you want the type to begin, and click. You can type along the path when it's a path you drew with the Pen tool, or on the outside of a path that surrounds a shape or frame.

The Type on a Path mouse pointer looks like a T with a slash and a plus sign appended to it, as shown in Figure 12-25. Once you see that pointer, click and begin typing. The text will flow along the path until it runs out of path or you run out of type. If you type more than will fit on the path, the

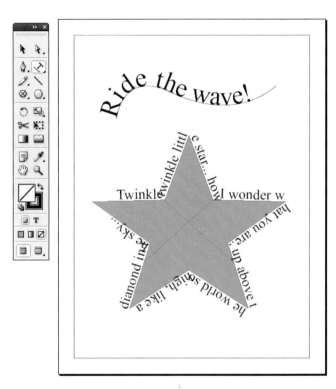

FIGURE 12-23 Type can follow a Pen-drawn path, the path created by the edge of a shape, or the bounding box of a photo or other graphic content.

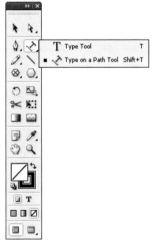

FIGURE 12-24 Activate the Type on a Path tool.

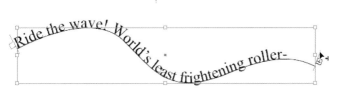

FIGURE **12-25** Click to tell InDesign where the type should begin following the path.

red overset text icon—the same one you'd see in a text frame that couldn't house all the text—appears at the end of the path.

Once you've typed your text, you can edit it and format it, just as you would type in a regular text frame. To edit the text, click within the text (with either the Type or Type on a Path tool), press DELETE or BACKSPACE or use your mouse to select text you want to remove, and then press the appropriate key. If you want to add text, click where it should go, and type it. It's no different from adding or removing text in a frame.

Where the process does differ is in your ability to move the type along the path. If, for example, you don't have room for the last word, but you would if you'd clicked just a bit closer to the start of the path when you started typing your text, what to do? Point to the box handles at the beginning of the text, and when your mouse pointer appears as a black arrow with a smaller arrow beneath it (shown in Figure 12-26), drag in the direction you want to "push" the text. You can drag to the right to push the text farther along the path, or to the left if you want to pull the text and make it start closer to the beginning of the path.

FIGURE **12-26** Push or pull your text along the path.

Did You Know?

You Can Handle the Path and Text Separately

You don't have to let the path show after you've used it to provide a shape for your text. Use the Swatches panel to apply either None as the color of the stroke, or if your text will be appearing on a colored background, choose that color for the stroke so that it's invisible against that background. If you want the path to show but don't want the text to touch it, adjust the baseline shift using the Control panel when the Type or Type on a Path tool is active and the text is selected. If you're not sure how to adjust the baseline shift, check out Chapter 6.

Use Align and Distribute

If you've got more than one object on your page, chances are you'll be paying close attention to the relative positions of those objects. Sometimes you can adjust their locations "by eye," and sometimes that's fine—it doesn't matter if something is precisely placed in relation to something else as long as an overall pleasing composition is achieved.

When you have several objects on a page, however, it can be important that they line up in some way—captions lined up underneath photos, graphic items lined up along a margin, or a series of advertisements on a page lined up so that their bottom edges are all the same distance from the text or the bottom of the page. You may also need to know that a series of items are all evenly spaced or distributed, which can be quite difficult to do without careful measurement. What makes all this much easier than you might think? The Align panel.

Shown in Figure 12-27, the Align panel allows you to control the placement of a group of objects, lining them up by their tops, bottoms, middles, or sides. This can include distributing them evenly or solely affect their alignment. To use the panel, simply select the objects to be aligned and/or distributed, using the SHIFT key to click each one and select them as a group, or use the Selection tool to draw a box around the objects and select them all at once, as also shown in Figure 12-27.

Once the objects are selected, use the panel's buttons to determine the way the objects should align, choosing which common side should be used as the basis of their alignment and/or distribution. After you've aligned them, if you don't want their alignment and/or distribution to change, group them using the Object | Group command. The command requires that all the objects you want grouped be selected, and it can be undone with the Object | Ungroup command.

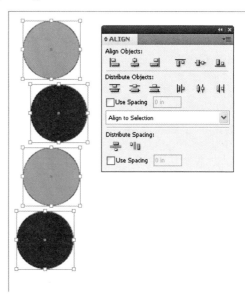

FIGURE 12-27 Align and distribute your selected objects.

InDesign gives you handy guides that pop up as you drag objects around on your pages. These green lines show you your alignment with regard to adjacent shapes or frames, appearing whenever you're lined up vertically, horizontally, or by the center of another object.

Specify Text Wrap

The Text Wrap panel—along with some of its buttons that also appear on the Control panel when an object is active—makes it possible for images and text to coexist in an InDesign document. Without text wrap, you would have to manually size and position text boxes to fit around your images and shapes so that they didn't overlap. Thankfully, this isn't necessary, and you can set up your text frames and graphical objects to work with each other and so that text flows around objects on the same page.

As with any panel, if you don't see it in the dock, choose it from the Window menu. Once displayed, its buttons apply to whichever object or group of objects is selected. You can set text wrap for multiple text frames or photos, for example, which can be handy if you want the same wrap settings for all the objects on a single page or spread.

FIGURE 12-28 Make your text flow around objects by establishing text wrap settings for the adjacent or overlapping items.

The Text Wrap panel, shown in Figure 12-28, is quite simple to use. Its buttons allow you to determine how much space, if any, will appear between your text and the object(s) around which it flows and to determine how that flow occurs.

Choose the kind of wrap you want, none or some.

Choose the amount of wrap and on which sides.

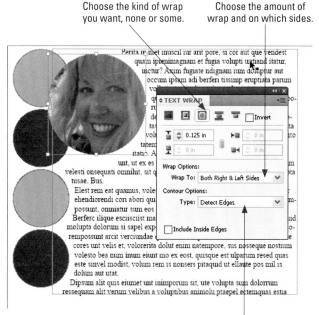

Set your wrap options and fine-tune how the wrap is applied.

The panel is broken down into three main areas. First, starting at the top, you choose the sort of wrap you want: none at all, wrap around one or more sides, or wrap that's based on the object itself. You can also set the wrap to force the text to jump over the object or to the next column, if there's no room for the text to wrap around the object in its current location.

In the next section, you fine-tune the wrap setting you've chosen by incrementing or decrementing the wrap distance on one or more sides of the object. You can also choose whether the wrap settings for all four sides of an object are constrained (using the chain icon).

Last, in the Wrap Options section of the panel, you can tell InDesign what to "wrap to," meaning which parts of the object are important to the wrap settings you've selected. The drop list includes all the sides of the object and allows you to wrap around the object with respect to the proximity of your document's spine once it's bound.

When you have a photo or other graphic image in place, the Contour Options portion of this last section of the panel is available whenever the Wrap Around Object Shape option is in use. This allows you to ask InDesign to detect the edges of the image, ignoring, for example, a white or light background and letting text wrap up to the edges to the image's main content, or to follow the clipping path you may have already established in Photoshop or through the InDesign Object menu's Clipping Path command.

Tip If you need to ignore, but not eliminate, text wrap settings for a particular object, while a text frame is selected, right-click the text frame and choose Text Frame Options. Select the Ignore Text Wrap check box, and the frame will do just that—ignore any text wrap settings for any other objects in the document.

Work with Object Styles

Like paragraph and character styles, object styles enable you to quickly apply a variety of formats and settings to an object. You can create object styles that apply to text frames, images, or shapes, including the appearance of just about any aspect of the object itself.

Object styles can also contain other styles, which means you can nest your styles for maximum impact. An example? Imagine an object style for creating pull-quotes—those snippets of text from an article that are used like a graphic to draw attention to a salient point within the text. You can set up a paragraph style that formats how the text looks, including font size, color, and perhaps a drop cap, as shown in Figure 12-29. That style can

FIGURE 12-29 Include a paragraph style within the settings for your object style to make sure that every aspect of a particular object can be quickly applied.

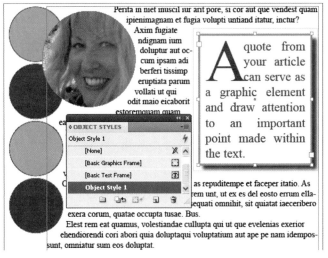

then be made part of, or set to be included in, an object style that applies a stroke to the text frame, a background color, and a text wrap value.

Not sure how to create a paragraph style? Check out Chapter 7.

FIGURE **12-30** The Object Styles panel

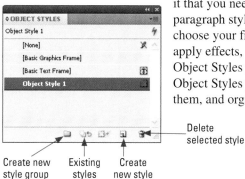

Delete selected style

Create new style group Existing styles Create new style

Create and Apply a New Object Style

Creating an object style is easy. The quickest way to do it is to take an object in your document and apply all the formatting to it that you need. If the object style should include an existing paragraph style, be sure that's applied to the object and then choose your fill colors, gradient (if any), stroke width and color, apply effects, etc. Then click the Create New Style button in the Object Styles panel. Shown in Figure 12-30, you can use the Object Styles panel to apply styles as well as create them, delete them, and organize them into groups.

In response, InDesign creates a generically named "Object Style 1," and you see it appear in the Object Styles panel. Once it appears there, you can click it to apply it to any selected object.

You can also create an object style from scratch using the Object Style Options dialog box for a blank style, which is created by clicking the Create New Style button with nothing selected. Use the dialog box lists and settings to establish the features your style will apply, give the style a name, and click OK. The downside? You won't know if it's what you want until you apply it to something, and invariably, you'll need to make changes.

Manage and Edit Object Styles

One of the first things you'll want to do to a new style is rename it. "Object Style 1" (or Object Style 2, if you've created more than one in a row), after all, won't be useful to you a week later when you can't remember what that style was meant to do. To rename a style—and to make other changes to its settings—simply double-click the style in the Object Styles panel, and view the Object Style Options dialog box, shown in Figure 12-31.

Through this dialog box, use the Style Name box to rename the style, and use the Basic Attributes and Effects for lists to change the way the style works. These two lists break the style

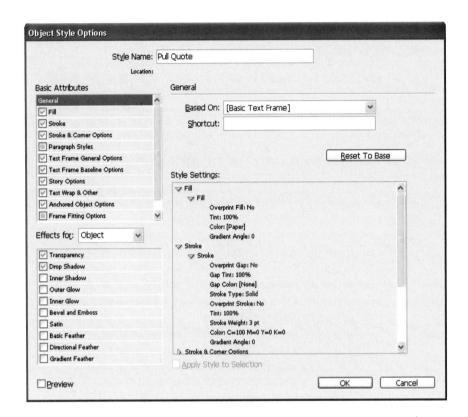

down into its components. By viewing the check boxes next to
each listed item, you can tell what is and what isn't part of the
style and make changes by adding or removing check marks.
Note that in the Effects for list, you can choose an option from the
drop-down list to choose Object, Fill, Stroke, or Text to get a look
at all of the features of the active style. The Style Settings section
is used to view the features of the style as it currently works, and
you can click the triangles to display more detail about each aspect
of the style.

Once you're happy with the settings in place, click the
OK button to apply them. From that point on, you can use the
style by name simply by clicking it in the Object Styles panel
whenever you want to apply it to one or more selected objects.

FIGURE 12-31 The Object Style
Options dialog box

Tip   You can group your styles by creating a group and then dragging the styles into that group. Using your
mouse, click the Create New Style Group button, and then drag an existing style into that group (as
desired), or make sure that group is selected when you add new styles later. To rename the group,
double-click the generic Style Group 1 name and use the Style Group Options dialog box to rename it.

13

Work with Layers and Effects

How to...

- Make your own layers
- Add content to layers and control layer visibility
- Group and ungroup objects
- Work with transparency
- Apply special shadows, glows, and other effects

The use of layers in an InDesign document can't be underestimated in terms of the power it gives you to control where things appear on the page and how effects are applied to them. You can design an InDesign document without using multiple layers (there's always one layer in use, so even if you haven't added any, you have been using a single layer all along), and if you're unfamiliar with their use, you may have been avoiding them. Once you get a sense of how much they can free you to structure and edit your pages, however, you'll find them essential to your productivity.

When it comes to effects, InDesign offers quite a few, enabling you to add shadows, glows, strokes, and transparency effects, all within the application. While you can apply these same effects—and many more, of course—in Photoshop or some other image-editing application, it's convenient to have so many of them right there in InDesign. For Photoshop users, the comfort of seeing familiar tools for adjusting most of the effects will shorten your learning curve considerably. For everyone else, the effects are quite easy to master, and thanks to a Preview option, you can see the impact of an effect before you commit to it.

Create Layers

Creating layers is simple, and requires just one thing—the Layers panel, as shown in Figure 13-1. Of course, if you don't see the panel in your InDesign dock, you can display it by selecting Layers from the Window menu.

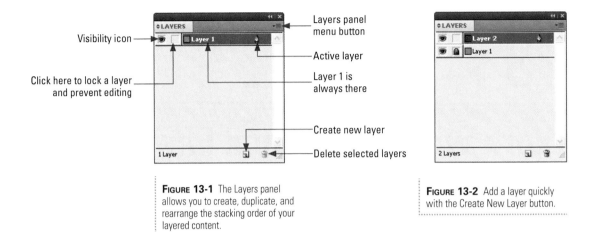

Layers panel menu button
Visibility icon
Active layer
Click here to lock a layer and prevent editing
Layer 1 is always there
Create new layer
Delete selected layers

FIGURE **13-1** The Layers panel allows you to create, duplicate, and rearrange the stacking order of your layered content.

FIGURE **13-2** Add a layer quickly with the Create New Layer button.

To create a new layer, click the Create New Layer button. A layer instantly appears, with a different-colored box next to it, in the Layers panel. Figure 13-2 shows a new layer, its red box differentiating it from the default blue Layer 1. Also shown in the figure, Layer 1 is now locked and a lock icon appears.

You can add as many layers as you want simply by clicking the Create New Layer button whenever you need one. When you add a new layer, any content you add to the document while that layer is active is added to that layer.

 If you're ever not sure which content is on which layer, simply click the visibility icon to hide a layer, and look at your page to see what disappeared.

Put Content on Layers

In InDesign CS4, like its preceding versions, you don't so much put content on layers as choose which layer is active before adding content to the document. This means, therefore, that it's good to have a plan for your layers before you begin building the document—if you intend to use layers, that is. As stated before, there's no explicit need to use the Layers feature at all. You can design a document and have everything on the one default Layer 1 and encounter no significant problems.

If you want to have your content on separate layers, however, you can create the layers first and then activate layers as you add content to the document. If you want, for example, all of your text frames to be on one layer, add a layer and be sure to activate it each time you add a text frame. If you forget and add a text frame without activating the designated layer, you can cut the text frame (Edit | Cut) and then add it back to the desired layer by selecting that layer and then issuing the Paste command. This cut and paste procedure works for any content that you want to move to a different layer. You can also use the Paste in Place command, also found in the Edit menu, if you want to be sure that the item appears in the same position on the new layer that it was in the old one.

Speaking of pasting, the Layers panel menu offers a unique command: Paste Remembers Layers. If you select this command from the menu, whenever you cut or copy and then paste, InDesign remembers which layer the content was on originally and keeps it on that layer when the content is pasted. Because this setting is off by default, however, you can leave it off and then use the cut and paste (or Paste in Place) procedure to move content to a different layer at any time. Figure 13-3 shows the Layers panel menu and the Paste Remembers Layers command selected.

FIGURE 13-3 If you want your content to remain on its designated layer, regardless of cutting or copying and then pasting that content, turn Paste Remembers Layers on.

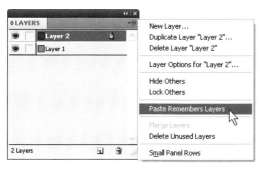

Adjust Layer Positioning

One of the primary reasons for placing content on a separate layer is so you can rearrange it easily. Instead of using the Object | Arrange menu to send objects forward, backward, to the top, or to the bottom, you can restack multiple objects (if they're all on one layer) simultaneously, or if you have each object on its own layer, use the Layers panel to adjust their stacking order individually.

Here's an example of how this works. If you look at Figure 13-4, you see three objects. Two of them, the star and the rectangle, are on Layer 2. The circle is on Layer 1. If we want to bring the circle to the top of the stack so it's overlapping the other two objects, all we need to do is put Layer 1 on top of Layer 2 by dragging it up in the panel. Just such a move is in progress in the figure, as indicated by the little "fist" icon, which shows we've grabbed the layer and are moving it.

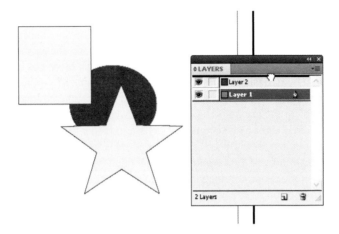

FIGURE 13-4 Drag layers up and down in the Layers panel to change the stacking order of the content on those layers.

Manage Layers

Managing layers includes several tasks: naming layers (so they have more relevant names than "Layer 1" or "Layer 2"), hiding layers, deleting unwanted layers, duplicating layers with content you want repeated, and changing the way layers are displayed in the Layers panel. All of these tasks can be conveniently performed using the Layers panel itself, either within the main panel or its panel menu, which was shown in Figure 13-3.

To rename a layer, simply double-click the current name. The Layer Options dialog box opens, as shown in Figure 13-5, and you can type a new name for the layer, pick a new display color for the layer (as it will appear in the palette), and choose from several check boxes that allow you to control the appearance and function of the layer's content.

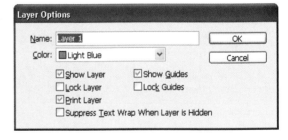

FIGURE 13-5 The Layer Options dialog box gives you nearly total control over your layers and their content.

The options shown checked (on) in Figure 13-5 are in their default positions—only Show Layer, Show Guides, and Print Layer are on without you having to do anything. The other options allow you to control editing of the layer (Lock Layer) and the movement of guides (Lock Guides).

The Suppress Text Wrap When Layer is Hidden option is handy if you want to essentially have two versions of your document, one with a particular layer and one without, and have laid the page out so that when a layer is hidden, the impact on surrounding text is accommodated by the placement and size of the text frames that are affected by the content.

Once you've renamed your layer, chosen a new color for it, and applied the desired options for the layer, click OK to apply them. Of course, a layer's locked status can be changed from right on the Layers panel, as can the visibility of the layer, so you don't need to reopen the dialog box should those aspects of the layer change in the future.

Tip If you have many layers in a particular document and you find that the Layers panel is filling up, you can shrink the display of each layer slightly, thus making more room for them to all be visible in the panel. Choose Small Panel Rows from the Layers panel's menu, and each layer's row in the panel is condensed.

Group and Ungroup Content

In addition to placing multiple objects on a single layer so that they can be restacked, hidden, displayed, or printed together, you can group objects so that InDesign allows them to be moved and resized together. A collage or grouping of shapes on a page, for example, might function better as a group for the purposes of keeping them all together and in a particular arrangement and/or for the simplification of setting up text wrap for the group. As shown in Figure 13-6, a group of shapes that's been literally grouped can be easier to manage on the page.

FIGURE **13-6** This group of objects can be moved, resized, and otherwise managed as a single unit because the individual objects have been combined into a group.

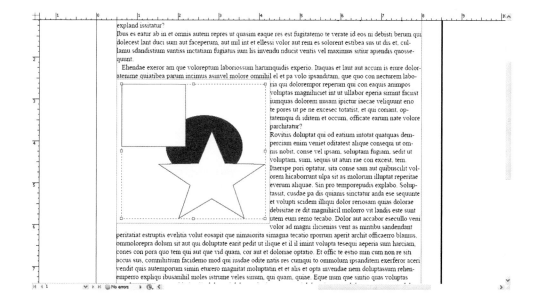

You can spot a group, should you be working with a document created by someone else or if you forget what you have and haven't grouped in your document, by observing the dashed line that appears around the grouped objects when any one of them is clicked. Note that the group has a single set of handles, unlike a group selection, where each object remains separate and has its own distinct corner and side handles for resizing and moving.

 Of course, you can resize and move several objects at once by selecting them together with the SHIFT key, but they won't move as a unit unless they're all selected. One false move, and you can move one of the objects out of the desired arrangement.

To group two or more objects, select them by pressing and holding the SHIFT key as you click the objects you want to group. Each object's individual handles appear around it, indicating that the object is selected. When all the desired objects are selected, choose Object | Group. You can also press CTRL-G. Figure 13-7 shows a group in progress.

 After grouping objects, the text wrap settings you may have had in place for the individual objects are gone, and you have to set a new text wrap for the group.

To ungroup a group of objects, click the group to select it, and choose Object | Ungroup. You can also press SHIFT-CTRL-G (or SHIFT-COMMAND-G on the Mac). After ungrouping, the individual objects will need new text wrap settings if there are adjacent text frames affected by the placement of the objects.

Apply Transparency and Effects

InDesign's effects options are quite extensive. Their diversity and the ability InDesign gives you to adjust how they're applied makes it easy to stay within the application for much of your document's development. Applying shadows, glows, strokes, and transparency need not send you hopping out to Photoshop and then back to place the edited image. Instead, assuming the image is already sized and in the right color mode for your ultimate printing or display goals for the document, you can place it once and then use InDesign's

FIGURE 13-7 Each object is selected, and the Group command will unite them.

Click an effect's name to see its controls.

The Effects button

Selected objects behind the dialog box

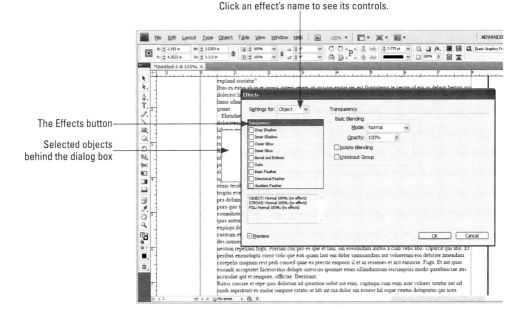

FIGURE 13-8 Click the Effects button to open the Effects dialog box.

Effects dialog box (shown in Figure 13-8) to apply one or more effects to the active object(s).

To apply an effect, select the object or objects (as a group or by pressing SHIFT and clicking multiple objects), and then click the Effects button on the Control panel. The button is available whether you have the Selection, Direct Selection, or Type tool in use. A menu appears, as shown in Figure 13-9, from which you can pick the first or only effect you wish to apply. Once you make your choice, the dialog box appears.

Tip   Because it's such a common effect, the Drop Shadow button applies a 75 percent opaque shadow to selected objects without requiring you to use the Effects button and dialog box.

Once the Effects dialog box is open, you can begin applying effects. Just select the check box to the left of each effect you want to apply, and the effect is applied in its default state.

Click an effect's name to see its controls.   The cumulative list of effects is displayed here.

Select a check box to apply the effect.

Turn on the Preview feature to see the effects in place before you click OK.

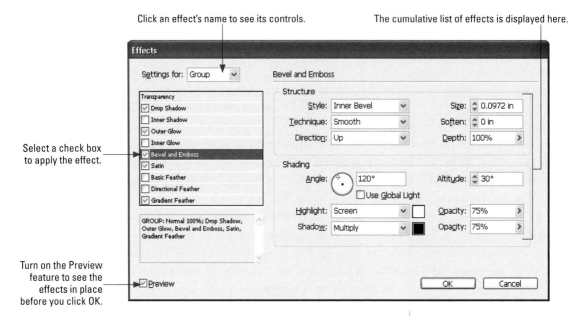

FIGURE 13-9 The Effects dialog box offers ten different effects, each with their own set of controls for manipulating the results.

To see what that state is or to change it, click the effect's name to display the controls for that effect. Use the various settings to change the intensity, size, color, and overall impact of each effect. Figure 13-10 shows the Drop Shadow controls.

If you want to see how the effect will look, click the Preview button in the lower-left corner of the dialog box and move the dialog box aside so that the selected object(s) are visible onscreen. You can move the dialog box by dragging its title bar.

FIGURE 13-10 Control the intensity of your drop shadow by changing its opacity, size, position, and spread. The default settings are shown here.

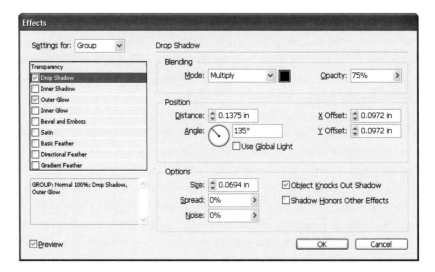

Once you like the effects you see through the Preview feature, click OK to apply them to the selected objects. You can always undo this action if you change your mind (CTRL- Z or Edit | Undo), or you can reopen the Effects dialog box to adjust the settings for one or more of the effects you applied.

Work with Transparency

Transparency is the first effect listed in the Effects dialog box, and it's always "on," in that 100 percent opacity and a normal blend mode are applied by default to all content in your document. As shown in Figure 13-11, if you want to change these settings, you can click the word Transparency in the Effects dialog box and manipulate the following controls:

■ **Basic Blending**   In this section of the dialog box, you can choose a blend mode to make your selected objects darker, lighter, or to make their colors change and/or more intense. You can also choose to make the selected objects more or less opaque, or see-through. By dragging the Opacity slider to the left, you make it possible to see through the selected objects.

■ **Isolate Blending**   This option, which is off by default, will prevent anything beneath the selected object or group of objects from being changed by the mode you choose.

FIGURE 13-11 Transparency effects include 16 different blend modes, an Opacity slider, and two options for controlling how much impact the transparency of your selected object(s) has on surrounding content.

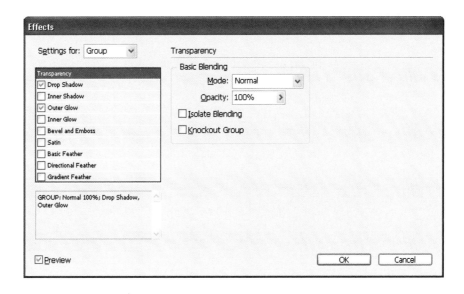

This is important, because most blend modes depend on layering of text and photos or filled shapes to determine their results. Isolating blending eliminates the selected mode's effect on anything beneath the selected objects, but doesn't prevent those overlapped items from affecting the way the mode is applied to the selected objects.

- **Knockout Group**   This option prevents the elements of a group from showing through each other.

Flatten Transparency

Flattening an image takes your photo or other graphic content and divides it into vector-based sections and rasterized sections, based on its content. You may not need to flatten your objects, depending on how you'll be exporting or saving your document. If you choose a format that doesn't support transparency, you'll have to apply a Transparency Flattener preset, available through the Print dialog box in the Advanced section (shown in Figure 13-12).

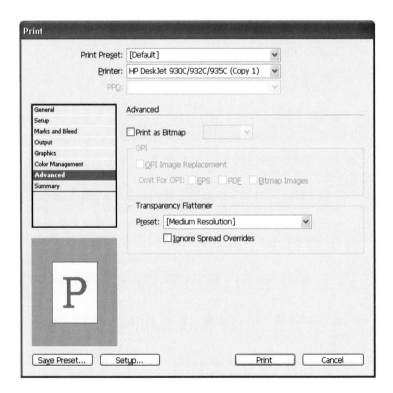

FIGURE 13-12 Using the Advanced section of the Print dialog box, you can choose a Transparency Flattener preset.

If you'll be exporting your document as a Portable Document Format (PDF), you can avoid having to flatten the document's images by choosing to save in Adobe Acrobat 5/ PDF 1.4 or later.

The available presets for transparency flattening include Low, Medium, and High Resolution. Make your choice according to the following considerations:

- Choose Low Resolution if your output is going to be printed on a black and white printer (a low-end inkjet or laser printer, for example) or if your document is headed for the Web or other onscreen viewing only.

- If you're going to print on a color and/or PostScript printer and the documents will be considered "proof" quality (not final or high-end), choose Medium Resolution.

- Choose High Resolution for final prepress documents or for proofs that have to be near final in quality. If you're printing separations, you'll also want to choose this preset.

Summary

In this chapter, you learned all about layers—from how to create them to *why* you'd create them, and how to add and rearrange content within them. You also learned how to control layer visibility, and in keeping with the idea that your InDesign documents have lots of objects in them, you learned to group and ungroup objects so that the results of your efforts to arrange and position the objects are preserved.

In addition to working with layers, this chapter showed you how to work with transparency, and how to apply other special effects, such as drop shadows and glows, to your InDesign objects and to the containers that hold content—text, pictures—created in other applications.

In the next chapter, you'll discover how to work with color—how to apply color, to create swatches, and to store your swatches from one document and be sure they're accessible in any other document.

PART IV
Use and Manage Color

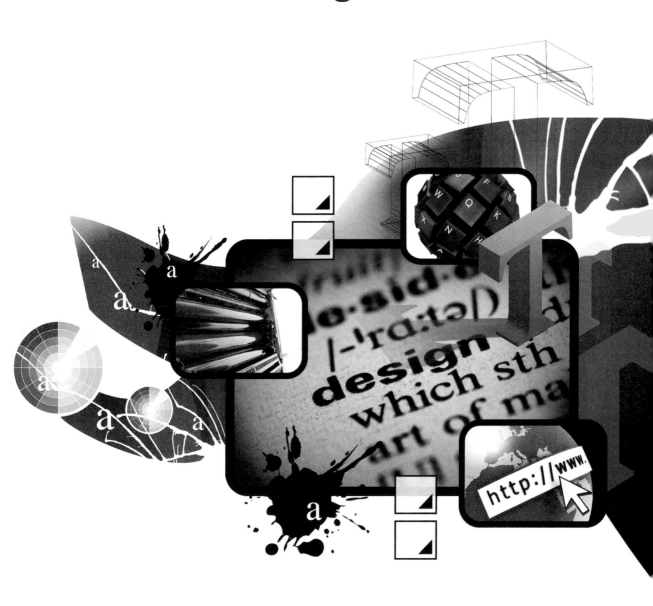

14

Get a Handle on Color and Swatches

How to...

- Choose colors
- Create color swatches
- Select color tints
- Design and store gradient swatches

Color can stimulate, soothe, and enhance your message. On the other hand, controlling color in a project can be frustrating, annoying, disappointing... Insert your own pejorative term, if you like.

In this section, see how to take some of the mystery out of color. You won't find a repeat of the Adobe printing or color management specs. Those documents are tomes unto themselves, and definitely worth the investment of your time to read through them. Perhaps on your next vacation?

Whether an image background, text, a collection of swirls, or some flashy text, there's no doubt color enhances a document.

InDesign offers several methods for choosing and storing color. For a casual color choice, use the Color panel or equivalent tools in the Toolbox and pick your colors from the Color Picker. For precise matching, you can choose and apply custom colors sampled from images on the page.

Define specific colors and store them for reuse in the Swatches panel, or import/export color swatches for use in a series of publications in multiple programs. Color swatches are convertible and transferable, ideal for designing publication suites.

Manage a Project's Colors with Swatches

The Swatches panel acts as a color manager in InDesign. From the panel, you can create and name colors and other color items such as gradients and tints. If you make a change to a swatch's color, all instances of the color update in the document automatically, making it easy to modify a color scheme.

FIGURE 14-1 InDesign includes several default colors as well as commands for creating and managing color.

Get Around the Swatches Panel

The InDesign Swatches panel stores information about the color swatches used in your project.

Check Out the Default Swatches

When you open a document, you'll see ten swatches in the default Swatches panel (see Figure 14-1). The colors include four CMYK swatches, three RGB swatches, and three special swatches.

Program default colors

Personalized default colors

Show All Swatches

Show Color Swatches

Show Gradient Swatches

New Swatch

Tip

In Figure 14-1, notice the additional three swatches at the bottom of the panel—these are personalized default swatches. Read about them in the sidebar, "Include Additional Default Swatches."

InDesign stores a group of default swatches and shows icons in the Swatches panel, including:

- The None swatch removes the stroke or fill from an object. You can't edit or remove this swatch.

- The Paper swatch simulates your printing paper color, good for previewing your output. You can't remove the Paper swatch.

- Black is a default CMYK 100 percent process color that overprints underlying inks by default. You can't edit or remove the Black swatch.

- PostScript printers use the Registration swatch to print objects like registration marks on separations. You can't edit or remove the Registration swatch.

- Icons on the Swatches panel identify the spot and process color types, as well as Lab, RGB, CMYK, and Mixed Ink color modes. (Read about color modes in Chapter 15.)

- A percentage next to a swatch in the Swatches panel indicates a tint of a spot or process color.

- An icon on the Swatches panel indicates whether a gradient is radial or linear.

Customize the Swatches Panel's Appearance

Change the swatches' appearances in the Swatches panel's menu. Select Name, Small Name, Small Swatch, or Large Swatch options. If you use the swatch-only options, a triangle/ dot combo at the lower-right area signifies a spot color; the triangle sans dot identifies a process color.

Use the buttons at the bottom of the Swatches panel to filter what types of swatches display (shown in Figure 14-1). Regardless of your choice, the None swatch always displays. Click Show All Swatches to view all color, tint, and gradient swatches; click Show Color Swatches to view process color, spot color, mixed ink color, and tint swatches; and click Show Gradient Swatches to show only gradient swatches.

How to. . .

Include Additional Default Swatches

If you use the same colors repeatedly (like the ones in your logo), you can add them as default swatches. Close any open publications, and choose the appropriate command from the Swatches panel's menu to display the dialog boxes for selecting color. You can add new color, tint, or gradient swatches in RGB or CMYK color and as process or spot colors, as you see in Figure 14-1.

Create New Swatches

The Swatches panel displays a variety of swatch types, including CMYK, RGB, Lab colors, gradients, tints, and spot/process/ mixed ink colors (Read about working with spot and process colors and mixed inks in Chapter 15.)

To add a new color swatch, follow these steps:

1. Select New Color Swatch from the Swatches panel's menu to open the dialog box. Or, you can press ALT-CTRL (Windows) or OPTION-COMMAND (Mac OS) and click the New Swatch button on the Swatches panel.

2. Specify a name for the color. For process color, you can leave the default selected, which shows the color values as the color name, or deselect the Name with Color Value check box and type a name in the Swatch Name field, such as **aqua** in the example shown here. If you choose a spot color from the Color Type dropdown list, type a name in the Swatch Name field.

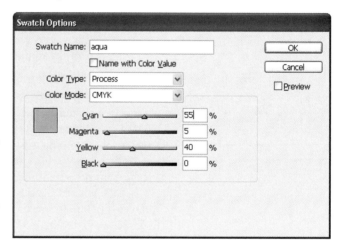

3. Click the Color Mode drop-down arrow, and choose an option, including Lab, CMYK, or RGB color. You'll also see dozens of color system choices for spot colors. Read more about using color libraries in Chapter 15.

4. To set the color, drag the sliders to modify the values or type numbers in the text boxes. If you're using the color value as the swatch's name, you'll see the Swatch Name field change as you modify the values.

If you see an alert icon, the color value is *out-of-gamut,* or beyond the color range allowed by the chosen color mode. Click the color box next to the alert icon to use the *in-gamut* color closest to your choice.

5. When you're finished, click OK to add the swatch and close the dialog box. To keep the dialog box open to select additional colors, click Add instead. When you're finished, click Done.

Manage Swatches

Color swatches come from various sources, aside from those you define in the Swatches panel. You'll find additional swatches added with imported graphics, for example, or created as unnamed colors or gradients. Here are some ways to handle color swatches.

Modify Swatch Colors and Names   When you use default naming for color swatches, the color components make up the color's name, such as C=55 M=5 Y=40 K=0 to represent a color swatch containing 55 percent cyan, 5 percent magenta, 40 percent yellow, and 0 percent black. If you double-click a swatch to open the Swatch Options dialog box, any adjustments you make to the color values update the name automatically.

FIGURE 14-2 Select a different color to replace the deleted one.

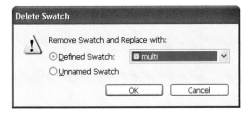

Replace a Used Color Swatch   If you change your mind about a particular color, you can easily replace a swatch with another. Select the swatch and click Delete at the bottom of the Swatches panel. You'll see a prompt asking how you want to replace the swatch. Click Unnamed Swatch to remove the swatch from the Swatches panel but maintain the color in the items, or click Defined Swatch and choose a swatch from the list (see Figure 14-2).

Delete Swatches   Select an unused swatch in the Swatches panel, and drag it to the trash can icon. To clean up all your swatches, choose Select All Unused in the Swatches panel's menu to select all defined (but unused) swatches. Click Delete to remove them from the file.

Merge Swatches   When you import swatches, add unnamed colors, or copy items from other documents, you may end up with duplicate swatches. Select the swatches in the Swatches panel, and choose Merge Swatches in the Swatches panel's menu.

Duplicate a Swatch   Define a variation of an existing color to use for a shadow or highlight. Select the swatch and drag it to the New Swatch button on the Swatches panel. Double-click the copy to open the Swatch Options dialog box and make the color adjustments. Duplicating a spot color generates another spot color printing plate (described in Chapter 15).

Track Down Unnamed Colors You can create colors in the Color panel or the Color Picker to use immediately, without saving them in the Swatches panel. To clean up the document and prevent generating multiple colors with nearly identical values, choose Add Unnamed Colors from the Swatches panel's menu. Every color you've defined and used in your document appears on the Swatches panel, named by their color values, like the five colors shown here.

Share and Reuse Swatches

Save your swatches for reuse in other projects, to share, or for import into other programs as Adobe Swatch Exchange (ASE) files. If your color settings are synchronized (find out how in Chapter 16), the colors are exactly the same across applications.

The following sections describe your swatch-sharing options.

Save Swatches for Reuse Select the swatches you want to save, and choose Save Swatches in the Swatches panel menu. Name the file, define the location, and click Save. The swatches are stored in an ASE file.

Import Another Library To import another library file, choose New Color Swatch from the Swatches panel's menu, and select Other Library from the Color Mode list. Select the library file, and click Open.

Load Swatches from Another InDesign Project Choose Load Swatches from the Swatches panel's menu to open a dialog box. Locate and select the InDesign document containing the swatches or the ASE swatches file, and double-click to close the dialog box and import the swatches.

Copy Swatches Share swatches among open files in two ways. Either copy an object using the desired color and paste it into the document, or drag the swatches you want to copy from the Swatches panel in one document and drop them in the document window of the other document to add to the Swatches panel automatically. If you want to copy a swatch's tints and gradients, you need to copy the original object, not just the swatch.

Check Out Kuler Colors

If you have problems defining color schemes—or are interested in keeping up with current color trends—check out Kuler,

You Can't Share Everything

Unfortunately, you can't share and share alike all your swatches from different programs. Patterns, gradients, tints, and mixed inks don't play well together. You can't share the Registration swatch from Illustrator or InDesign. Nor can you reuse numerous Photoshop file formats, such as duotone, monitorRGB, webRGB, or book color reference swatches from Photoshop. Fortunately, InDesign takes care of excluding swatches for you.

On the other hand, you can share swatches from a number of files and sources, including InDesign Document (INDD) and InDesign Template (INDT) files; AI and Encapsulated PostScript (EPS) Illustrator files; and ASE files from InDesign, Illustrator, or Photoshop.

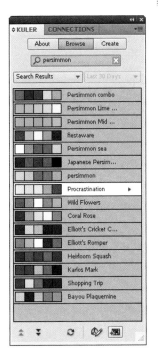

FIGURE 14-3 Tap into online color themes in Kuler.

an InDesign panel linked to an online application where you can create, save, and share themes.

Kuler requires an active Internet connection to browse themes. To use it, choose Window | Extensions | Kuler to open the panel. Click the Browse panel, and type a theme name, tag, or creator in the Search box. Click Search to show a list of returns (see Figure 14-3). Select a theme, and click the triangle on the listing to open a menu. Choose View Online in Kuler.

If you'd like to include a theme in your project, click Add to Swatches Panel at the bottom of the panel.

Apply and Save Tints

Color tints are screened versions of a color. From an ink perspective, the lighter the tint, the less color applied to the paper. Tints range from 0 percent to 100 percent; the lower the number, the lighter the tint. Tints offers variations on spot color without adding the cost of additional spot color inks as tints of the same color print on the same plate.

You can either apply a swatch color to an object and then adjust its tint using the Swatches panel's slider, or create a new swatch for the tint. Keep in mind that colors and their tints update together. If you edit a swatch, all tints based on that color update as well.

You'll find Kuler in several Creative Suite 4 (CS4) applications, including Photoshop, Flash, Illustrator, and Fireworks, as well as InDesign. Read more about creating, uploading, and sharing themes in the Kuler online service at http://www.kuler.adobe.com.

If you plan to reuse a tint, select the color in the Swatches panel and choose New Tint Swatch from the Swatches panel's menu to open the New Tint Swatch dialog box. Use the controls to specify the tint value, and click OK to close the dialog box. On the Swatches panel, you'll see the new swatch at the bottom of the Swatches panel listed by the parent color's name and a percentage.

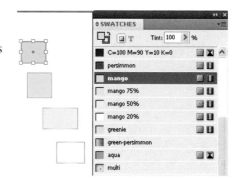

 You can either create unnamed tints in the Color panel or create the tint and click Add To Swatches from the Color panel's menu.

Make Quick Color Selections

In addition to designing color via the Swatches panel, InDesign lets you quickly pick colors from other panels or directly from content on the page. In all cases, when you pick a color, known as an *unnamed color*, you can add it to the Swatches panel for reuse.

You can add new colors at any time. Right-click the color swatch, and choose Add to Swatches Panel, or simply drag the color swatch to the Swatches panel. At the end of your project, choose Add Unnamed Colors from the Swatches panel's menu to add all colors you've picked outside of the Swatches panel. Of course, once the color is listed on the Swatches panel, it's no longer an unnamed color.

Specify Color in the Color Picker

The Color Picker lets you choose colors from a color field or specify colors numerically. You can define colors using RGB, Lab, or CMYK color models. Follow these steps to choose a color:

1. Double-click the Fill or Stroke box in the Toolbox or Color panel to open the Color Picker.

2. To choose a color spectrum to display, click any value in the different color model fields. For example, click L, a, or b to switch to the Lab Color Space View, and so on (see Figure 14-4).

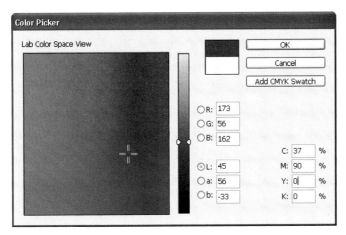

FIGURE 14-4 Click a value to display a color space, such as CMYK.

3. To pick the color, click in the spectrum, click or drag along the slider to increase/decrease intensity, or type values in the fields.

4. Once you've made your selection, click Add [Lab] [RGB] [CMYK] Swatch to add the swatch to the Swatches panel if you want to save it.

5. Click OK to close the dialog box and fill a selected item, or set the color as the default stroke or fill color.

Choose Colors in the Color Panel

Use the Color panel to create color on the fly simply by sampling. You don't have to work in any dialog boxes, like the Swatches panel. On the other hand, you don't name and save the color automatically to your document as with the Swatches panel.

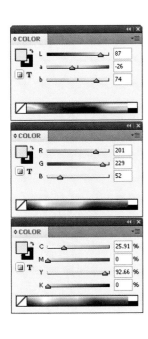

To create a color in the Color panel, follow these steps:

1. Choose Window | Color to open the Color panel, or press F6.

2. Choose Lab, CMYK, or RGB from the Color panel's menu to specify the color gamut you want to use. You'll see different color controls for each color model, as well as a color bar at the bottom of the panel.

3. Click to sample a color from the color bar, drag the sliders, or type values for the color settings.

4. The color applies to the selected object on the page. If you don't have a selection, the sampled color becomes the default for the fill or stroke for new objects, depending on whether the Fill or Stroke icon is active in the Color panel.

If you decide you'd like to reuse the color, add it to the Swatches panel.

Sample Color with the Eyedropper Tool

The Eyedropper tool offers a simple way to copy fill and stroke attributes, such as color, from any object, including an imported image. The Eyedropper tool loads all attributes, such as type and transparency, as well as color, although you can limit the copied content to a stroke or fill color.

Click either the Stroke or Fill icon in the Toolbar to make the icon for the color you want to select active. Select the object you want to change on the page. Finally, SHIFT-CLICK the object with the Eyedropper tool to sample the color you want to use. The selected object updates with the sampled color. If you simply click the object for sampling, all attributes are stored and applied.

 Tip   If you want to reuse the loaded Eyedropper tool, press ALT/OPTION to display the empty Eyedropper tool. Continue to press ALT/OPTION and click the object for sampling. Release the key and drop the new attributes on your desired object.

If you're sampling a color from an imported image, zoom in to a high magnification as the Eyedropper samples one pixel. Clicking an RGB image creates an RGB color; clicking a CMYK image creates a CMYK color.

 **Produce One-Off Color**

Here's one practical way to use the Color panel in InDesign rather than the Swatches panel: to generate a one-off color. The process works much the same as using linked content and breaking a link to an instance.

Suppose you've defined a color swatch for your project and applied it throughout. Then you decide you'd like to use a version of the color with more magenta in it for an object. Changing the color swatch modifies all items using your original color (shown in the left shape in the illustration). On the other hand, if you change the selected color in the Color panel, only that instance changes (as you see in the right shape).

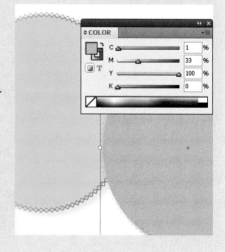

Design Gradients

Gradients can add movement and interest to your document, and serve as visually unifying elements. A gradient blends two or more colors gradually from one to the other across a specified distance. In InDesign, you can design gradients with a minimum of two and as many colors as you like, and use them as fills and strokes. You can work from the Swatches panel, or create a swatch on the fly in the Gradient panel.

Build and Store a Gradient

It's simplest to design a gradient from the Swatches panel and then use it in your project. Follow these steps to specify a gradient:

1. Choose New Gradient Swatch from the Swatches panel's menu to open the New Gradient Swatch dialog box.

2. Type a name for the gradient in the Swatch Name field, and choose Linear or Radial from the Type drop-down list.

You define the colors on the *Gradient Ramp.* The colored squares below the ramp, the *stop colors,* specify the colors used. Above the ramp, look for small diamonds that identify the midpoint between two colors. In a gradient with two colors, you'll have one midpoint; with three colors, you'll have two midpoints; and so on.

3. Click the color square at the left of the Gradient Ramp to activate the color bars. Click the Stop Color drop-down arrow, and choose a color system. Your choices include CMYK, Lab, RGB, and Swatches. For any of the color systems, choose a color using the controls in the Stop Color area. If you choose Swatches, scroll through the list of swatches and select a color.

4. Repeat for the square at the right of the Gradient Ramp. Click the stop color square, and choose the color from the Stop Color area, using the same color options as for the left stop color.

5. Click just below the ramp to add another color stop if you want a third color. Use the controls again to add the next color (see Figure 14-5).

6. Modify the gradient as desired with as many color stops and colors as you wish. To delete a color, drag the color stop downward from the Gradient Ramp and release the mouse. Drag color stops and midpoints horizontally to adjust the degree of color blending.

7. Click OK to close the dialog box and add the gradient to the Swatches panel, or click Add to add the gradient to the Swatches panel and keep the dialog box open.

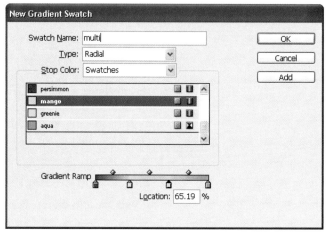

FIGURE 14-5 Specify the colors to use for a gradient.

 You can modify gradients pasted from Adobe Illustrator, provided that the gradient was pasted using Adobe Illustrator Clipboard (AICB) format. To select the gradient, use the Direct Selection tool.

Design One-Off Gradients

You can bypass the Swatches panel to design a gradient, just as you can a color. Choose Window | Gradient to display the panel. You work in the Gradient panel in much the same way as in the new Gradient Swatch dialog box, with one exception: To add a color stop, drag a swatch from the Swatches panel and release it on the ramp. Release the swatch on an existing color stop to replace it. The Type and Location options are the same as those in the New Gradient Swatch dialog box. The Reverse button lets you flip a gradient, and the Angle field lets you rotate a linear gradient.

Your gradient applies to selected content on the page. If you don't have anything selected, the gradient becomes the default stroke or fill for new drawn objects. To save your gradient, drag the color from the Fill box on the Gradient panel to the Swatches panel.

Adjust a Gradient's Position

You don't necessarily want a gradient to follow a finite and constant path. Fortunately, you can customize the gradient's position using the Gradient tool.

Apply your gradient to an object's fill or stroke, such as the stroke in the objects here. Make sure the object remains selected, and then click and drag with the Gradient tool. The location you click defines the start point, and the location where you release the mouse defines the end point of the gradient. In the right object, you see both the modified gradient stroke as well as the Gradient tool's path used to revise the gradient location.

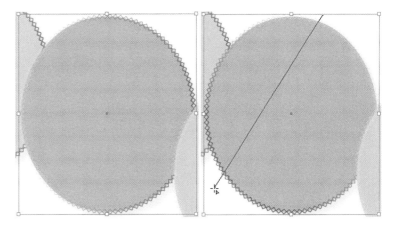

Apply Gradients to Text

Try using multiple gradients the next time you need something different for a text heading or title. Select the ranges of text and apply the gradients (the text in Figure 14-6 uses three gradients). Characters in the text frame show the gradient that corresponds to their area of the frame as the gradient's endpoints anchor to the text frame. When you make changes to the text frame, the colors of the characters change according to their position along the anchored gradient.

FIGURE 14-6 Type shifts position relative to the gradient, although you can control it using the Gradient tool.

Note   You can also convert the text to outlines and apply a gradient. The gradient anchors to the text outline rather than the text frame, so it won't shift, although you can't edit the text.

Summary

There's a lot to learn about color! This chapter covered the swatches gamut (pun intended), from choices for displaying swatches in the Swatches panel, to building and using gradients. Swatches contain information of various types about a particular color, and can be shared, exported, and reused. Swatches can be stored or used as unnamed colors. You can design and store tint and gradient swatches, along with solid colors.

The color saga continues in the next chapter. You'll see how to work with spot color, mixed inks, and how to handle trapping, a technique to prevent gaps in printed content.

15

Control and Manage Color

How to...

- Use spot and process colors
- Manage swatch libraries
- Mix inks for custom colors
- Specify color settings

For those who work online or in nonprinting media, the idea of manipulating color based on inks seems restrictive. On the other hand, for print-based designers, the reality of ink never strays far from the front of the mind.

In this chapter, learn the basics of approaching color from a print perspective and see how to keep color consistent using color management settings.

Define Spot and Mixed-Ink Colors

Color for printing comes in two versions—process or spot color. A *process color* prints from a combination of the four standard inks on separate color plates in cyan, magenta, yellow, and black (CMYK). Using a *spot color* in addition to or instead of process inks requires an additional printing plate. To make your inks go further, you can design a *mixed-ink* color, a combination of process and spot colors.

Your project and budget generally define the type of color used. Spot colors produce precise color matches, often chosen from color-matching systems. In common practice, you'd use a spot color to color-match a logo or other trademarked symbol and a process color for continuous tone images, such as color photos, where using multiple spot inks on separate plates would be extremely expensive.

Specify Spot Color Swatches

In InDesign you primarily work through the Swatches panel to define, create, and control colors in your publication. The methods for adding a spot color or a process color are the same. To add a spot color, select the option from the Color Type drop-down list in the New Color Swatch dialog box (see how to build swatches in Chapter 14).

Select Library Colors

Rather than specifying color values in the New Color Swatch dialog box, you can select colors from one of the many color libraries included with InDesign, such as the PANTONE Process Color System, Focoltone color system, and Trumatch color swatch system.

Choose New Color Swatch from the Swatches panel's menu to open the New Color Swatch dialog box. Click the Color Mode drop-down arrow, and choose a library file. Scroll through the color swatches, and click Add to include them in your project's swatches, as you see here. Click OK when you're finished to close the dialog box.

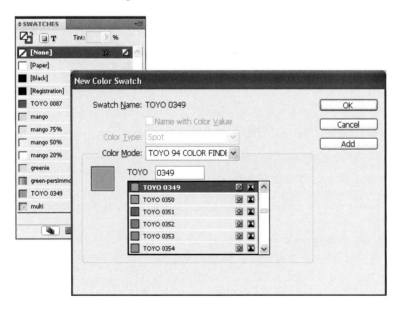

Import Spot Colors with Images

Imported Encapsulated PostScript (EPS), Portable Document Format (PDF), Tagged Image File Format (TIFF), and Adobe

Photoshop (PSD) files import spot colors to the Swatches panel. You can apply these swatches to objects in your document, but you can't modify them. You can't delete the colors unless you first delete the graphic.

Tip   Occasionally, the spot color stays even after the graphic is removed. Use File I Export and export the document in InDesign CS3 Interchange (INX) format. Reopen the INX file in InDesign, and the spot colors are gone.

Create Mixed-Ink Colors

When you're looking to achieve the maximum range of print colors with the fewest number of inks (and dollars!) you can create new swatches by mixing spot inks and process inks together. You can create a single mixed-ink swatch or use a mixed-ink group to generate multiple swatches at once.

Produce a Mixed-Ink Swatch

Once you've added at least one spot color to the Swatches panel, you can design mixed-ink swatches. A mixed-ink swatch contains two or more colors, one of which must be a spot color. To define the swatch, follow these steps:

1. Choose New Mixed Ink Swatch from the Swatches panel's menu to open the New Mixed Ink Swatch dialog box, and type a name for the swatch.

2. Click the box to the left of an ink's name to select it, as indicated by the ink icon.

3. Drag the sliders or type values to adjust the amount of ink in the swatch. In the example, the mango color uses 100% Process Yellow and 18% TOYO 0087 (see Figure 15-1).

4. Click Add to include the new swatch in the Swatches panel and keep the dialog box open, or click OK to close the dialog box and add the swatch.

FIGURE 15-1 Mix process and spot colors to produce a mixed-ink swatch.

New Mixed Ink Swatch		
Name: Mango-mix		
Inks		
Process Cyan	———————	%
Process Magenta	———————	%
Process Yellow	———————	100 %
Process Black	———————	%
TOYO 0349	———————	%
TOYO 0087	———————	18 %

OK   Cancel   Add

Assemble a Mixed-Ink Group

Rather than creating mixed-ink swatches individually, create a group using a sequence of colors based on varying percentages of process and spot inks, following these steps:

1. Choose New Mixed Ink Group from the Swatches panel's menu to open the New Mixed Ink Group dialog box. Type a name for the group: this name is used as the prefix for the numbered swatches.

2. Click the box to the left of an ink you want to use. Define the percentages for the amount of ink to use at the start (Initial); the number of times to increase the ink (Repeat); and the percentage of ink to add for each repeat (Increment). In the example shown here, Yellow starts at 40% and increases twice at 25% each time—that is, 40%, 65%, and 90%.

3. Click Preview Swatches to view a sample of the swatches and make adjustments as necessary.

4. Click OK to close the dialog box and add the ink group to the Swatches panel.

Edit and Manage Mixed Inks

Like other sorts of swatches, you can modify and edit mixed inks and mixed-ink groups. Here are some issues to be aware of, due to the relationships between parent and child swatches and process and spot inks:

- Changes to a swatch in a mixed-ink group apply to the swatch only; changes to the parent of a mixed-ink group apply to all swatches.

- To delete a single swatch or several swatches, select a swatch or swatches, and click Delete. If you want to delete an entire mixed-ink group, select the parent swatch, and click Delete.

- Converting a mixed-ink swatch to a process or spot color swatch breaks the relationship between the swatch and the mixed-ink group.

Convert Mixed Ink to Process Color   If you find you don't need the precision of a spot color, or if the cost is prohibitive, simply convert mixed-ink color to process color. For an individual swatch, double-click to open the Swatch Options dialog box, and choose Process from the Color Type drop-down list. To convert a mixed-ink group, double-click the parent swatch to open the Mixed Ink Group Options dialog box, select Convert Mixed Ink Swatches to Process, and click OK.

Add Another Swatch to the Group   Select the swatch for the parent of the mixed-ink group, and choose New Color Swatch from the Swatches panel's menu to open the New Color Swatch dialog box. You'll see the group's name, followed by the next number in the swatches sequence. For each ink, drag the slider or type a value for the percentage. When you've found the perfect color, click OK to close the dialog box and add the new swatch.

Handle Document Colors with the Ink Manager

The Ink Manager controls what happens to your colors when the document is output. In the Ink Manager, you can match one spot color to another, convert spot colors to process color, and define ink behavior for printing separations.

Choose Ink Manager from the Swatches panel's menu to display the dialog box, where you'll see the four process colors and any spot colors you've defined in the document, regardless of whether you've used them or not.

Alias Spot Colors

When you open the Ink Manager, you're most likely looking to alias one spot color to another. You might import graphics with different spot color names than those listed in the Swatches panel for the same color, resulting in extra plates for the same ink. Or, you might have two or three spot colors and decide to decrease the spots for cost savings.

The Ink Manager shows a list of your inks (see Figure 15-2). Select the ink you want to alias, such as the TOYO 0349. Then click the Ink Alias drop-down arrow and choose the ink to alias it to, such as the aqua ink shown in the example. The Type column for TOYO 0349 reads *<aqua>*, indicating aliasing to that ink.

FIGURE 15-2 Alias one ink to another to decrease the number of plates.

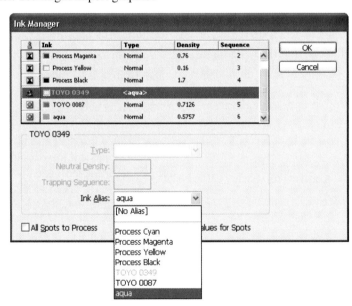

You can check the alias using the Separations Preview, discussed in Chapter 16.

Note

Convert Inks

Along with setting ink aliases, you can convert inks in the Ink Manager in one step. Your options include:

- To convert a spot color ink into a CMYK process color, click the spot color icon to the left of the ink name. You'll see the icon change to CMYK and that the ink controls are disabled. Click the icon again to revert to spot color.

- Select the All Spots to Process check box to convert all spot colors in the document to process color; deselect the check box to restore the spot colors again.

- Select the Use Standard Lab Values for Spots check box to convert spot colors in some systems (such as TOYO, PANTONE, and others) to Lab color rather than CMYK for the most accurate output.

Tip   The CMYK options provide backward compatibility for older versions of InDesign.

Work a Little Color Magic

Once you've gone to the effort of defining and tweaking your ink colors, consider using them for some special image coloring, such as duotones, tritones, and tints. In InDesign, you can make duotones from both grayscale and color images, although you use different techniques.

You won't get the same level of control working in InDesign as you would in Photoshop, where you can assign spot and process colors to a black and white image, and control curves for each color and black. But if your job doesn't require critical image control, try some of these coloring techniques in InDesign.

Color a Monotone to Look Like a Duotone   A simple way to simulate a duotone is with a grayscale image. Import the grayscale PSD, TIFF, or JPEG image into InDesign. To add a punch of color, select the graphic frame with the Selection tool and click a swatch in the Swatches palette to fill the frame, adding a tint to the grayscale image, as you see here.

Monotones can be monotonous. For a better duotone look, use a mixed-ink swatch and your grayscale image. Apply a mixed-ink swatch composed of one spot color and 50% black. Adjust the combinations of inks to produce the best duotone effect.

Create a Tritone Effect Using a Gradient   Take the overprint method to the next level and create a tritone using a gradient. Simply fill the frame with a gradient instead of a flat color. To see the effect, choose View | Overprint Preview (see Figure 15-3). Read more about overprinting in the next section.

Tint Color Images   If you're starting from a color image, you have to use a blend mode to add a tint. Select the image frame with the Selection tool, and add a color swatch (you can use most colors and tints). Then, use the Direct Selection tool to select the image. Finally, choose the Luminosity blend mode from the Effects panel to see the outcome. The example shown here uses a TOYO 0087 tint.

FIGURE 15-3 Overprinting a gradient produces an interesting tritone effect.

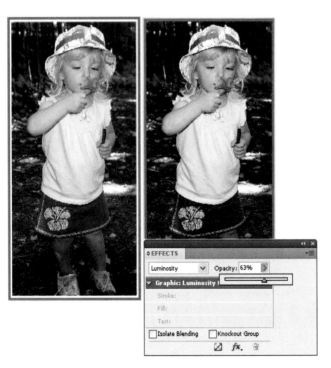

Prevent Errors with Traps and Overprints

Offset printing runs paper through a press multiple times, laying one ink down after the next. If the inks print with perfect alignment, or *in register,* there's no problem. However, the odds against perfect registration are high, resulting in *misregistration,* or gaps between inks.

By default, when one ink overlays another ink, any ink underlying the top ink is removed, or *knocked out,* to prevent color mixing. *Trapping* is the opposite: Trapping prevents ink gaps by expanding one object slightly to overlap another area, known as *overprinting* (see Figure 15-4).

Choose a Trap Method

In InDesign, there are several ways to trap a document, ranging from avoiding the situation altogether to using full internal or external trapping. The areas you'll find that need trapping most are vector art and text. In other content, such as images, the varying overlays of color are usually spread sufficiently to prevent gaps.

FIGURE 15-4 Use trapping to manage ink misregistration.

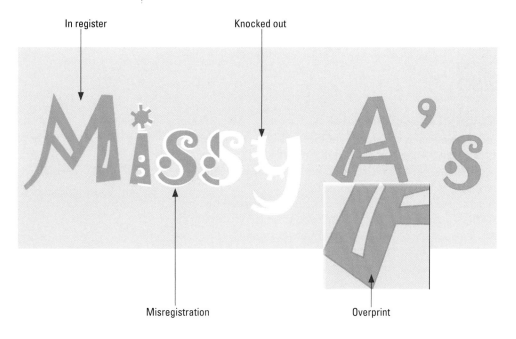

In register

Knocked out

Misregistration

Overprint

Use Common Inks

Sometimes, you can avoid trapping altogether by making sure that overlapping or abutting colors contain the same inks, such as the backgrounds with gradient fills and text in various colors used in the sample project, shown in the illustration.

The yellow separation plate shows that all of the text and background contain some yellow, while the image background has large areas that don't print on the yellow plate due to the blue-yellow gradient applied to the image. As you see in the inset shown here, the background and text contain different colors, but the common yellow makes any misregistration gaps virtually invisible.

Read more about viewing separations in Chapter 16.

Overprint Strokes and Fills

InDesign includes commands for the automatic overprinting of strokes and fills, or you can add them yourself. To add manual trapping, simply include a thin stroke around an object that matches the fill color.

You can set any object's fill or stroke to overprint by setting its attributes. Choose Window | Attributes to display the Attributes panel. Select the content for overprinting, and select the Overprint Fill or Overprint Stroke check box in the panel.

When the image shown at the top of Figure 15-5 prints on a PostScript printer, the red text would mix with the yellow and green background. However, when you apply the overprint settings, you don't see a difference on your monitor, as overprints aren't visible onscreen. Choose View | Overprint Preview to

FIGURE 15-5 The onscreen view of the page (top) has more depth and looks more like the print version using the Overprint Preview (bottom).

simulate the appearance, shown in the bottom image in Figure 15-5. The Overprint Preview darkens the red color, and you see the underlying color in the "Togs for Tots" label.

Apply Trap Presets

InDesign includes a trapping engine and can use the Adobe In-RIP (Raster Image Processor) Trapping engine on Adobe PostScript output devices that support it. Automatic trapping, as the term suggests, calculates relative levels of darkness/lightness (or *neutral densities*) at the edges of type and graphics, and creates traps by spreading lighter colors into darker colors.

Choose Window | Output | Trap Presets to open the Trap Presets panel. To apply a preset, choose Assign Trap Presets from the panel's menu to open the dialog box. Choose the entire document, range of pages, or individual pages, and click Assign.

You can't use a preset for an individual object.

You can modify trap settings for your document. The simplest way is to double-click the Default preset to open the Modify Trap Preset Options dialog box.

Most settings produce great output using the default settings. Leave the defaults, unless you are a prepress whiz or have instructions from your prepress bureau. For your information, here's the scoop on what makes up a trap preset:

- The Trap Width field shows two values. Default sets the trap width for all inks except black, while Black, as you might expect, defines the trap width for black.

- The Images options control the trapping of objects and images. Built-in trapping can't trap placed bitmap images or EPS vector graphics.

- The Trap Appearance settings define the style used for joining and ending edges of trap areas. Unless you have specialized requirements, leave the default Miter preset.

- Trap Thresholds define how and when to apply trapping. For example, Step defines the difference in percentage between process colors to apply trapping.

Summary

This chapter built on the color discussions started in Chapter 14. You learned how to work with spot, process, and mixed colors. Along with defining single spot colors, InDesign offers an option to create a group of mixed inks at one time. You saw how the Ink Manager helps you reduce the number of plates by using ink aliases.

For something different, we showed you a few ways to use some color to finesse the appearance of an image without having to work in Photoshop—great for a quick change. In the last part of the chapter, you saw how traps and overprints help generate better-quality output.

Coming up in Chapter 16—you guessed it—more color. Learn the ins and outs of color management and the tools InDesign offers to preview your work before sending it out for print.

16

Color-Manage Your Publication

How to...

- Control color in InDesign
- Soft-proof color
- Preview color separations
- Preview transparency flattening

At first glance, the idea of managing color may seem overwhelming. How can you possibly see the same shade of blue in an illustration, a chart, or an image background when you print it from your desktop, send it to an offset printer, or have someone halfway around the world print from your PDF file?

The answer, of course, is a color management system (CMS). As part of the CS4 suites, InDesign uses color management via Bridge. Within InDesign, you can use color profiles and other color settings to comply with different output requirements. Then turn to a number of proofing and preview features to make sure the content looks the way you intend.

Set Up Color Management

InDesign, along with many other programs, uses color management to compensate for different devices and how they interpret and display color. The goal is to achieve color consistency throughout your workflow. Color management is active by default in InDesign. If you work with Adobe Creative Suite, you can use Adobe Bridge to synchronize color settings across the various products.

Make Sense of CMS

If you could produce content in one way and output to one device, there wouldn't be any need for color management, but the reality is far different. Humans, devices, and graphics use different color gamuts that overlap but don't match. At the top of the heap are human eyes, capable of viewing a spectrum of 16.4 million colors; at the other end are low-cost inkjet printers. Your CMS attempts to compensate and create the best matches.

- First, the CMS translates the colors from your computer's color space into a device-independent color space, such as Commission Internationale d'Eclairage (CIE) Lab color. At this point, the color doesn't belong to any particular device or process.

- Then the CMS maps the color to the output device's color space and adjusts the colors based on differences in color gamut.

Synchronize Color Management Settings in Bridge

Synchronizing your color using the color management feature in Bridge provides consistent color settings in your work. For example, when you're working on a suite of products, such as marketing materials, it's particularly important that color remain consistent across documents, images, and software.

Specify a Color Setting

Open Adobe Bridge, and choose Edit | Creative Suite Color Settings to display the Suite Color Settings dialog box, shown here.

Choose a color setting that describes your working space from the list, and click Apply. If you don't see the color setting you want to work with, select Show Expanded List of Color Settings Files.

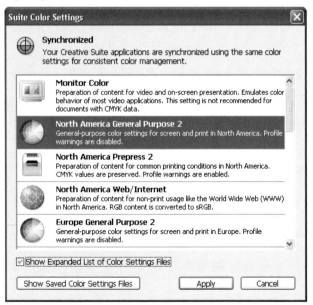

Your color-setting options include:

■ Monitor Color for designing publications for onscreen or video use.

■ North America General Purpose 2 for publications printed from desktop laser and inkjet printers and onscreen publications in North America. This space adjusts the RGB working space in InDesign (along with the rest of the Creative Suite) to standard red-green-blue (sRGB), and the CMYK working space to U.S. Web Coated (SWOP) v2.

■ North America Prepress 2 (or other regional prepress) for typical printing press settings in North America. This space uses the same CMYK working space as North America General Purpose 2, but resets the RGB working space to Adobe RGB (1998).

Adobe RGB (1998) has a wider gamut than sRGB and converts readily to CMYK for output.

■ North America Web/Internet for typical settings for onscreen presentation in North America.

Bridge synchronizes all of your Creative Suite applications with the chosen setting. If the color settings in a file aren't synchronized, you'll see a warning message in the application's Color Settings dialog box.

Color-Manage Imported Content

When you place content in a document, the characteristics of the files and the active color settings define how InDesign manages the color. Placed images and PDF files bring their own criteria in some circumstances. Color management policies for images are the same for both North America General Purpose 2 and North America Prepress 2 settings.

RGB Profiles Preserved   InDesign preserves the RGB profiles in imported images. Conversions for both proofing and output to CMYK use the embedded profile.

CMYK Profiles Ignored   InDesign ignores CMYK profiles for imported images to preserve image data, called a *safe CMYK workflow.* Use the safe CMYK workflow with untagged CMYK images or images using the same profile as your document color space.

For more precise control of output color when you manage and control your source images, use "Preserve Embedded Profiles" as the CMYK policy.

Color in Placed PDF Files   In a color management workflow, InDesign uses the embedded profile in a placed PDF file as long as the PDF file contains an embedded International Color Consortium (ICC) or PDF/X (graphics standard) profile. Otherwise, the PDF file uses the InDesign document's color profile. When it's time to print or export the document, you can use the embedded ICC profile or replace it with the InDesign document profile.

Check Color Settings in InDesign

If you use InDesign as part of Adobe CS4, color management settings are synchronized, although you can change them if you want. Choose Edit | Color Settings to open the Color Settings dialog box. You'll see a message at the top of the dialog box explaining the colors are synchronized, and the setting selected as the default in Bridge is shown in the Settings field (see Figure 16-1). If you modify any settings, the message changes to Unsynchronized.

FIGURE 16-1 The settings include working spaces and information about color management.

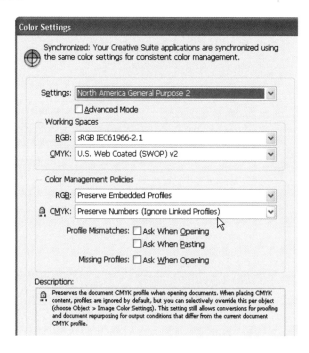

You Don't Always Need Color Management

Color management may help synchronize your output, or it may make little difference. Its value depends on your output characteristics, as in these examples:

- If you work with multiple output devices, printers, and color separations
- If you work with a number of color graphics from different sources
- If you use content in different media, especially print and online
- If your work may be printed anywhere on any sort of printer, such as printing from an online PDF source

Use Stand-alone Management

If you use InDesign as a stand-alone product, you can set color management within InDesign. Choose Edit | Color Settings to open the Color Settings dialog box (shown in Figure 16-1). Regardless of whether your CMS is universal or document-specific, InDesign offers the same color settings.

Choose an option appropriate for the kind of work you do in InDesign, with the same choices as those listed in the previous section, "Synchronize Color Management Settings in Bridge."

Publication Previews

It takes a lot of work to get a publication ready for output. I'm sure we all know that! To decrease disappointment and save time and money, be sure to run your publication through some previews before sending it off. InDesign includes several ways to evaluate and simulate how the document looks when printed.

Chapter 15 includes a discussion on trap presets, another important part of previewing. Chapter 17 describes using Preflight, a method for evaluating document content to comply with specific requirements, standards, or types of output.

Soft-Proof Color

Before the days of color-managed workflows, you'd have to preview your publication using printed, or *hard copy*, proofs. Using color management, you can use your profile to simulate how color looks on your monitor.

Select a Profile

A soft proof follows a sequence. First, you create your document as usual in the working color space. Then the colors in your document recalculate to comply with the color space of your output device's profile. Finally, your monitor shows the proof profile's color values.

Choose View | Proof Setup and select one of two presets. Your choices include:

- Choose Working CMYK to use the CMYK working space defined in the Color Settings dialog box.

- Choose Document CMYK to use the document's CMYK profile.

Customize and View the Preset Results

To customize a preset for more accuracy, choose View | Proof Preset | Custom to open the Customize Proof Condition dialog box shown here. Click the Device to Simulate drop-down arrow, and make a selection from the dozens of options. You'll see numerous offset print choices and a range of RGB options. You can also select from a wide variety of onscreen display options, ranging from HDTV to SDTV, to camera settings, and basic video display options.

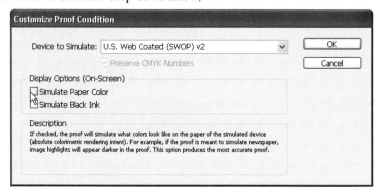

By default, the Device to Simulate field shows U.S. Web Coated (SWOP) v2. The Preserve CMYK Numbers check box is active and disabled by default. Choose these customization options, and then click OK to close the dialog box:

- Select the Simulate Paper Color check box to display a simulation of the soft white of paper, rather than sharp pixel white.

- Select the Simulate Black Ink check box to display the actual dark gray color printed on paper instead of solid black.

Tip You can simulate black ink alone, but if you choose to simulate paper color, the black ink simulation is selected automatically.

Choose View | Proof Colors to toggle the soft-proof display on and off. When soft proofing is on, a check mark appears next to the Proof Colors command and the name of the proof preset or profile appears at the top of the document window. As you see here, when simulating paper and black ink colors (top) the difference from onscreen color (bottom) is obvious (see Figure 16-2).

FIGURE 16-2 Using the simulated paper and black ink colors (top) shows a significant difference from the default onscreen display (bottom).

Preview Color Separations

It's important to preview your layout as separations before sending it to your printer to assess your overprints (described in Chapter 15), as well as amounts of ink used on the page. You can preview each ink separately and print the separations as well.

 Tip Colors display properly in separations, whether or not they have names. Read about choosing and naming colors in Chapter 14.

 **How to...**

Improve the Quality of Your Soft Proofs

Here are a few tips for soft proofing—and decreasing print disappointments:

- Make sure to calibrate your monitor, and take the ambient lighting in your workspace into consideration.

- If you're proofing for offset printing, choose View | Overprint Preview to see overprints.

- For comparisons, choose Window | Arrange | New Window to view two copies of the document. Leave the original image in one and soft-proof the other.

View Ink Plates

To check out your document, choose Window | Output | Separations Preview to open the Separations Preview panel, and choose Separations from the View drop-down list. Click the eye icons to toggle visibility for the inks, shown here. If you hide all inks except one, the page renders in black to show the appearance of paler inks, giving you a better idea of what the actual plates look like.

 Tip   Move your cursor over an object on the page to see the amount of ink shown in the panel for visible colors. You'll see the values whether or not the separation for that color is visible.

Check the Ink Limits

Along with viewing color plates, you can see how much ink is used for printing. Choose Ink Limit from the View drop-down list. Type the value for the total ink recommended by your printer, or leave the default, 300%.

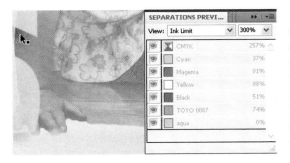

When you move your cursor over an area on the page, the amount of ink for each color shows on the panel and the total CMYK ink value shows in the CMYK listing. Areas with more than 300% total ink are highlighted on the screen (see Figure 16-3). In the figure, notice that the CMYK total is only 257%, well below the threshold, but the spot TOYO 0087 ink adds another 74%, bringing the total to 331%.

FIGURE 16-3 Highlights indicate areas that exceed the ink limits for the document.

Preview Transparency Flattening

Transparency and blending modes give your InDesign projects all sorts of creative possibilities. However, transparency also creates a significant problem when it comes to output, whether you're exporting to a PDF file or a high-quality PostScript printer. The PDF format—as well as most professional printing workflows—is based on the PostScript page description language, which doesn't support transparency at all.

That doesn't mean you won't have your lovely gradient or drop shadow on your printed document, like the example you see here.

To get around the issue, InDesign creates a flattened replica of the transparency using a combination of fills, bitmaps, and other elements.

Transparency behaves differently in RGB mode than in CMYK mode. Choose Edit | Transparency Blend Space, and choose either Document RGB or Document CMYK, depending on where you intend to use your publication.

Flattening takes place when creating a PDF or Encapsulated PostScript (EPS) file, or when printing. InDesign offers three transparency presets for flattening: Low Resolution for checking onscreen or rough draft prints, Medium Resolution for desktop proofing or print-on-demand content, and High Resolution for commercial print output.

Note   Read about transparency flattener presets in Chapter 13.

Preview Flattening

Take a few minutes to check out flattener previews as part of
your document proofing workflow. Previews show areas of
concern to check carefully before sending a layout to print.

Follow these steps to preview flattening:

1. Choose Window | Output | Flattener Preview to open the
   panel.

2. Click the Highlight drop-down list, and choose an
   option. Once you make a selection, the remaining
   settings on the panel are activated. The layout renders
   in grayscale and any areas that are affected by flattening
   are highlighted in color (see Figure 16-4).

Click Ignore Spread Overrides if you want to specify different flattener presets for different
spreads, such as a spread with high-resolution images and transparency, or a spread containing
only text and line graphics.

3. Select another Highlight option. To view the affected
   areas, click Refresh, or click Auto Refresh Highlight to
   save mouse clicks.

4. Click Apply Settings to Print to use the preset as part of
   your document's print settings.

FIGURE 16-4 Use flattener
preview highlights to identify
affected areas on the page.

Where to Get the Transparency Guide

For guidance on using transparency in your InDesign print jobs, download this Adobe reference, "Transparency in Adobe Applications: A Print Production Guide."

At the time of writing, the paper for Creative Suite CS3 is available at this location: www.adobe.com/designcenter/creativesuite/articles/cs3ip_printprodtrans.pdf

Check for other resources on your Creative Suite installation CD.

Build Another Preset

You can create your own presets, if necessary. Choose Transparency Flattener Presets from the Flattener Preview panel's menu to open the dialog box, and click New to display the Transparency Flattener Preset Options dialog box, shown here.

Choose a raster/vector graphic balance, resolutions, and whether to modify other content on the page. Click OK to close the dialog box and add your preset to the default preset options.

Summary

This chapter looked at working with color management. If you're working with CS4 design suites, Adobe Bridge can apply and synchronize color management across products for consistent output. Whether working in Bridge or in InDesign, color management lets you specify settings for the type of work you're doing.

The second part of the chapter dealt with previewing your publications. In this chapter, we looked at soft proofing, previewing color separations, and transparency flattening.

There's more color information to come. Part V, starting with Chapter 17, looks at different forms of output. In Chapter 17, see how to use Preflight to evaluate your documents, how to print, and how to export PDF files from InDesign.

PART V

Outputs and Exports

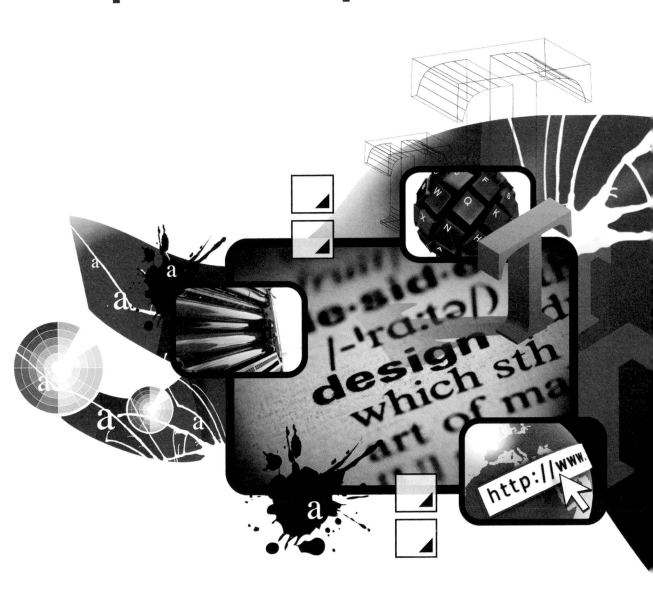

17

Prepare Print Output

How to...

- Preflight files
- Package content for output
- Select printing options
- Work with export presets
- Convert files to PDF

Just as InDesign offers many ways to create and manage publications, the program offers a number of ways to preflight documents and export the finished product.

InDesign lets you control printing using a variety of controls. PDF files have become synonymous with documents that preserve the layout characteristics of the original files. As an integral part of a print publishing workflow, InDesign includes direct export to PDF using a variety of presets.

Printing your InDesign layout can be as simple as choosing File | Print and clicking OK, or it can involve careful tweaking of various options in the Print dialog box panels—either to solve a problem or to generate a specific type of printout. Most of the time, your jobs fall somewhere in between.

Preflight and Package Files

Live Preflight, a new feature in InDesign CS4, gives you a heads-up on errors as you develop your publication. If you've ever been faced with 80 or 90 preflight errors and a looming deadline, you're sure to appreciate on-the-fly notifications!

When the project is complete, use the Package feature to create a copy of your document and all its resources, ready to send off for production—or to send off to someone else for further work.

Track and Repair Errors Live

Live Preflight includes one default setting, which is active by default. To accommodate projects with special requirements, you can easily construct your own profiles.

Track Ongoing Errors

The Preflight indicator sits on the Status bar at the bottom of the document window. The icon is either green when the document is error-free or red when errors are detected. Double-click the icon to open the Preflight panel (see Figure 17-1).

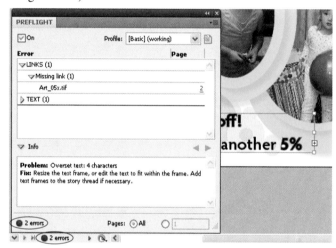

FIGURE 17-1 Identify and correct errors in real time using Live Preflight.

The panel displays a list of errors. Click the drop-down arrows to identify the location and characteristics of the errors. For the ultimate convenience, click the link on the panel to select the object on the page containing the error.

The default function evaluates all pages, but you can click the page range option at the lower-right corner of the panel and type a page number or range, restricting the testing to the pages identified.

Note For some errors, such as a color mismatch, the Preflight profile doesn't identify a particular swatch in the Swatches panel. Instead, it identifies an object using the offending item or a program feature, such as the Ink Manager. Click the Info drop-down arrow at the bottom of the Preflight panel to see concise information about the problem.

Create Custom Profiles

InDesign offers the [Basic] profile, which can't be embedded or modified. Instead, create a custom profile following these steps:

1. Choose Define Profiles from the Preflight panel's menu, or click the arrow on the Status bar and select the command from the Preflight pop-up menu to open the Preflight Profiles dialog box.

2. Click the plus sign (+) below the Profiles column at the left of the dialog box to activate the Profile Name field. Type a name for the new profile.

3. Click the arrows to open the different categories and reveal the settings, as shown here. You'll also find some nested items, such as Spot Color Setup.

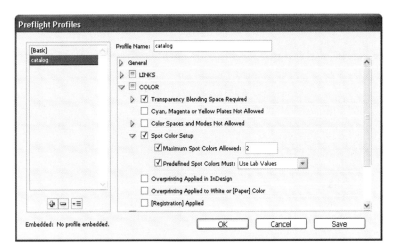

4. Make your choices in these areas:

- In the General category, type a description for the profile.

- In the Links category, select or deselect link status, such as missing, modified, or Open Prepress Interface (OPI).

- In the Color category, specify a variety of items, ranging from transparency blending space, whether specific color spaces or modes are disallowed, number and value requirements for spot color, and how to handle overprinting.

- In the Images and Objects category, choose test items, such as image resolution, transparency, scaling, stroke width, and layer visibility.

- In the Text category, choose items such as overset text, missing fonts, minimum type size, and disallowed font types.

- Finally, in the Document category, specify page size and orientation requirements, number of pages, how blank pages are defined, and bleed and slug setup.

5. Click Save to store the profile and keep the dialog box open to construct another profile, or click OK to close the dialog box and save the profile.

Specify Preflight Options

Once you've constructed a profile, or if you decide to use the default, you can configure how the profile operates within your document. Choose Preflight Options from the Preflight panel's menu. In the resulting Preflight Options dialog box, shown here, set how you want the profile to function.

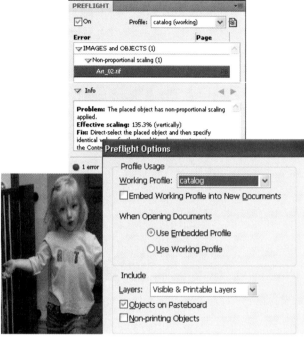

When you've made your selections, click OK to close the dialog box and return to the Preflight panel. Here are your choices:

- Select the profile to use as the default for new documents from the Working Profile drop-down list. If you want the working profile to be embedded in new documents, select Embed Working Profile into New Documents.

- Select either Use Embedded Profile or Use Working Profile to define the preflight profile applied when you open a document.

- Make layer selections specifying whether items on hidden layers are tested.

- Select the Objects on Pasteboard check box to report errors on content stored on the pasteboard. If you just use the pasteboard for storage, there may be little value in including the option. On the other hand, if you configure items before adding them to the page, you can check the pasteboard items just like the regular document pages for errors, as in the non-proportional image shown in the illustration.

- Select the Non-printing Objects check box to report on master page objects using the Hide Master Items command or objects defined as non-printing in the Attributes panel.

Limit the Number of Errors Displayed

Look for one more useful display option. In the Preflight panel's menu, click Limit Number of Rows Per Error, and choose a value from the list, ranging from 25 to No Limit. Why bother, you ask? All you need is a document using an incorrect font type when the profile tests for that font type, and you'll have hundreds of errors.

Manage Profiles

Like many settings systems in InDesign, you can manage preflight profiles in a number of ways. Your choices include:

FIGURE 17-2 Use the menu to manage preflight profiles.

- Select a profile and then click Embed to the right of the Profile list. An embedded profile becomes part of the document's metadata and travels with the document. You can send a document with an embedded profile for the recipient to use if desired. If not, a different profile can be used.

- If you want to unembed a profile, choose Define Profiles from the Preflight panel's menu. Select the profile from the list, and choose Unembed Profile from the Preflight Profile menu (see Figure 17-2).

- To export a profile to reuse or share, choose Export Profile from the Preflight Profile panel's menu, choose a name and location, and click Save to save the profile as an InDesign Preflight Profile (IDPP) file.

- Profiles can be loaded from a stored profile or from a document containing the embedded profile. Choose Load Profile from the Preflight Profile menu, select the IDPP file or document, and click Open.

Consider copying your custom profiles for future use. In the event you have to restore your preferences, you can easily load your profile copy.

Save an error report for future reference as text or PDF, listing the errors shown in the Preflight panel. If you want an inventory of your document and items such as fonts and inks, create a report from the Package feature. Read more in the next section.

Package and Ship Your Project

If you're a freelance designer, expect some last-minute changes, or aren't sure what the printer wants, you can send your publication and its components as a tidy package, complete with output instructions. Before packaging, be sure to check that contents are linked properly in the Links panel and that you're not showing any preflight errors.

To produce a package, follow these steps:

1. Choose File | Package to open the Package dialog box. InDesign automatically runs Preflight to check the file. Results of the check are displayed in the Summary pane of the dialog box, along with any warnings or errors found.

2. Click through the panes of the dialog box by selecting titles in the left columns. Here's what you'll find:

- On the Fonts pane, look for fonts used, their type, a status for the font, and whether it's a *protected* font, which prevents you from including the font information in the document. As you see here, the sample project uses five fonts; the font used for the selected text on the page is highlighted in the pane.

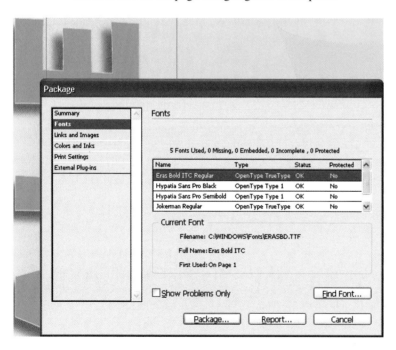

- On the Links and Images pane, find a list of links to images and other media, such as SWF files. You'll see a list of the images in the document, along with basic information, such as the page on which the image displays and resolutions.

- On the Colors and Inks pane, look for a list of process and spot inks, as well as whether the document uses a color management system (CMS).

- On the Print Settings pane, find a list of print settings for the file, such as scaling, trapping, color, and so on. The settings you see are the ones chosen the last time the file was printed.

- Finally, the External Plug-ins pane lists any third-party plug-ins installed in the program.

To save a copy of the package review, click Report. In the resulting Save dialog box, you'll see the file's name as the text file's name. Click Save to store the report. The contents of the report and printing instructions text files are the same.

3. Click Package to replace the Package dialog box with the Printing Instructions dialog box. Add contact information for the recipient of the package, as well as other information, such as extra instructions. Click Continue to open the Package Publication dialog box.

4. Choose a name for the folder, named using the file's name by default, and select the location. Choose the items to include with the package. The default choices include Copy Fonts, Copy Linked Graphics, and Update Graphic Links in Package.

5. Click Package/Save to close the dialog box, then read and click OK to close the Warning dialog box regarding copying font software. Finally, generate the finished material and produce the content.

Print Your Publication

InDesign offers an extensive range of print settings and features, as you'd expect. Fortunately, if you've used Preflight and done different previews (outlined in Chapter 16), you can minimize errors and get your publication printed.

Choose Print Options

To start your printing adventure, choose File | Print to open the Print dialog box. Make your choices from the column headings at the left to display the panel at the right of the dialog box (see Figure 17-3). Regardless of what panel you're working with in the Print dialog box, you'll see a Preview window showing a proxy page with a large "P" on the preview at the lower-left area of the Print dialog box.

 If you choose PostScript as the printer and device-independent PostScript Printer Description (PPD), you won't see the proxy.

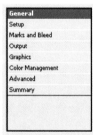

The Print dialog box includes eight panels of settings. Depending on choices made for your printer, the available settings vary from panel to panel. For example, if you choose a desktop printer, you won't have any output choices other than Composite Gray and Composite RGB. On the other hand, if you're printing a PostScript file, you can choose from a number of separation options, depending on the PPD chosen for the file. Once you've made your choices, click Print to close the dialog box and process your publication.

Given that the settings are so variable, in this section, look for information about features on the different panels, rather than a click-by-click narrative.

Define the Mechanics of Your Print Job

The first three panels in the Print dialog box deal with mechanical issues of printing the publication, such as how many copies and the scale used.

FIGURE 17-3 Choose a heading to display the settings panels and view updated previews.

 **Save Print Settings**

Defining print settings can be time-consuming. If you've made a number of customizations, click Save Preset at the bottom of the dialog box and store the settings. The next time you need to process the same type of publication, simply click the Print Preset drop-down arrow, and choose your custom settings.

Choose General Settings

You see the General Settings panel when the Print dialog box appears. You'll see the last printer you selected, as well as the last Print Preset option chosen. If you haven't used a preset, you'll see [Default] listed.

Along with other printers you're networked to, you'll find Adobe-specific items in the Printer drop-down list. Installing InDesign also installs a PostScript print driver used to print the file to disk as PostScript for handoff to a print shop. If you've installed Acrobat, you'll also find the Adobe PDF print driver installed.

Specify the usual types of print options, such as the numbers of copies, page range, and so on. Finally, select items for printing that are generally non-printing or those you've specified as non-printing in the Attributes panel. You can print visible guides and grids, for instance, or include blank pages.

 If you want to print items on hidden layers, choose All Layers to print the hidden layers along with visible layers.

Define the Document Setup

Click the Setup heading in the column at the left of the dialog box to show the Setup panel. Here you select a paper size and orientation. Only the sizes allowed by the selected printer are available.

By default, your document prints at 100% scale; click Scale To Fit to resize your design for a quick proof of the document. Identify where to place the content relative to the paper using the Page Position options if you don't want to use the default

How to. . .   Use Printed Master Pages and Guidelines

If you're designing, sharing, or documenting templates for future use, include the non-printing elements for extra information. Select the Print Master Pages and Print Visible Guides and Baseline Grids check boxes on the General panel of the Print dialog box. Your reference material then includes the guides and grid information as well as the template.

position at the upper-left area of the page. You can center the page horizontally, vertically, or along both axes.

For a quick reference of your entire project, select the Thumbnails check box, and select a configuration from the drop-down list. As you see here, the preview updates the page proxy with the thumbnail layout. Click Print to close the dialog box and print your thumbnails. InDesign adds the page numbers along with the thumbnails.

If your document page size exceeds your paper size, click Tile and specify how to divide the page into sections and how much to overlap the pages. After printing, you must manually reassemble the content to display the complete page.

Set Marks and Bleeds

On the Marks and Bleeds panel, set the options for displaying printer's marks as well as bleed and slug margins. In order to show the marks, your paper has to be large enough to contain the content and the marks and bleeds, or you can select the Scale To Fit check box on the Setup panel.

InDesign offers a collection of standard, commonly used printer's marks (see Figure 17-4).

FIGURE 17-4 Apply standard printer's marks to the page for alignment and calibration.

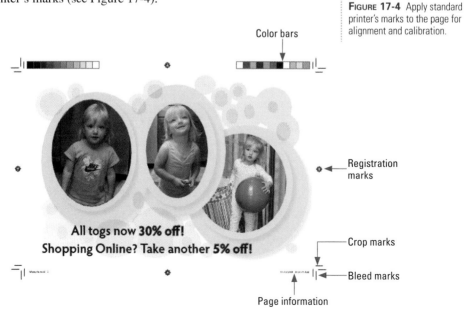

Color bars

Registration marks

Crop marks

Bleed marks

Page information

All togs now 30% off!
Shopping Online? Take another 5% off!

Standard printer's marks include these items:

- Crop marks identify the trim boundaries of the page.
- Bleed marks are offset from the crop marks using the settings specified in the document or on the Marks and Bleeds panel, and indicate how much of the bleed area to print on each side.
- Registration marks align color-separated film plates.
- Color bars add ink bars composed of small squares of CMYK and grayscale ink used to calibrate ink density on the printing press.
- Page information includes the filename, page number, and time stamp for the printout.
- The slug area isn't defined on the Print dialog box. If you included a slug area in the document settings, select the Include Slug Area check box to display the marks (not shown in the figure).

 You can customize the appearance of the lines used for the marks. Click the Weight dropdown list, and choose a thickness or leave the default: .25pt. You can also click the up or down arrows to increase/decrease the offset value, which is the amount of space between the edge of the page and the crop marks.

Determine Print Settings for Page Elements

The next four panels on the Print dialog box include settings for the page elements, including color output, graphics, fonts, inks, and transparency. The Summary panel lists the options you've selected in the previous panels.

Define Output

In the Output panel, choose the Color option from the dropdown list, and make a selection from the composite and separations options. The choice you make influences the content of the panel. For example, if you choose any of the composite color output, the Inks panel is disabled. The separations and

In-RIP separations let you select inks and frequency/angle settings, as you see here.

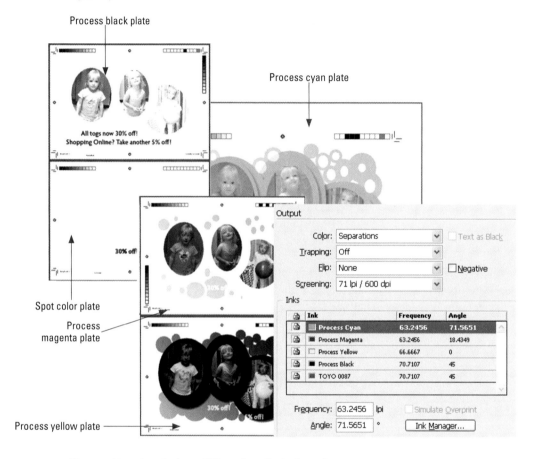

Process black plate

Process cyan plate

Spot color plate

Process magenta plate

Process yellow plate

Composite color choices differ primarily in how they interpret the color values in your document. Color conversion from the print process converts imported raster images and colors chosen for items you draw in InDesign. The options include:

- The Composite Leave Unchanged option is best when you want InDesign to reproduce original colors precisely and you're using a color-managed system.

- The Composite Gray option converts all color into grayscale, with the exception of placed PDF and EPS files containing RGB or Lab colors. Use this option for quick proofs.

Imported vector and EPS artwork isn't affected unless the objects are associated with transparency and blending on the document.

- Composite RGB converts all color to RGB, good for some printers like inkjets that produce optimal color using RGB color information.

- Composite CMYK is the default choice and best for printing proofs and separations on PostScript printers. This choice converts RGB or Lab colors to CMYK.

If your printer supports PostScript, you can choose from two separations options to print color separations with one page per process color or spot color. Separations always print in black, as they're designed for making printing plates. Speaking of black, select the Text as Black check box to convert colored type to 100% Black in any of the composite modes.

Select screening options supported by your printer, including Linescreen (lines per inch, or lpi) and Resolution (dots per inch, or dpi) modes.

You don't usually need to change frequency and angle settings except when two spot colors are included in a mixed-ink swatch or are applied to the same area. The inks will print atop one another. Ask your printer for an alternate angle setting to use for one of the colors.

Tweak the Graphics

Adjust the Graphics panel defaults for the optimal combination of print quality and speed. On this panel, choose settings for images and fonts.

Select one of four methods for handling image data in the Send Data drop-down list (see Figure 17-5). Your choices include:

- Optimized Subsampling (the default), which down-samples high-resolution images as part of the print process.

- All sends all of the image data to the printer and requires a significant amount of printer memory if you have many high-resolution images (not shown in Figure 17-5).

- Choose Proxy to send low-resolution images for a rough proof.

- Choose None to substitute gray boxes for images for a quick layout proof.

None   Proxy   Optimized subsampling

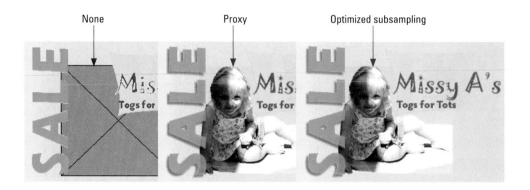

FIGURE 17-5 Choose a method for sending image data depending on your requirements.

Select one of three fonts options from the Download drop-down list. The Complete option downloads every glyph in every font used in your document to the printer at the start of the printing process. Don't choose this option without a lot of available printer memory.

You do want to download PPD fonts rather than the printer fonts to avoid error.

Choose Download a Subset to send the characters used for a page with the rest of the page's data on an individual page basis. If you choose None, that's what you get. No font data downloads to the printer; the printer's font data is relied upon instead.

For PostScript output, choose the highest level available in the drop-down list, and select Binary rather than ASCII from the Data Format drop-down list, as binary files print faster. Occasionally, the output may be garbled, in which case, change to ASCII format.

Assign Color Management

Click the Color Management heading to display the panel settings. Here you'll define a print choice, as well as color and printer profile options.

In the Print area, select either the Print or Proof options. Leave the Print option selected by default if you're simply printing your document. Choose the Proof option to simulate different printers.

In order to use the Proof option, specify printers in the View | Proof Setup | Custom menu.

Warning
Remember to disable color management in the printer driver dialog box.

FIGURE 17-6 InDesign offers warnings about required modifications.

There are three options for color management, which you may or may not need to change. The Color Handling drop-down menu lets you specify whether InDesign manages color for most printers. If you choose to let InDesign manage color for you, a warning kindly reminds you to disable color management in your printer's dialog box (see Figure 17-6). A PostScript printer adds a choice to let the PostScript printer manage the color.

By default, the Printer Profile matches the Document CMYK profile in the Color Management panel. The options for Preserve CMYK Numbers (on by default) and Simulate Paper Color (off by default) can be changed if you've selected any option other than Document CMYK. You generally leave the defaults as-is.

Select Advanced Features

Click Advanced in the heading column at the left of the Print dialog box to display the Advanced panel. You may or may not have to make any selections on this panel, depending on your server and printer environment.

For a network using an OPI image server that swaps low-resolution for high-resolution images for printing, select the OPI Image Replacement check box. You can also specify whether to print EPS, PDF, or bitmap images. If you don't use an OPI server, not all printers allow for image swapping, so the settings aren't available.

The eighth and final panel is the Summary panel. Here you'll see a list of all the settings selected on the other panels.

Print Your Page as a Single Bitmap

Attention Windows users: The high-end graphics and color manipulations possible in InDesign can potentially wreak havoc with your printed output. If you are having problems printing a document with numerous shading and gradient objects, click the Print as Bitmap option on the Advanced panel, available when you're using a non-PostScript printer. Choose a resolution from the drop-down list. Your choices depend on your printer's resolution.

The same scenario is possible when printing from Mac. In Mac OS 10.3 and later, InDesign prints the pages as PostScript, rendered by Mac OS printer drivers.

Generate PDF Files from InDesign

InDesign CS4 relies on the same presets, called *joboptions,* as those used for generating PDF content using Adobe Printer and Adobe Acrobat.

Generating a PDF export prints the contents of the publication to a PDF format. To produce a PDF file, follow these steps:

1. Choose File | Export to open the Export dialog box. Name the file and select a storage location.

2. Click the Save as Type/Format drop-down arrow, and choose Adobe PDF. Click Save to close the Export dialog box and replace it with the Export Adobe PDF dialog box.

3. Choose the export settings for the document. Select a preset, and make modifications as necessary. As you see here, the dialog box includes a description of the chosen preset.

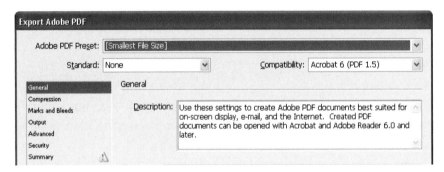

4. Specify the lowest PDF version capable of opening your document.

5. Click Export/Save to close the dialog box and process the exported file.

Use a PDF Preset

A PDF preset is a group of settings designed to balance file size with quality, depending on how the PDF will be used. PDF presets can apply to printing or comply with international standards for consistent output. You can also create and share custom presets for your unique output requirements.

The names and descriptions of the basic presets are listed in Table 17-1.

Preset Name	Description of Features
Smallest File Size	Best for use online or sending via e-mail. Fonts are embedded, all colors are converted to sRGB, and images are down-sampled.
High Quality Print	Use for printing PDF files to your desktop printer. Fonts are embedded and subset.
Press Quality	Use for printing PDF files to a high-quality prepress printer. Fonts embed and subset.

TABLE 17-1   PDF Presets for Exporting PDF Content from InDesign

In addition to the presets listed in the table, InDesign offers exports in PDF standards-compliant formats. The PDF/X standards are international standards for graphic content exchange as defined by the International Organization for Standardization (ISO). When you select a standard, the file is tested against the standard. A file meeting the requirements is considered standards-compliant.

InDesign offers presets for PDF/X-1a:2001 and PDF/X-3:2002, as well as the newest standard, PDF/X-4:2008. Several other PDF standards for archival, engineering, and so on are available only through Acrobat 9 Pro.

You Can Export Layered InDesign Documents to PDF

If you choose an export compatibility of Acrobat 6 (PDF 1.5) or higher, you can export your InDesign document's layers to PDF layers, viewable in Acrobat. Select the Create Acrobat Layers check box on the General settings panel, and proceed with the rest of the export settings.

When the document opens in Acrobat or Adobe Reader, you can display the Layers panel and toggle layer visibility, as you see here.

Locate and Load Adobe PDF Presets

New PDF presets (.joboptions files) that you create automatically appear in the Adobe PDF Presets menu. The presets are stored in the Settings folder in these locations:

- **Windows XP**   Documents and Settings\[username]\Application Data\Adobe\ Adobe PDF

- **Windows Vista**   Users\[username]\AppData\Roaming\Adobe\InDesign\Adobe PDF

- **Mac OS**   [username]/Library/Application Support/Adobe/Adobe PDF (Mac OS)

Supplementary InDesign PDF presets are installed in the Adobe PDF\Extras folder. Use your system's search utility to locate additional .joboptions files. You may also receive custom PDF presets from service providers and colleagues. For these presets to be listed in the Adobe PDF Presets menu, they must be moved to the Settings folder manually or using the Load command in the Adobe PDF Presets dialog box.

Define Custom Presets

The set of default PDF presets are appropriate for most circumstances. However, you or your printer may have specialized settings that aren't included in the existing presets. Fortunately, you can save a new preset based on a default one or build new presets from scratch.

You can't edit the default presets, although you can certainly save a modified copy of one. Follow these steps to customize an existing preset:

1. Choose File | Adobe PDF Presets | Define to open the Adobe PDF Presets dialog box. Select the preset you want to start from, and click New to open the New PDF Export Preset dialog box.

2. Name the preset, called *Adobe PDF Preset 1* by default. Choose a PDF/X standard if desired, and choose an Acrobat/PDF version from the Compatibility drop-down list.

3. Choose the options you want, and click OK to close the dialog box. You'll see your new preset added to the default list of presets.

If you have made some changes in the Export Adobe PDF dialog box as part of the export process, click Save Preset at the bottom of the dialog box. Name and save the new preset, which is also added to the other preset files.

Summary

This chapter covered printing in all its forms. As you no doubt realized, printing from InDesign can be a complex topic! It helps to keep in mind that many of the features and processes you work with are based on presets and that many items chosen in other parts of your workflow influence choices you can make for printing.

InDesign CS4 introduces the new Live Preflight feature, a great timesaver to keep on top of errors and issues in your document as you develop your content. Once your document is prepared, you can use the Package feature to bring together all of the file's assets to send to a colleague or your print shop.

Printing options vary considerably, depending on the type of printer you're using and the general characteristics of the document. The print settings fall into two general categories, including the mechanical aspects of the pages and the elements on the pages.

The final area of discussion centered on PDF output integrated into InDesign. You can choose from several default presets or define your own for online, print, or standards-compliant output.

Coming up, an entire chapter devoted to PDF files. You'll see how to use a variety of interactive and dynamic features to add navigation and interest to your PDF output.

18

Create Interactive PDF Content

How to...

- Include PDF navigation features
- Design bookmarks
- Configure hyperlinks and cross-references
- Add movies to a file

InDesign Creative Suite 4 (CS4) includes features for exporting your publications as interactive PDF files. There are several dynamic and interactive features you can use in Acrobat or Adobe Reader, many of which also export to Shockwave Flash (SWF) (read more about SWF in Chapter 19).

In this chapter, see how to get the most from PDF files produced from your InDesign publications. Discover how to insert navigation features such as bookmarks and hyperlinks, or add some pizzazz with a movie or two.

Create Dynamic PDF Documents

You can export dynamic Adobe PDF documents that include a variety of interactive and navigation features. Insert bookmarks linked to a page or a graphic to navigate in the PDF file; link items to a table of contents; or link to other documents, online sources, or e-mail. If you plan to use your PDF file in full-screen mode, use page transitions to animate the change from one page to another. For more action and excitement, add movies and sound to the file or link to streaming Internet-based files.

 Note   To ensure that the interactive elements function in the PDF, make sure that you specify bookmarks, hyperlinks, and interactive elements in the Export Adobe PDF dialog box.

Bookmark PDF Content

Bookmarks are common navigational features in PDF documents that link to a page, text, or graphic in the document. For more organized navigation, you can nest bookmarks in a hierarchy in the Bookmarks panel.

 If your publication has a table of contents, the entries automatically convert to bookmarks. Read about tables of contents in Chapter 9.

Generate Bookmarks

Choose Window | Interactive | Bookmarks to display the Bookmarks panel. Each new bookmark needs both a label in the Bookmarks panel and a destination.

- To identify the destination, place the text cursor within some text, select a graphic frame, or display a full page (double-click the page's icon in the Pages panel).

- To define the label, click Create New Bookmark on the Bookmarks panel, and type the name.

- To do both simultaneously, select some text on the page, and click Create New Bookmark on the Bookmarks panel to use the selected text as the bookmark, as you see here.

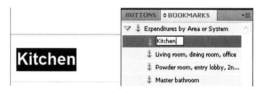

 New bookmarks appear at the end of the list unless you click the bookmark above where you'd like to add the new one.

Modify Bookmarks

You can manage and customize a basic bookmark list in a number of ways. For example, triple-click the label to activate the name field and change it, select a bookmark and drag it to move its location, or drag it to the trash can icon for deletion. You'll see a black indicator bar that identifies the new location when you release the mouse.

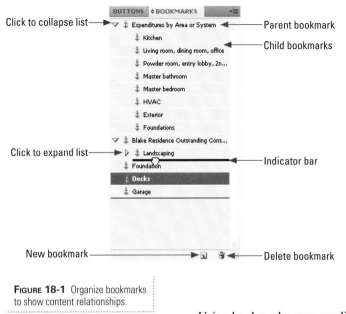

Click to collapse list — Parent bookmark

Child bookmarks

Click to expand list — Indicator bar

New bookmark — Delete bookmark

FIGURE 18-1 Organize bookmarks to show content relationships.

One important modification lets you arrange and nest bookmarks to define a hierarchy. Select one or more bookmarks and drag them to the bookmark you want to use as the parent bookmark. Release the mouse to nest them as child bookmarks. The parent bookmark shows a triangle to the left of the icon, indicating the presence of nested bookmarks. If you want to "un-nest" bookmarks, select them, and drag the icon(s) below and to the left of the parent bookmark. Release the mouse to promote the bookmarks in the list.

Using bookmarks, you can list all applicable content together in the Bookmarks panel (see Figure 18-1).

Reordering your list of bookmarks doesn't affect the document's order in any way. Select a bookmark's name and drag it to a new location. If you'd like to list the bookmarks according to the page locations they display, choose Sort Bookmarks from the Bookmarks panel's menu.

Insert Hyperlinks in an InDesign Document

InDesign offers hyperlinking to a number of destinations using a number of sources. Text, a text frame, or a graphics frame can be a hyperlink *source,* used to jump to a specific entity. You can use different items as *destinations,* including a file, e-mail address, Uniform Resource Locator (URL), page, or named anchor on a page.

The existence of hyperlinks doesn't mean they'll export with your content. You have to specify hyperlink exports in the Export Adobe PDF and Export SWF dialog boxes. Read about PDF exports in Chapter 17 and SWF exports in Chapter 19.

Hyperlink Basics

You can produce different types of links in InDesign. Regardless of the type of link you're creating, follow the same general steps to get started:

1. Choose Window | Interactive | Hyperlinks to open the Hyperlinks panel, which is tabbed with the Cross-References panel by default.

2. Select the text, frame, or graphic to serve as the hyperlink's source.

3. In the Hyperlinks panel, click Create New Hyperlink on the panel's toolbar, or select it from the panel's menu, to display the New Hyperlink dialog box.

4. Specify the Link To item. Choices include a URL, as you see here, File, E-mail, Page, Text Anchor, or Shared Destination, described in the following sections.

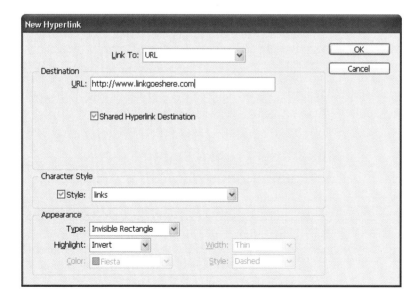

5. Choose the destination, which varies according to the type of link you're defining, as shown in the following sections. For example, a URL offers a single field to type the URL, while Shared Destination offers two fields for selecting the document and the shared destination.

6. Define an appearance for the link, either by applying a style (as in the example) or choosing appearance options. The options vary, depending on whether you choose a visible or invisible link.

7. Once you've configured the link and defined the appearance, click OK to close the dialog box and complete the link.

Hyperlink Specifics

Choose from several different types of hyperlinks and configure the options accordingly, following the steps outlined in the "Hyperlink Basics" section.

Hyperlink to a URL   You can base your URL hyperlinks on any Internet resource protocol, such as `file://`, `ftp://`, `http://`, or `mailto://`. In the Hyperlinks panel, type or paste the URL, including the protocol. Leave the Shared Hyperlink Destination check box selected to include the URL in a list to reuse.

Hyperlink to a File   Often, you'll have ancillary information that readers can access for more information. For example, in a monthly sales report, you may have Microsoft Excel spreadsheets showing the raw data. You can insert a hyperlink to an external file that opens it in its native program when you click the link in the PDF or SWF file. Choose File from the Link To drop-down list. Click the Path icon to open a Browse dialog box, then locate and select the file to link.

Tip   InDesign uses relative links, so when hyperlinking from one document to another, put the files in the same folder.

Hyperlink to an E-mail Message   Choose E-mail from the Link To menu in the New Hyperlink dialog box. Type the address in the Address field, and insert text for the subject line.

Hyperlink to a Page   There are different ways to hyperlink to a page, either with or without a named destination. In the New Hyperlink dialog box, click the Document drop-down arrow and choose a file from the list of open documents, or click Browse to open a dialog box where you can locate and select another file. Click the Page up and down arrows to select a page in the document. Logically, you can only select a page number that exists in the selected document. Click the Zoom Setting drop-down arrow and specify a view setting, such as Fit View to show the visible part of the current page or Fit Width to display the page's width in the window.

Hyperlink to a Shared Destination   When you create a hyperlink to a URL, file, text anchor, or e-mail address, you can reuse the same destination. Choose Shared Destination from the Link To menu. In the Destination area, choose a document containing the links from the drop-down list of open and saved documents. Then, click the Name drop-down menu and choose a link. You can select external hyperlinks or text anchors you've inserted in the file.

 If the document you want to use isn't open, click Browse in the Destination drop-down list, locate the file, and then click Open.

Hyperlink to a Text Anchor   Choose Text Anchor from the Link To drop-down list. In the Destination area, select the file containing the anchor from the Document drop-down list. Click the Text Anchor drop-down arrow to show the list of anchors you've defined in the selected document.

Link to Named Destinations

You don't always want to link to an entire file or page. You may have a table of contents and want to link to the beginning of each section. Or, as in the example project, link from the introductory table to specific tables.

In order to make the specific page location show in the exported file, you have to construct named locations in the destination document first, which you then link to from the source document. Of course, if you're working in one document, the source and destination documents are the same thing.

Specify a Hyperlink Destination

Build hyperlink destinations for hyperlinks or cross-references to a text anchor, page, or URL. You don't see a list of destinations as you're building it, unfortunately. The only place you'll see the list is when you're creating the hyperlink.

Follow these steps to create a destination:

1. Use the Type tool to place the insertion point, or select the range of text that you want to be the anchor. You can't use text on a master page for an anchor destination.

2. Choose New Hyperlink Destination from the Hyperlinks panel's menu to open the New Hyperlink Destination dialog box.

3. Click the Type drop-down arrow, and choose Text Anchor, Page, or URL.

   - For a Text Anchor destination, text selected prior to starting the process shows in the Name field; otherwise, type a name for the anchor.

   - For a Page destination, type a name for the page, select its actual page in the document, and specify a zoom setting (see Figure 18-2).

   - For a URL destination, select URL from the Type drop-down menu. Text selected on the page prior to starting the destination process displays in the Name field. Otherwise, type a name for the link. Specify the URL in the field.

4. Click OK to close the dialog box. Once you've constructed the destinations, you can create the hyperlinks.

FIGURE 18-2 Define characteristics for destinations, such as the page and zoom view.

You Can Sort and Test Your Hyperlinks List

When you want to check your links, click the forward/backward arrows at the bottom of the Hyperlinks/Cross-Reference panel. Select a link on the panel, and then click the right arrow to view the link's destination; click the left arrow to see the link's source.

Keeping track of dozens of hyperlinks can be tricky. Choose Sort from the Hyperlinks panel's menu, and choose one of the following options to view your links in different ways:

- Choose Manually to see the links listed chronologically.
- Choose By Name to display the links alphabetically.
- Choose By Type to display the hyperlinks grouped by type.

Cross-Reference Document Contents

InDesign offers cross-references that you can insert as a variation of hyperlinks. In a cross-reference, you define a reference between text or an insertion point to other text in the same or another document. Cross-references work especially well with styled text. The example project includes one cross-reference from one document to another and one within the same document.

You don't have to preconfigure linking items such as anchors or destinations as you work with the document contents. To set up a cross-reference, place the text cursor at the location where you want the cross-reference and follow these steps:

1. Click Create New Cross-Reference at the bottom of the Hyperlinks panel to open the New Cross-Reference dialog box.

2. To specify your linking choice, click the Link To drop-down arrow and choose Paragraph or Text Anchor from the list (the example uses Paragraph).

3. Choose an open file from the Document drop-down menu, or click Browse to locate and select another file you'd like to use. The document's styles are listed in the left panel on the dialog box.

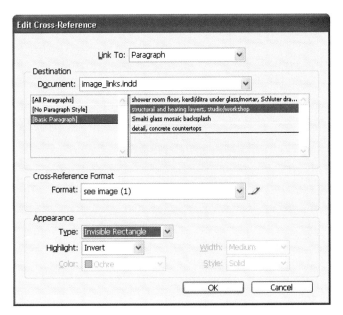

FIGURE 18-3 Specify the format and features of a cross-reference link.

4. Select a style to display the paragraphs using that style in the subject document.

5. Choose a cross-reference format from the drop-down list. You can choose many options, ranging from the full paragraph to the page number. Or, click the icon to the right of the Format field to customize your own format (see Figure 18-3).

6. Add appearance features as desired; if you use a custom format, you can specify a character style for the cross-reference instead.

7. Click OK to close the dialog box and complete the cross-reference.

You'll see the new cross-reference added to the panel and shown on the page according to your formatting choices, such as the custom style shown here.

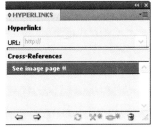

Define Page Transitions

Both PDF and SWF files can show animated transitions as you move from page to page (in SWF, you're actually moving from keyframe to keyframe—read more later in the chapter). You can apply and modify transitions for one or all of your spreads in InDesign.

To add transitions to a document's pages, follow these steps:

1. Select the pages or spreads in the Pages panel. You can't apply a transition to a single page of a double-page spread, nor can you apply a transition to a master page.

2. From the Pages panel's menu, choose
Page Transitions | Choose to open the
Page Transitions dialog box. Move
your mouse over the thumbnails of the
transitions for a preview.

3. Select the transition from the dialog box,
and deselect the Apply to All Spreads
check box, active by default, if you want
to apply transitions only to selected
pages.

4. Click OK to close the dialog box. You'll
see icons next to the pages/spreads that
include transitions.

If you want to change the transition's
options, such as the type, direction, or speed,
choose Window | Interactive | Page Transitions
to open the Page Transitions panel. As you see
in Figure 18-4, you can change the options of
an applied transition in the Page Transitions panel.

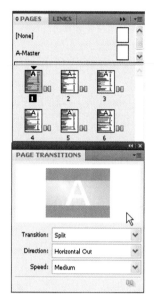

FIGURE 18-4 Modify directions
and speed for your transitions.

 The transitions in the exported PDF file are viewable only in full-screen mode. Press CTRL-L/COMMAND-L
in Adobe Acrobat or Adobe Reader to invoke the view; press ESC to exit full-screen mode.

Add Movies and Sound
Files to Documents

InDesign lets you insert movies and sound clips into a document
for export to PDF. You can insert and configure the file, although
you can't play the movie in the source InDesign file. You can
also link to a streaming Internet video file instead of embedding
the media in the document.

There are restrictions on what types of media you can use in
your publication. You need QuickTime 6 or later. Movies can be
in QuickTime, Audio Video Interleaved (AVI), Moving Picture
Experts Group (MPEG), and SWF formats. Sound files can be
Waveform Audio format (WAV), Audio Interchange Format
(AIF), or Audio (AU) formats. WAV files must be uncompressed
8- or 16-bit files.

Insert a Movie or Sound File

Inserting a media file is like adding any sort of file in many ways. Follow these steps to get started:

1. Choose File | Place, and select the file.

2. In InDesign, click the loaded cursor where you want to place the object. You don't see an image of the movie in the frame—instead, you'll see an object linking to the media file.

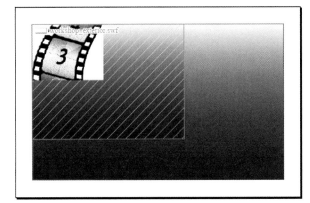

3. If you want to preview your movie, press ALT/OPTION and double-click the object with the Selection tool.

4. Double-click the object to open the Movie Options dialog box, where you can edit the settings.

5. Select the options you want to use, and click OK to close the dialog box. You'll see a frame like the one shown here that displays the movie's dimensions, its name, and the standard poster.

Link to an Online Movie   Instead of linking to a local object, you can link to and test a streaming video file online. When you're configuring the movie's settings in the Movie Options dialog box, click Specify a URL and insert the address in the URL field. Then click Verify URL and Movie Size to make sure that the URL is valid.

Link to a Sound File   Sound files link the same way as movie files, following the same steps for selection and insertion. Double-click the object on the page to open the Sound Options dialog box, where you can specify many of the same features as for movies. For example, type a description, specify a poster image, have the sound play on page turns, and embed the sound in the exported PDF file.

Specify Your Movie's Features

The Movie Options dialog box offers a range of customizations to consider. If you're planning to use movie files as part of a larger layout, check out the options as you're planning the layout. You may want to use the movie poster as part of your document, or use another image instead of a poster (see Figure 18-5).

Embedding the movie or sound file increases the size of the PDF document, but you don't have to worry about including the file with the PDF document for distribution.

Pick a Poster, Any Poster

A movie or sound clip placeholder poster is an image, but you don't place it like a regular image. Instead, specify the poster as you configure other movie or sound options.

You can choose from several poster sources, including:

- Choose None to omit a poster altogether, although the movie's frame exists. Use this option when you want a more complex design beneath the movie to show instead of the poster.

- Choose Standard to use the generic options provided by InDesign.

- Choose the default poster to display either a poster image included with the movie file or the first frame of the movie.

- Select Choose Image as Poster, and click Browse to locate and select a bitmap image.

If you decide to use a different image later, select the poster frame with the Direct Selection tool and use the Place command to insert the new image.

- If you want to use a frame from the movie as a poster, choose Movie Frame as Poster to display a preview window and slider. Drag the slider to display the frame you want, and click OK. You can't select a frame from an SWF movie.

Movie Export Issues

There are a few things to keep in mind when you work with movies in InDesign to ensure a smooth export, including:

- Unlike placed images, when you export a movie to a PDF file, the movie's boundaries define the size of the object, not the frame or poster size. Plan your design around this behavior to avoid disappointment and annoying layout issues.

- If you use an imported image as the poster and use the Fitting commands, you'll see a dialog box on export saying the clipping needs adjusting. Not to worry—the content exports well.

- The PDF file shows movies in the top layer. If you overlay a movie with other content in InDesign, that content displays behind the movie in the PDF.

- If you want to use an interesting layout including the movie, place your content on the page first, and then add the movie without a poster. As you see here, the mouse indicates that a movie exists, but it doesn't show on the page.

You Can Communicate in Real-time

The CS4 products include an option to collaborate online using Adobe ConnectNow, a free web conferencing service from Acrobat.Com. Choose File | Share My Screen to display the Adobe ConnectNow login screen. Log in using your Adobe ID, and take advantage of the different features to communicate with colleagues.

■ ConnectNow requires a Flash player; you must have an Adobe ID to use the service, but your invited participants don't need to be registered.

■ Send e-mail invitations to invite two other participants.

■ Set up a customized display using a variety of pods, such as Shared Notes and Chat.

■ Use video conferencing or talk using Voice over Internet Protocol (VoIP)

■ Share your screen with your participants. As you see here, a shared screen shows the group of ConnectNow pods, but no other interface elements.

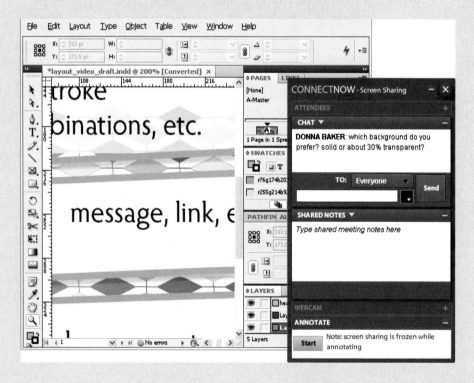

For more information, visit the online site at http://www.adobe.com/acom/connectnow.

- Keep track of the media files you add to an InDesign document in the Links panel. Restore the links if you move or rename the file.

- The InDesign document links to the movie. If you need to share the source InDesign file, include movie and media files as well.

Summary

It's fascinating to consider how software develops over a few short years to accommodate an ever-expanding range of media and other new developments. InDesign CS4 has kept up with the times, as you've discovered in this chapter. For the most part, interactive and media types described in this chapter are for PDF export.

The chapter started out with some common navigational features you'd use in an interactive PDF file, including bookmarks and hyperlinks. We looked at cross-references, useful as a feature in long documents, but usable in a shorter project, too. For interest, you can add page transitions or insert movie and sound files.

There's still more interactivity you can use in a document. Up next, continue delving into motion and responsive documents with discussions on using buttons and Flash.

19

Create Buttons and Flash

How to...

- Configure buttons and button states
- Add interactivity to buttons
- Design a Flash-ready publication
- Export InDesign files for Flash

InDesign CS4 lets you produce content in Flash-ready formats, including Shockwave Flash (SWF) files ready for distribution or Flash Exchange (XFL) format for further manipulation in Flash.

In this chapter, see how to work with the new button design features and program buttons for PDF and SWF use. InDesign lets you easily create buttons from scratch and add different states and actions to make them interactive. In the latter part of the chapter, see how to organize and design files for SWF playback or to export into Flash for incorporation in another project.

Control the Action Using Buttons

Using text as links to content or for actions like opening files is fine, but sometimes your page needs a little more zip and visual impact. How about using some buttons? Buttons are easily configurable from existing content on the page, or you can work with buttons from the new Buttons library.

The Button tool in older versions of InDesign produced an object that worked much like a frame. InDesign CS4 takes your button-building bonanza to a new level, producing an object that works like a group. The new buttons let you define button states and assign actions that export to PDF; some also export to SWF.

For a quick way to add simple navigation, such as Next Page or Previous Page, put the buttons on the master page. The buttons appear on all document pages using the master.

Create a Multistate Button

Most objects in your InDesign document are button material, with the exception of movie posters, movies, and sound files.

Use any sorts of objects you like as a button source. You can type some text and add a colored background to the text frame to define a named button, like *Exit* or *E-mail.* If you like, place an image and select it to convert to a button. You can use one object or a group, such as a drawing and text.

When working on buttons and designing dynamic documents, select the Interactivity workspace.

Select the object or objects to convert. Choose Window | Interactive | Buttons to open the panel. Click [Normal] to define the button, or click Convert Object to a Button on the Buttons panel's toolbar.

The State of the Button

A button—whether a single object or a group—can display three variations, depending on the user's interaction. The appearances, called button *states,* include:

- Normal, the way a button looks on a page unless the mouse is within its area

- Rollover, the way a button looks when the user moves the mouse over the button's bounding box

- Click, the way a button looks once the user has clicked and released the mouse over the button's bounding box area

You don't need to use all three states. For example, you might only want to use Normal and Click states, in which case the button object has two groups (one for each state) instead of three.

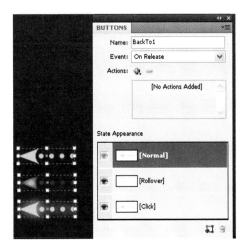

FIGURE 19-1 Configure the appearance for each button state.

Change the Appearance of a Button's States

To configure the Rollover and Click states, follow these steps:

1. Select the button on the page with the Selection tool. You'll see the button identified in the Buttons panel (see Figure 19-1).

2. Click [Rollover] in the Buttons panel to activate the Rollover state. Now you'll see a copy of the Normal appearance in the Rollover section of the panel.

3. Make the changes as desired to the button's appearance, like the inner shadow in the example shown in Figure 19-1.

4. Click [Click] to activate the Click state, which copies the Normal state appearance to the Click state. Again, make changes as desired to the button's appearance. In the example, the arrow uses an outer glow.

Once the buttons' appearances are complete, you can add the actions.

Assign Events and Actions to Buttons

Something has to happen to initiate an action in a document. The "something" is an *event*. When your user moves the mouse over your button, they see the Rollover appearance; when they click the button, they see the Click appearance. The mouse movements that trigger the changes in the appearance are the events. Along with visual changes on the page, you can attach actions that occur with the mouse actions.

Add Actions to Buttons

When the user clicks your button, they see the Click appearance. In order for the button to have value, attach one or more actions that occur as the user releases the mouse after clicking the button, such as opening a file. Follow these steps to choose an event and its actions:

1. Select the button using the Selection tool. You'll see its name in the Buttons panel.

2. Click the Event drop-down list, and select an event, such as On Release.

3. Click the Actions plus sign to open a list of actions. The list offers many choices, as you see here.

4. Click the action you want to assign to the event. Depending on the action, you'll see different choices in the panel. A few actions, such as Go To Next or Go To Previous, don't have any settings.

5. Add additional actions to the event if you like; add additional events and actions as desired.

Use the Sample Button Library

InDesign CS4 offers the Sample Buttons panel, an object library shown in Figure 19-2. The panel displays as part of the Interactivity workspace. Otherwise, you can choose Sample Buttons from the Buttons panel's menu to open the panel. Drag the button you want to use from the panel, and drop it on the page.

The panel includes several dozen preconfigured buttons you can use. The buttons contain effects for identifying different states as well as actions. All the left-pointing arrow buttons include a Go To Previous Page action, while the right-facing arrow offers a Go To Next Page action.

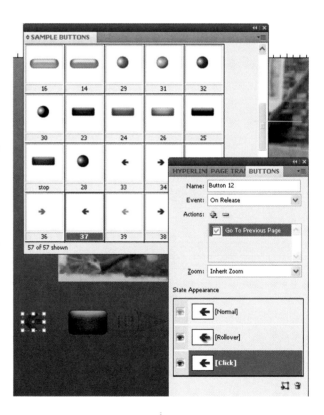

FIGURE 19-2 Use preconfigured buttons from the library.

How to... Modify Button Actions

Your buttons and their actions aren't static. Select the button with the Selection tool. Here are some changes you can make:

- Deselect the check box for an action to deactivate it for testing. If you're not sure if you want to keep an action, deselect it and test it, rather than deleting it outright.

- Select an action in the list, and click the minus sign next to the Actions label to delete the action.

- Your actions are easy to edit. Select the appropriate event from the drop-down list, select the action in the list, and then modify the settings.

- Drag-and-drop the actions in the list to reorder the sequence in which they are applied.

Note Like other library files, open the InDesign application folder and you'll find the library files in the Presets folder. Also, like other library files, you can add or delete buttons.

Set the Button Tab Order

Before exporting a publication, be sure to check the tab order. Users working with assistive devices like screen readers use tabs to move from field to field in a top to bottom, left to right pattern. You can include buttons on hidden layers in your tab order list, but not those on master pages.

You set the tab order on a page-by-page basis. Open the page you want to check, and choose Object | Interactive | Set Tab Order to open the list of fields (buttons) on the page. Review the list and drag buttons to the proper locations, or select a button and click Move Up and Move Down. Click OK when the order is correct to close the list.

Open the next page you want to check, and repeat. Continue until you've finished ordering your entire document's fields.

Tip If you decide you like the appearance of an object but don't want to use it as a button, choose Object | Interactive | Convert to Object. The content remains, minus the states and actions.

How Flash Interprets InDesign Content

How do you know whether your document works as a Flash file or not? In this section, learn how different aspects and features of a document translate to SWF or XFL. Knowing beforehand logically cuts down the amount of troubleshooting and reworking necessary later.

If you're unsure about online vs. page sizing, keep this in mind: 1pt in an InDesign publication equals 1px in the SWF file.

Export an InDesign Publication to Adobe Flash Formats

InDesign offers two ways to export your content for Flash use. You can export a publication directly to Adobe Flash (SWF) for online use or as an XFL file to take into Adobe Flash for further manipulation.

For either type of export, choose File | Export to open the Export dialog box, and choose SWF or XFL from the File Type/Format drop-down menu. Click OK to close the Export dialog box and open the Export SWF, or Export XFL dialog box, as shown here.

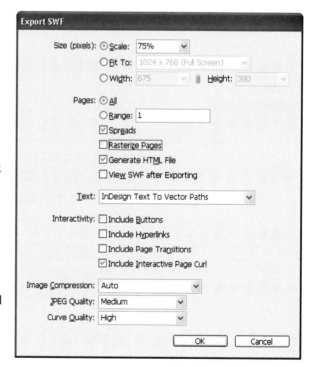

Export to SWF

When you export a file to SWF, you can define the output size of the file and which pages to include, as you see here. The default SWF uses the original document's dimensions. Then choose the type of text, interactivity, and image compression options and click to export the document.

Export to XFL

The new XFL format in InDesign CS4 lets you export a file exclusively for use in Flash using a subset of the SWF export

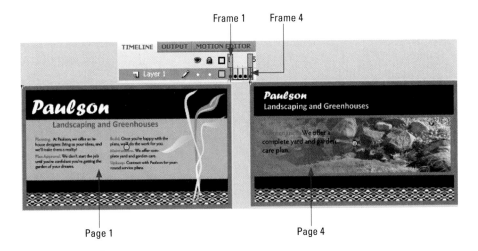

FIGURE 19-3 Each spread becomes a keyframe in Flash.

options. When you select XFL as the export format, choose the page size and range, whether you want to manage transparency and page content as a single raster image, and a text option. There aren't image conversion choices, as XFL converts images only to Portable Network Graphics (PNG). Click OK to process the file.

Convert Pages and Page Items

Flash has no concept of a page, which makes the idea of exporting a page-based InDesign document seem impossible at first glance. The solution is quite elegant: Flash recognizes symbols, and the export process wraps each page or spread in a symbol for use in the program.

Flash translates each page to a keyframe in a single layer on the timeline, similar to slides in a slideshow (see Figure 19-3). In response to an action such as clicking a button or link, another keyframe—and another page—shows on the screen.

Images and other high-resolution content automatically convert to low-resolution content when you export to either SWF or XFL. Choose a scale size or common page size, such as 1024 × 768, during the export process.

Handle Text Exports

InDesign offers different ways to export text as part of the SWF export process. Choose the type of text conversion you want to use, depending on what you want to do with the text later, as well as how it appears. Here you see examples of each type of text output.

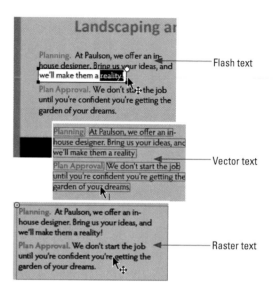

- Exporting as editable Flash text translates your InDesign text to text you can manipulate in Flash. This text, along with being editable, is available for indexing by search engines.

- Vector text displays multiple vectors using (DefineShape) tags. The text frame breaks up into smaller units to maintain visual appearances.

- Raster text displays one or more raster images representing the text. The text is rasterized at the text frame level, with one raster image per frame. Inline or anchored objects in the text frame rasterize with the text.

Translate Interactive Features

Buttons and hyperlinks can export on a limited basis from InDesign to Flash, while movies don't export at all, and transitions always export.

Control the Action

Some actions associated with buttons work in SWF files, while others don't. You can attach Next Page and Previous Page actions to buttons that export to the SWF file. SWF exports don't include other common actions, such as Exit, Open File, and Close, and XFL files don't recognize actions at all. The solution: Add the buttons in InDesign, and then program them in Flash after export.

Handle Hyperlinks

In a SWF file, links to external websites or other pages in the same document are supported. XFL files, on the other hand, don't support hyperlinking.

Use Page Transitions

Page transitions, similar to those you see in online presentations, work well when exported to SWF. Along with the regular transitions, you can use a special page curl that lets you drag page corners to turn the pages (see Figure 19-4).

FIGURE 19-4 Use a page-curl transition for navigating a SWF document.

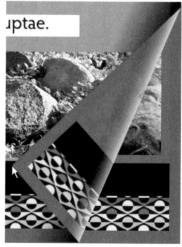

Insert Movies and Sound

Movies and sound clips aren't included in an exported SWF or XFL file, but their posters are displayed. You can add media posters to your layout in InDesign, export the document to XFL, and use Flash to make them dynamic.

Prepare Images for Predictable Export

In InDesign CS3, each image in a document is exported to SWF as a separate image asset, regardless of whether the image recurred or not. For both SWF and XFL export from InDesign CS4, multiple uses of the same image are stored as a single image asset, with a few exceptions. These include:

- If you copy and paste the same image multiple times, each instance saves as an individual asset.

- If you place two instances of a raster image on a document and scale or transform one differently, the SWF contains separate assets for each instance.

- Non-placed content, like gradients you add to drawn objects on the page, aren't seen as image assets.

SWF Image Exports

SWF exports include JPEG pass-through. That is, a JPEG image added to an InDesign document and used as-is (without modifications or effects) isn't compressed again when exported. On the other hand, if you insert JPEG files and then transform the image in some way or add effects, the image reprocesses as part of the export.

XFL Image Exports

In an XFL export, all images are converted to uncompressed PNG. Take care with Illustrator files. If you place an illustration, such as a PDF file exported from Illustrator, the XFL file

  identifies it as a single item, like the example on the left shown here. Using drag/drop or copy/paste from Illustrator to InDesign results in one Flash object per Illustrator object, along with all their editable paths in the exported file, as you see in the right example.

Make it simpler to use copied content in a SWF file. Choose Edit | Preferences and click Clipboard Handling preferences. Select the Prefer PDF When Pasting and Copy PDF To Clipboard check boxes.

Preserve File Names

When you export a document from InDesign to SWF or XFL, names of your placed image files are stored along with the rest of the file data. Rather than a collection of images numbered image01.jpg to infinity (or the number of images used), you'll see your files maintain their original names. Where you have duplicates due to changing scales, each instance uses the name and a number, such as tree1.png, tree2.png, and so on.

The preserved names apply to both raster and vector images. Not only that, but if you import an image in one format, such as tree.tif, and then export in another format, the name still stands, such as tree.png. How cool is that?

Control Color and Transparency

SWF and XFL files use red-green-blue (RGB) color. When a document is exported to SWF or XFL, InDesign converts all color spaces (such as CMYK and Lab) to sRGB and spot colors to equivalent RGB colors.

 To avoid color changes with transparency, choose Edit | Transparency Blend Space | Document RGB.

Transparency groups, some blend modes, and simple alpha channels translate to unflattened XFL content. You can't export all InDesign blend modes for use in Flash, as you see in Figure 19-5. However, you can use several blend modes, including Normal, Multiply, Difference, Hard Light, Screen, Overlay, and Lighten.

 **Transparency Affects Interactivity**

Before exporting to SWF or XFL, make sure that transparent objects don't overlap any interactive elements such as buttons or hyperlinks. If an object with transparency overlaps an interactive element, you'll probably lose the interactivity. The workaround is to flatten transparency before exporting.

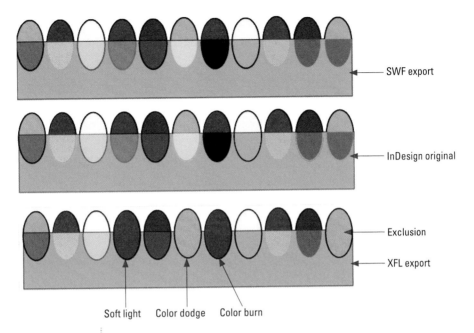

SWF export

InDesign original

Exclusion

XFL export

Soft light   Color dodge   Color burn

FIGURE 19-5 You'll see different results when exporting blends to SWF or XFL formats.

Summary

There's a lot more to interactivity in InDesign CS4 than you may have imagined, isn't there? Continuing from Chapter 18, we looked at buttons, available in both PDF and SWF files, although PDF supports more button actions than does SWF.

Speaking of SWF, the latter part of the chapter described how to use InDesign in concert with Flash. You can export content from InDesign directly to SWF format for playback, or export in the new XFL format for further manipulation in Flash. To help make your results more predictable, I included sections on handling the elements that make up a file, including text, images, interactive objects, and color and transparency.

Up next, delve further into several types of InDesign output. Learn about using datamerges, working with XML, exporting content for use online, and exporting image content.

20

Create Other Forms of Output

How to...

- Datamerge documents
- Generate XML
- Export online publications
- Export content as images

A long with the multiple ways to export your InDesign publications to print, PDF, and for Flash, InDesign offers more ways to repurpose and reuse your documents (is there no end to this program's abilities?).

Many programs, including InDesign, are now capable of using and exchanging data via XML to allow the data to be used in other ways. For a more specific export, try a datamerge, where a list of records automatically populates fields in an InDesign document to generate a finished product.

If you want to use your content online, InDesign includes features to export your document as an eBook or XHTML page—complete with optimized images. Speaking of images, you can export your pages themselves as images, too.

Merge Data to Create Output

One common word-processing task you can readily take care of in InDesign is a datamerge. Datamerges are used to create form letters, mailing labels, and so on where you have information that varies in specific fields, such as names or addresses.

To perform a datamerge, you need to compile the *data source,* a table holding your information. You also need an InDesign *target document* containing data-field placeholders that will receive the data. Once both parts are ready, you merge one data record from the data source into one copy of the target document to generate one iteration of the final document.

	A	B	C	D	E	F
1	Location01	address02	address03	address04	Title	Contacts
2	122-4668 14th St. West	Bennington	PB		01122 Executive Director	Jane Sharpe
3	122-4668 14th St. West	Bennington	PB		01122 Intake Coordinator	Lois Trufault
4	122-4668 14th St. West	Bennington	PB		01122 Office Manager	Caroline Bishop
5	122-4668 14th St. West	Bennington	PB		01122 Finance Officer	Jack O'Neil
6	122-4668 14th St. West	Bennington	PB		01122 Counselling Services	Samantha Carter
7	122-4668 14th St. West	Bennington	PB		01122 Medical Liaison	Daniel Jackson
8	122-4668 14th St. West	Bennington	PB		01122 Educational Liaison	Edna Pope

FIGURE 20-1 Configure the data source file.

Define the Data Source

Design your data source in a database or spreadsheet. Be sure your field names are logical to you. Collect your data in *fields*, such as names or job titles. In a spreadsheet, you'd see the fields as titles for your columns. Each entry, called a *record*, contains data for each of the fields, like a row in a spreadsheet (see Figure 20-1).

Data source files separate the items by commas in a comma-separated value (CSV) file or by tabs in a tab-delimited file, stored as a .txt file.

Prepare the Target Document

Design or open the file you're using as the target document to hold the merge fields. Include the text and images to appear in each copy of the finished product.

InDesign offers prompts as you work on a datamerge. Choose Window | Automation | Datamerge to open the panel. From the Datamerge panel's menu, choose Select Data Source to open a dialog box for you to locate and select your file. When you click Open, the fields are listed on the panel.

Data fields function on the document page or the master page (as in the sample project), but not both. Read more about using a master page in the sidebar, "Add Data Fields to a Master Page."

Drag text frames on the page to the locations where you want the fields, and then drag a field from the list in the Datamerge panel to the text frame on the page. You'll see the field's location on the Datamerge panel. When the fields are placed, configure the text frames for the merged content, as you see here.

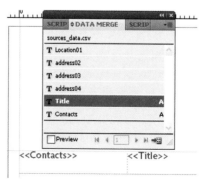

Add Data Fields to a Master Page

If your record data changes often, put the fields on the master page, select them, and choose Allow Master Item Overrides on Selection from the Pages panel's menu. This way, the merged output includes the placeholders on the master page and merged results on the document page as overridden master page items.

The merged document maintains links to the data source if the fields are on the master page. To update your sources, choose Update Content in Data Fields from the Datamerge panel's menu.

Preview and Generate the Merged Output

Be sure to check out the merged files before you complete the merge. Check for accuracy, as well as any layout issues you may have missed, such as extra spaces.

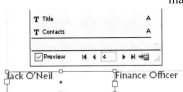

FIGURE 20-2 Preview the data in the fields before merging.

Before performing the merge, click the Preview check box at the bottom of the Datamerge panel. You'll see the first record displayed in the fields on your target document (see Figure 20-2). Click the navigation buttons on the Datamerge panel to cycle through data from different records.

Once you're ready, choose an export option from the Datamerge panel's menu. Choose Create Merged Document or Export to PDF to open the Create Merged Document dialog box. Choose settings on the Records and Options tabs as necessary, and click OK to process the files.

Look for these options on the Records tab:

- Specify the extent of the merge: single, multiple, or all records.

- Choose the number of records per page, or leave the default single record. If you choose Multiple Records, specify the layout features, such as margins and spacing.

- Select the Generate Overset Text Report With Document Creation check box if your records contain variable amounts of text. The report displays only if fields on the merged document include overflow text.

On the Options tab, choose from among these options for placing images:

- If your records don't include data for every field, select the Remove Blank Lines for Empty Fields check box on the Options tab to improve the layout.

- For large datamerge runs, you can change the default 50 records per document. Select the Record Limit per Document check box, and specify a number.

Incorporate XML into Your Workflow

InDesign can import and export XML files used to structure, store, and transport information. XML data stores in plain-text files, which offer a software- and hardware-independent way of storing data.

Think of XML as similar to a datamerge. An XML file contains the data and its values, and your document contains equivalent XML tags that hold incoming data, like data fields in a merge document.

Using XML is a complex process, far beyond the scope of this book. The following sections use a DVD collection as an example to give you an idea of how XML can be integrated into different InDesign files and workflows. The XML file was constructed in Notepad, although you can use any program that lets you save the file as XML, including InDesign.

You can compile an XML file from an InDesign document through the Structure panel.

Define and Assign Tags in InDesign

You can reuse the data stored in an XML file anywhere, such as the labels in the example InDesign project. Placeholder frames are assigned tags that match the XML tags. To make the labels, follow these steps:

1. In InDesign, configure the labels as desired, and insert placeholder text frames to hold the data; you can add placeholder text if you like, as shown here.

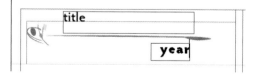

2. Choose Window | Tags to open the Tags panel, showing a single tag named *Root*.

3. Choose View I Structure to open the Structure panel. You'll see a single parent element named *Root*. Leave the element as-is, or rename it. In the sample, the root is renamed *collection*.

4. On the Tags panel, click New Tag on the toolbar. In the resulting dialog box, name the tag, choose a color, and click OK to close the dialog box and add the new tag. Repeat as necessary. The two tags in the sample are named *title* and *year*, and the parent tag is named *dvd*.

InDesign includes several ways to define tags, including manually tagging content, loading tags from another file, and mapping tags to styles.

5. Each label in the InDesign document corresponds with a parent <dvd> tag in the source XML. Insert one parent <dvd> tag in the Structure panel for each label.

6. To assign a tag to a placeholder frame, select the <dvd> parent tag in the Structure panel. Then select the frame on the page and click the tag's name in the Tags panel, or drag the label from the Tags panel and drop it on the frame (see Figure 20-3).

7. Duplicate the content to create the desired layout on the page. Each copy includes copies of the tagged frames. In the Structure panel, you'll see duplicates of the placeholder frames for each copy of the label added.

FIGURE 20-3 XML tags added to placeholder frames show in the document's structure.

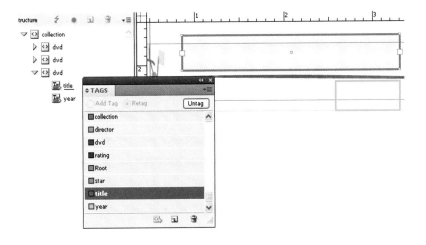

Import the XML Data

The final step is to import the XML file. Only the tags in the document are matched; the remaining tags aren't used. Follow these steps to complete the labels using imported XML data:

1. Choose File | Import XML, or choose Import XML from the Structure panel's menu. Locate and select the file (the sample project uses *dvd_collection.xml*).

2. Click Open to add the tags from the XML file to the Structure panel. Values for imported tags that match the tags in the document populate automatically.

3. As you see here, additional tags are added to the Structure panel that correspond with the imported elements.

You can select whether to merge content or append content. The *append* mode adds the XML as content in the Structure panel for you to place manually. The *merge* mode compares the imported XML with content on your page and attempts to place elements.

Repurpose Content for Online Use

InDesign offers several ways for you to get your documents online, ranging from a simple copy and paste to exporting for different media, such as an XHTML-based eBook. You can reuse exported content in Dreamweaver or another HTML editor, and create JPEG images from objects on your page or the entire page.

Interactive PDF outputs are explained in Chapter 18, and Flash exports and outputs are described in Chapter 19.

Design an eBook

Your documents or book files can become eBooks viewable in Adobe Digital Editions software. The finished product is an XHTML file, complete with your images and layout. Download and auto-install the Adobe Digital Editions viewer at www.adobe.com/products/digitaleditions.

Create the eBook

An eBook file contains several types of content, including the XHTML conversion of your page layouts. A JPEG thumbnail generated from the first page in the file displays as the eBook's link in the Digital Editions Reader library view.

To produce an eBook, open the file in InDesign and choose File | Export for Digital Editions to display the Save As dialog box. Leave the default name, storage location, and file format options, and click Save to close the dialog box. The three-tab Digital Editions Export Options dialog box appears. Make your choices from the three tabs (described next), and click OK/Export to export the file.

Don't change the file's name. If you try to use another name, you'll receive an error message.

Specify eBook Export Options

The Digital Editions Export Options dialog box contains three tabs. Look for several export choices on the General tab, such as:

- Choose a Cascading Style Sheet (CSS) style option for exported text and paragraphs, ranging from none to defined styles.

- Decide how to map bullets and numbers: as tagged lists or text. Using tagged lists produces XHTML tags for the list and its elements, while converting to text creates paragraphs using text characters instead of bullets or numbers.

- Select the View eBook After Exporting check box to open the exported file immediately after processing.

Click the Images label to display the images settings in the dialog box. On this tab, specify the following settings for image conversions:

- Choose Optimized or Original copies. Since your images are copied to store in the .epub file, you can choose Optimized to decrease the image files' sizes for faster downloads, or leave the originals as-is.

- Select GIF or JPEG from the Image Conversion Mode drop-down list, or choose Automatic to let InDesign decide. Leave the default formatted selection to preserve formatting, such as image rotations and sizing.

Finally, click Contents to display the third tab of the settings. Here you can choose an export format, either EPUB or DTBook (XHTML and DTBook on Mac). Also, specify whether to include tables of contents generated in InDesign along with the ones generated for the eBook by default.

Read Your New eBook

In Adobe Digital Editions, choose Library | Add to Library to open the Select Items to Add to Library dialog box. Locate and select your file, and click Open to add your publication. Click its name to show details about the publication (see Figure 20-4). To read your eBook, double-click the name to open it.

Convert Your InDesign Files to XHTML

You can export web pages and corresponding folders of optimized images to work with in your favorite web editor.

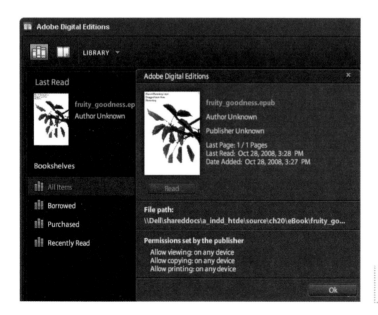

FIGURE 20-4 Read publishing details for your eBook.

Be Aware of Conversion Issues

Not all objects are converted, nor are all settings maintained. When you export contents to XHTML, you control image exports, but the formatting of text isn't preserved.

Figure 20-5 shows an example InDesign document before creating a web page (left) and the resulting web page (right). Content converts, but there aren't any exported images.

Here are some things to keep in mind as you prepare your files for converting to web pages (with reference to Figure 20-5):

- On a web page, you generally see hyperlinks to other pages and other sites or to internal anchors. An XHTML conversion of an InDesign document supports hyperlinks only to web pages and anchors in the same document. You won't find active links from one document to another, nor will you find table of contents links.

FIGURE 20-5 Export an InDesign document to XHTML for online use.

Pasted or drawn artwork

Active link   Bullet list

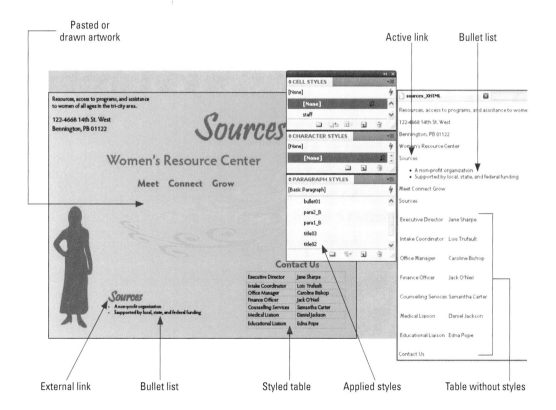

External link   Bullet list   Styled table   Applied styles   Table without styles

- Some InDesign features are excluded from conversion simply because they aren't supported in XHTML or are structures found only within InDesign's programming. For example, XML tags, books, bookmarks, page transitions, index markers, and text converted to outlines aren't included.

- As a general rule of thumb, content that's linked or embedded in your document converts to images in the exported web page. That means images and graphics in all formats export as either GIF or JPEG files. SWF movie files export, while other types of movie files aren't supported.

- In your output, InDesign preserves style names—but not the contents of the styles. You'll see character, paragraph, cell, table, and object styles appear in the markup as CSS style classes, as shown here.

```
<head>
        <meta http-equiv="content-type" content="text/html;charset=utf-8" />
        <title>sources_XHTML</title>
        <style type="text/css" media="screen"><!--
                div.story {}
                li.bullet01 {}
                p.main-title {}
                p.para1-b {}
                p.para2-b {}
                p.title02 {}
                p.title03 {}
                span.sources-label {}
                td.staff {}
        --></style>
</head>
```

- Items created using tools in InDesign aren't exported since they aren't discrete objects. Excluded items include anything drawn with the drawing tools or pasted on to a page, such as Illustrator content.

 You can export a JPEG image of the layout to use as a page background. See how in the upcoming section, "Export Your Publication as Images."

- Unless you purposely select objects on the pasteboard or an object touches the page, it can't be converted to XHTML simply because there's no way to define its position relative to the page. The same issue applies to master pages, but there's a simple workaround. Select the page thumbnails in the Pages panel, and choose Override All Master Page Items from the Page panel's menu.

InDesign bases the page layout on reading order, scanning top to bottom and left to right. In a complex document, you may find some content out of order that you'll have to repair. Try grouping items such as layered text and images to improve the exported layout. Items grouped in InDesign are grouped in XHTML in <div> tags.

The export options for XHTML and eBooks are identical for some features. Refer to the previous section for more on mapping bullets and image management options.

InDesign can redefine most text items on your pages with their HTML equivalents, including bulleted and numbered lists, footnotes, and table contents, shown here. Text frame content exports, including overset text. Table and cell styles export, although table formatting, such as borders (shown in Figure 20-5), doesn't export.

```
• A non-profit organization    <ul>
• Supported by local, state, a    <li class="bullet01">A non-profit organization</li>
                                  <li class="bullet01">Supported by local, state, and federal funding</li>
Meet Connect Grow              </ul>

Sources

Executive Director  Jane Sharp  <div class="story">
                                  <table>
                                    <tbody>
                                      <tr>
Intake Coordinator  Lois Trufau         <td class="staff">
                                            <p>Executive Director</p>
Office Manager      Caroline Bi        </td>
                                        <td class="staff">
Finance Officer     Jack O'Neil            <p>Jane Sharpe</p>
                                        </td>
                                      </tr>
Counselling Services Samantha Carter

Medical Liaison     Daniel Jackson
```

Reuse Your Content in Dreamweaver

You can export content from InDesign to use in Dreamweaver. Select specific items, such as text, tables, graphics, and so on, for export if you don't want to export the entire InDesign file. Otherwise, follow these steps to create the web page content:

1. Choose File | Export For Dreamweaver to open the Save As dialog box. Name the file and choose a storage location. Click Save to close the dialog box, and the XHTML Export Options dialog box appears.

2. In the XHTML Export Options dialog box, specify the options in the General panel. The Export Document option is active by default, unless you've selected content on the page. Choose a number list conversion. Your choices include converting numbered lists into their equivalent HTML tags, converting a numbered list into HTML and assigning a paragraph number, or converting to paragraphs.

3. Click the Images heading to show the images settings, identical to those found on the eBook export options. The sample file doesn't include any linked content, so images aren't exported with the XHTML.

4. Click the Advanced heading to show the Advanced panel of settings, and choose an option for connecting with your CSS rules. You can choose Empty CSS Declarations to list the styles' names in the <head> component of the page for later editing, No CSS (self-explanatory), or External CSS to work with a linked spreadsheet. Specify the Uniform Resource Locator (URL) to include in the link.

Note   To launch an external JavaScript when the page opens, select the Link To External JavaScript option, and type the URL in the field. InDesign makes the link, but doesn't check the script's functionality or validity.

5. Click Export to close the dialog box and start the conversion. When the files are processed, you'll have a web page and a web images folder if you export linked content. Be sure to check external CSS file, JavaScript, and image folder paths for accuracy.

Export Your Publication as Images

You can export a page or selected objects as images from your InDesign file, rather than as a complete file. For example, export some layers as an image for a Microsoft PowerPoint background, export text objects as images for a web page, export the page for a sample web page, and so on.

InDesign exports full-color or grayscale images of your pages or selected objects as JPEG files. To export your page, select specific objects if desired, and choose File | Export to open the Export dialog box.

Specify a location and filename, choose JPEG from the Save As Type/Format drop-down list, and click Save. The Export dialog box closes, and the Export JPEG dialog box appears. Make your choices (listed next) and then click Export to close the dialog box and create the image shown in Figure 20-6.

Choose your export settings from these options:

- If you selected objects, leave the default selection choice or assign a page range.

- Select an option from Maximum to Low from the Quality drop-down list.

- Specify Progressive format to show a low-resolution image that gradually draws more detail, or Baseline format to show a placeholder that downloads the image and then displays it onscreen.

- Choose a resolution from 72 to 2400 pixels per inch (ppi) from the Resolution drop-down list.

FIGURE 20-6 Select objects on the full page (left) to use for a background image elsewhere (right).

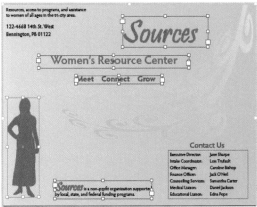

Summary

InDesign includes a range of advanced features and tools designed to streamline your workflow, as you learned in this chapter. Perform datamerges using a data source and an InDesign document containing matching fields. An alternative way to use data is working with XML files and a tagged document, as in the DVD label example.

InDesign lets you move your content online, as eBooks or as exported XHTML and optimized images. As a finale, the chapter included methods for converting pages or page content to images, for web use or otherwise.

Up next—wherever you want to go! InDesign is a fascinating program, and contains so many features to explore and experiment with. Enjoy, and thanks for reading!

Index